The Twilight of Unionism

Geoffrey Bell was born in Belfast and has written extensively about Ireland and British attitudes to the Troubles, past and recent, for print, television and exhibitions. These include *Protestants of Ulster*, and the documentary *Pack Up the Troubles* for Channel 4.

The Twilight of Unionism

Ulster and the Future
of Northern Ireland

Geoffrey Bell

VERSO

London • New York

First published by Verso 2022
© Geoffrey Bell 2022

1 3 5 7 9 10 8 6 4 2

Verso
UK: 6 Meard Street, London W1F 0EG
US: 388 Atlantic Avenue, Brooklyn, NY 11217
versobooks.com

Verso is the imprint of New Left Books

ISBN-13: 978-1-83976-693-0
ISBN-13: 978-1-83976-695-4 (US EBK)
ISBN-13: 978-1-83976-694-7 (UK EBK)

British Library Cataloguing in Publication Data
A catalogue record for this book is available from the British Library

Library of Congress Cataloging-in-Publication Data
A catalog record for this book is available from the Library of Congress

Typeset in Sabon by MJ & N Gavan, Truro, Cornwall
Printed and bound by CPI Group (UK) Ltd, Croydon, CR0 4YY

Contents

My mother read to me from the Bible. It says that God created the world, but it doesn't say anything about borders. You can't cross a border without a passport or a visa. I always wanted to see a border properly for myself, but I've come to the conclusion that you can't. My mother can't explain that to me either. She says, 'A border is what separates one country from another.' At first I thought borders were like fences, as high as the sky. But that was silly of me, because how could trains go through them? Nor can a border be a strip of land either, because then you could just sit down on top of the border, or walk around in it, if you had to leave one country and weren't able to get to the next. You would just stay on the border, and build yourself a little hut and live there and make faces at the countries on either side of you. But a border has nowhere for you to set your foot. It's a drama that happens in the middle of a train, with the help of actors who are called border guards.

Irmgard Keun, *A Child of All Nations* (1938),
translated by Michael Hofmann (2008)

This book is for Cassidy and Orla.
May you grow up to see fewer borders.

Ireland and Its Provinces

The grey line marks the historic boundaries of Ireland's four counties of Ulster, Connacht, Leinster, and Munster. The blacked dotted line is the political boundary of Ulster as created at partition in 1921.

Introduction

In *The Protestants of Ulster*, first published in 1976, I wrote that this community was the most misunderstood and criticised in western Europe. This intentionally provocative statement proved unintentionally prophetic.

I was referring to the Protestant community of what is known as Northern Ireland. Despite much collected evidence and many contested opinions, a lack of comprehension of this community remains common, certainly among those with only a passing interest in exploring the politics and history of the island of Ireland and its relationship with its nearest neighbour. Compounding this, in the last few years there has been a growing lack of empathy shown by the British, Europeans and Americans towards the most visible and vocal members of this community. As they have become more noticeable, they have also been more criticised for perceived misdeeds and backward ideas.

This book is not a re-run or an updated version of the portrait I attempted in 1976, though it does share the same insistence on the necessity of looking beyond daily headlines and instantaneous reactions. The difference is that what follows is a greater concentration on the dominant political creed shared by most Protestants within Northern Ireland. This is unionism: the support for the union between Great Britain and Northern Ireland. But this definition is insufficient: the nature and motivations of Northern Ireland unionism, and indeed British unionism, require further elaboration.

This is much more necessary now than it was even a decade ago, because British unionism in general and its Northern Irish variant have become more interrogated and less confident. Thus, it is contemporary dilemmas and predicaments that inform what follows, albeit while acknowledging that these have important historical roots: in Ireland there is no border between past and present politics. Historically, unionists in the north-east of the island have enjoyed marching, either in protest or in celebration: what this book asks is where they are now marching towards. It is a question many in that community are also asking, today more frequently than ever before.

The superficiality of judgement that too many observers have recently offered is actively unhelpful. Chapter 1 reflects on such verdicts, locating them in their time and political circumstances. It also traces how an optimism and sense of self-importance within Northern Irish unionism, as represented by the Democratic Unionist Party of Arlene Foster when it allied itself to the British Conservatives under Theresa May, ended in disillusionment and resentment – as well as ill fortune for the individual leaders concerned.

Chapters 2 and 3 offer some historical context that seeks a contemporary relevance by beginning with more general issues being addressed today in Britain and Northern Ireland. These are notions of exceptionalism and supremacism. In Britain, discussions on these have focused on the legacy of imperialism and colonialism. The context in respect to Ireland is assertions by unionists that the British were intellectually and morally superior to the Irish, and that Irish Protestants were similarly superior to Irish Catholics. Such thinking, I suggest, was a major part of the justification for northern Protestants' ideological and physical resistance to Irish self-determination in the late nineteenth and early twentieth centuries. For example, the willingness of English Tories at the start of the twentieth century to threaten civil war in support of 'Ulster' remaining British will be explored, as it should be whenever responsibilities for Ireland's 'troubles' of whatever generation are discussed.

The propaganda and self-justification for such behaviour has contemporary parallels with the growth of English nationalism and imperialist nostalgia, evident then and in the England of recent times. Accordingly, the continuation of the colonial mentality in Britain's approach towards Northern Ireland of today is a theme that will recur throughout the book.

Chapter 4 explores how the alliance between the British and Ulster unionist parties began to fall apart under the pressure of the challenges to their Northern Ireland from the 1960s onwards. The sense of estrangement that developed was particularly manifested within the Northern Irish Protestant community in its growing hostility towards their one-time Tory allies across the Irish Sea. This disenchantment, which was often reciprocated, remains profound and consequential.

Chapter 5 explores one of the effects of that estrangement: that is, how the unionist monolith that had enjoyed more than fifty years of one-party governance in Northern Ireland began to splinter and fall apart – and how and why Ian Paisley emerged from the sectarian shadows to become the most successful unionist politician of the past fifty years.

Part of this process was, for the first time, a significant questioning by the less well-off Protestants of their traditional upper-class leadership. This in turn led to debates, even excitement among some commentators and political activists, that provoked discussions of the Protestant working class and its position in relation to Irishness and to class. These discussions remain important, providing a significant key to an understanding of past, present and future in Northern Ireland. They touch on the ways in which the Protestant working class can play a progressive role in that future. This evaluation occupies chapter 6.

There follows an examination of the Good Friday/Belfast Agreement of 1998 and its aftermath. There have been many significant accounts of this, but chapter 7 will highlight the shrinking allegiance to it from within the Protestant community, and the current fragility of the Agreement. The chapter also evaluates the role of recent British politicians in contributing to these cracks and those in the wider peace process.

Chapters 8 and 9 discuss where all of this leads. Chapter 8 explores how determined the British state and its people now are to defend and promote their link with Northern Ireland. It also returns to the theme of British state colonialism, examining whether it still prevails in British political attitudes and policies in respect to Northern Ireland. The views and actions of such individual politicians as Boris Johnson, Michael Gove and Keir Starmer will be considered.

Finally, chapter 9 discusses whether the contemporary tensions and divisions within Ulster unionism threaten its continued coherence. It explores the question of whether today's crisis of unionism is a product only of recent accidents, unexpected political misjudgements and deceit, or whether there is also a deeper, more historical process at work. It also considers where Northern Irish Protestants' allegiances now lie, at a time when discussions of possible Irish reunification are more prevalent than at any time since partition in 1921.

This book addresses a number of themes that relate to each other, seeking to probe their relevance for Ireland, Britain and Europe both today and in the near future. Throughout the text, two implied questions are posed both to the English and to the Irish, in all their diversity: What have you created in Ireland's north-east corner? And what are you going to do about it?

In recent years British unity has become fractured. Aside from Northern Ireland, the most obvious challenge has come from the people of Scotland – although the Welsh people also seem at least to be starting out on a similar exercise of asserting themselves against the English leadership of the UK state. In that sense, the precarious future of British unionism in Northern Ireland, while having its own dynamic, is part of a wider uncertainty. The questioning – or alternatively, defence – of the record of worldwide British colonialism and imperialism that is now a live issue in Britain, surely should find a major reference point in Britain's first act of colonisation, in the island of Ireland.

In the seventeenth century, Protestants from Scotland and England were encouraged by the British state to settle in that colony to keep it and the rest of Ireland British. The plantation of Ulster was, for the British, the only successful part of that enterprise. Yet today, its legacy is often an embarrassment to the British – and a thankless, lonely cause for those in Northern Ireland who still adhere to its traditions. This book seeks to explain both what happened and its consequences.

1

'Crackpots'

There were few signs of tears when, on 14 June 2021, Arlene Foster finally resigned from the position of first minister of Northern Ireland. She had announced her intended departure several weeks before, when calls from within her Democratic Unionist Party (DUP) to quit had become overwhelming. She had been party leader since 2015 and first minister since January 2016, although she had been out of power from 2017 to 2020 because of the collapse of power-sharing in the six north-eastern counties of Ireland. Her subsequent permanent loss of office was because too many in her party had decided she had failed them.

In truth, she had. She had failed them with her on-off alliance with the Conservative and Unionist Party governments of the UK. She had failed them in mishandling the consequences of Britain's decision to leave the European Union. She had failed them through the decline of her party in opinion polls. Because of these and other mistakes, she had also failed because she had dithered over what sort of Northern Ireland she wanted to see: the old Northern Ireland of Protestant supremacy and solidarity, or a new Northern Ireland of reconciliation and mutual respect. It was these failures that meant Arlene Foster was not mourned.

Fulsome tributes from Irish and British politicians were noticeable by their absence. There is little likelihood her face will ever appear on the banners of the Orange Order, whose parades she watched with shows of satisfaction and pride. Nevertheless, in her farewell address she stood on her traditional ground, saying: 'I strongly believe in the good sense of the people of Northern Ireland to continue to recognise the value of our place in the United Kingdom.'[1] There were two problems with this. First, by the time she left office there were more people in Northern Ireland who lacked this 'good sense' than there ever had been in its history. Second, there were now also more people in the UK who doubted the good sense of the DUP and its electors.[2]

As it turned out, the overthrow of Foster did little good to either her party or the broader cause of unionism. Her successor, the easily lampooned Edwin Poots, was ousted after just six weeks in office because of perceived weakness in acquiescing to Irish-language legislation. His successor, Sir Jeffrey Donaldson, who had started his political life as the political agent in Northern Ireland for the English supremacist Enoch Powell, was unable to reverse the DUP's electoral decline. In May 2022, he led the party to unionism's greatest ever defeat, with Sinn Féin, the party of Irish republicanism, out-polling the DUP at elections for the Northern Ireland Assembly.

During that election campaign Donaldson had often declared that unionism was being betrayed by the British government of Boris Johnson, but few in Britain seemed to worry greatly about that. By then, not only had its citizens other things on their minds, from a pandemic to a European war to an accelerating rise in the cost of living, but they had grown irritated with the DUP and its self-portrayals of victimhood. The previous five years had helped to assure that.

It was only in the early summer of 2017 that the mainstream British public discovered the DUP. This was just after the UK general election in June, when the Conservative and Unionist Party secured the largest number of parliamentary seats, winning 318 out of 650, while – against many expectations, including their own – failing to secure a majority. The

Conservatives had stood against the DUP in the general election in Northern Ireland seats, so they were, in theory, political rivals. What they shared was a belief in the unionism referred to in both their titles: the union of Northern Ireland and Great Britain. They also both occupied the right of the political spectrum. Certainly, they shared a deep hostility to a Labour Party then headed by Jeremy Corbyn, who had a history of anti-unionism. Most importantly, at least for outgoing prime minister Theresa May, the DUP had won ten Westminster seats; if she could put those in her pocket, she would retain the tenancy of No. 10 Downing Street.

So a deal was negotiated, and the British public were introduced to the DUP. The newspaper headline that set the tone was in the *Daily Mirror*. The new Conservative and DUP alliance was, its 9 June front page shouted, 'A COALITION OF CRACKPOTS'. The paper gave several reasons for this. 'They oppose[d] abortion – even for rape victims', they were 'anti-gay', and had 'strong historical links with Loyalist paramilitary groups', and were thereby associated with the violence and terrorism of Northern Ireland's 'Troubles'. There was also, explained the *Mirror*, the matter of the DUP's world-view, which included 'a denial of climate change', at least on the part of some of the party's leading lights, while some also promoted creationism – that is, the literal belief that the world was created in six days by God. Case closed: crackpots.

Others made a similar judgement. Writing in the *Guardian*, Polly Toynbee, one of England's most influential liberal commentators, wrote that the DUP was 'a party of Christian fundamentalists whose laws force childbirth on raped underage children'. Accordingly, the Tories were guilty by association. It was a 'humiliation' for a country and party that 'pretends to a reputation for civilised values, that its Prime Minister signed up with such people'.[3] Similarly, *Observer* columnist Catherine Bennett raged against 'May's collusion with a gang of actively homophobic pro-lifers who genuinely regard women as two-legged wombs', adding for good measure that the elected DUP MPs were 'ten wannabe theocrats'.[4]

Such outrage was complemented by disdain from the *Economist*, which repeated a common Belfast quip that the DUP's election manifesto was 'the Bible with fortnightly bin collections'. It noted that the Conservatives 'have spent years trying to shed their "nasty party image"' and speculated that 'an alliance with the DUP could set that back'.[5] Even the *New York Times* chipped in, although not quite with the same emphasis as the British press. It described the DUP as 'socially conservative, a fundamentalist Protestant bloc that is fiercely loyal to dreams of Britain's lost Empire'.[6] Especially vitriolic was *Observer* columnist Stewart Lee, who called the DUP the 'Plague Monks' after computer game characters, who had been defined as 'zealots utterly dedicated to the spread of corruption and decay in the name of the great horned one'.[7] Lee elaborated: 'It's like going into partnership with the unevolved flesh-eating subterranean humanoids from Neill Marshall's 2005 horror film *The Descent*':

> Founded by gaberdine hate foghorn, Ian Paisley, the Plague Monks are opposed to abortion and deny the facts of climate change, evolutionary theory and even geology. Their former health minister, Jim Wells, supported attempts to lobby the visitors' centre of the Giant's Causeway into accepting that the ancient basalt may be only 6,000 years old, as that was when God created everything...[8]

On top of all that, *The Times* then published an offensive cartoon of Arlene Foster, depicting her with chin stubble, sitting in the speaker's chair in parliament, accompanied by a speech bubble that read: 'My Government ...'. The caption was 'New Queen's Speech'.[9] Given all of this, it was hardly surprising that an opinion poll, also commissioned by *The Times* recorded that only 8 per cent were 'favourable' to the Tory/DUP deal, while

48 per cent were 'unfavourable' – the remainder recorded as 'neither' (29 per cent) or 'Don't know' (16 per cent).[10]

These opinions also surfaced in Tory ranks. Just before the Conservatives/DUP deal was signed, the *Daily Telegraph* reported that 'more than a dozen Tory MPs have significant concerns about the prospect of the deal and have warned it could lead to the collapse of the Good Friday Agreement'. Tom Tugendhat MP was quoted as posing 'Three questions on DUP deal'. These concerned the deal's effects on the peace process, on 'equal rights' in Northern Ireland, and on Brexit.[11]

John Major also had his say. As a former prime minister, he had had dealings with the DUP under Paisley. He gave an interview with BBC Radio 4's *World at One*:

> I am concerned about the deal, I am wary about it, I am dubious about it … My main concern is the peace process. A fundamental part of that peace process is that the UK government needs to be impartial between all the competing interests in Northern Ireland. And the danger is that, however much any government tries, they will not be seen to be impartial if they are locked into a parliamentary deal at Westminster with one of the Northern Ireland parties.[12]

Another Tory and former government minister, Chris Patten, declared the DUP 'a toxic brand'.[13] There were even questions raised in the House of Lords by David Trimble – later Lord Trimble – a former leader of the Ulster Unionist Party (UUP) and co-recipient of the Nobel Peace Prize for his efforts in Northern Ireland. He noted, 'My Lords, the Prime Minister has been very generous to the Democratic Unionist Party to the point where she is open to criticism.'[14]

One of what turned out to be the more challenging comments came from Adam Moore, a member of the Conservative Party in South Belfast, who wrote to the *Daily Telegraph* saying the deal endangered the prospect of a return to power-sharing in Northern Ireland, because the DUP could now rely on the government's direct rule to get what it wanted and would not need to 'compromise in negotiations with the other parties in Northern Ireland'. He added: 'The Government is now ... beholden to one of the most reactionary parties in Europe.'[15]

What exactly provoked such reactions? What was the nature of the deal? Did it promise to confine all women to their kitchens, bedrooms and maternity wards? Or all gays to heterosexual education centres? Or all environmental campaigners to learning the Book of Genesis off by heart? Not exactly.

The DUP agreed to support the government in all confidence motions, on the Queen's Speech, the budget and finance bills, and 'supply and appropriation legislation'. It also agreed to 'support the government on legislation pertaining to the United Kingdom's exit from the European Union'. The Conservatives agreed to the DUP's conditions, including progressive promises that pensions would be fully protected against inflation and that winter fuel payments to pensioners would remain universal. These guarantees went against contrary suggestions in the Conservative manifesto. There would also be £1 billion 'for additional support for Northern Ireland', and there was a commitment to spend 2 per cent of the UK's GDP on the armed forces, in line with NATO commitments. The agreement repeated the promise made in the Tory manifesto that it 'would never be neutral in expressing its support for the Union', while it would abide by 'the consent principle and the democratic wishes of the people of Northern Ireland' on the union between Great Britain and Northern Ireland.

Possible confusion arose from the pledge that 'both parties will adhere fully to their respective commitments set out in the Belfast Agreement and its successors'. The Belfast Agreement was, to the rest of the world, the Good Friday Agreement; but the DUP had always objected to this phraseology, as it seemed to bestow a divine blessing on the 1998 agreement that had finally brought peace in Northern Ireland, and between the

IRA and the UK, after thirty years of the Troubles. Moreover, although the phrasing applied here spoke of 'commitments' in the Good Friday/Belfast Agreement (GFBA), that hardly applied to the DUP, which had made no commitments therein: the party opposed it at the time of its signing. Arlene Foster had even resigned from her previous party, the Ulster Unionists, to join the DUP because of the parties' respective positions on this question.

The DUP's divergence from what had by now developed into near-universal worship for a totem of peace and reconciliation in Northern Ireland might be another reason to consider it to be made up of crackpots; but, if so, that judgement should also have applied to a member of May's own government, namely Michael Gove, who had returned to May's cabinet after the 2017 election. In 2000, while working as a journalist at *The Times*, Gove had written *The Price of Peace* for the Centre for Policy Studies. It was a fifty-eight-page denunciation of the GFBA, which, said Gove, meant that 'Terror ha[d] been legitimised', and was 'designed to lever Northern Ireland out of the United Kingdom' and amounted to 'appeasement' of the IRA.[16] This analysis, which we will return to, suggested that the DUP had at least one ideological ally in May's cabinet – though the DUP had signed up to the GFBA supplementary, the St Andrews Agreement of 2006.

On Northern Ireland specifically, the deal between the DUP and May said it 'recognise[d] the need for early restoration of devolved government' there – while Gove's words in 2000 were critical even of this: 'But the devolved assembly in Belfast has not been designed to underpin the Union, it has been framed to facilitate a cross-border dynamic ... [I]t has given Irish republicans room and incentive to advance their goals without allowing Unionists the means to entrench, let alone enhance, Ulster's Britishness.'[17] Gove was to defend these views as late as July 2016.[18] All of which suggested that the GFBA was not exactly safe in the hands of the DUP and the Tories.

In reacting to the insults hurled at them by the British media and others, the DUP was restrained, offering a different version of itself. In a press statement issued on 12 June, Arlene Foster commented:

> For decades our party has played a full role at Westminster and increasingly in recent years our Members of Parliament have been prominent on the national stage. Against that backdrop some of the national commentary, and analysis about the party, and by extension its voters has been downright inaccurate and misleading. I have no doubt over time those responsible will look foolish in the extreme.
>
> People in Northern Ireland know that the DUP is the party of choice for many. Indeed, almost three hundred thousand people cast a vote for us on Thursday. For the past fourteen years we have been Northern Ireland's largest party and throughout we have worked to move Northern Ireland forward through political negotiations and the power sharing institutions. We have become Northern Ireland's main voice at Westminster since 2005.[19]

Whatever the strength of this general defence, Foster was correct in suggesting that the attacks on her and her party were, at least by implication, an attack on those she represented and those who had voted for the DUP. The general election had seen the party win 292,316 votes, which was 36 per cent of the total votes cast in Northern Ireland – an increase over the general election two years earlier of 10.3 percentage points. While the vote of her ultimate enemy, Sinn Féin, had also increased, by 4.9 per cent – securing a total vote of 238,915 and a total share of 29.4 per cent – the DUP was happy that it had gained heavily from its unionist competitors. Chief among these, the more moderate UUP, attracted just 83,280 votes, or 10.2 per cent of the total vote – representing a UUP-to-DUP swing of 5.8 per cent.

Thus, the insults hurled at the DUP from across the Irish Sea were indeed, by implication, targeting the majority in the unionist community. This was commented on in the *Belfast Telegraph*, where it was noted that the British press, had produced graphical as well as written invective:

> To be sure, the cartoonists are no longer as blunt as *Punch* magazine of a century ago wherein we were always depicted with simian features, shillelaghs and bizarre clothing ... Inevitably Ulster Protestant males are depicted as evil Orangemen. In one cartoon, four Orangemen – one of them sitting on a large bag marked 'SWAG' ... In a terraced street the Prime Minister is giving bags of money to a large Orangeman in front a mural which includes a Red Hand of Ulster with a £50 price tag. In a car nearby sits a smiling skinhead in a sweatshirt with tattooed arms. Money floats in the air ...
>
> The portrayals are vicious, and they are not simply of a politician, but of Ulster Protestants in their entirety ... The Belfast bar scene where Guinness is now free forever and the DUP are all lying on the floor in a catatonic state, suggests a lack of knowledge of the average Ulster Protestant, DUP member or supporter.
>
> Perhaps someday the English will mature and we will no longer face such racial abuse.[20]

The writer was Christopher McGimpsey; he added that he did indeed drink Guinness and had tattoos, but that also he held a BA (Hons) from Syracuse University, New York, and a PhD from Edinburgh University. He was also a member of the UUP, a one-time Belfast City councillor and an Alderman there. It could be argued that the notorious *Punch* cartoons he referred to did not depict Irish Protestants as he described, and that rather it was rebellious Catholics who were drawn thus; but his general complaint was not unique. A letter writer to the *Belfast News-Letter*, David McNarry, similarly complained:

People like me, voting DUP for the first time, were joined by 290,000 with no blame and certainly no shame attached in holding values which differ from other parts of the United Kingdom.

Yet I reeled from the headline 'Crackpots' spread across the front of a national tabloid in reference to DUP voters. Since when the ramping of vitriol by other Labour supporting luvvie media has gone overboard in bias and hype.[21]

Such sentiments were echoed by some in the British press. Tim Stanley, a columnist at the *Daily Telegraph*, in an article headlined, 'It Has Become Politically Toxic to Become a Christian', pointed out: 'It was forgotten that Labour's sister party in Northern Ireland [the SDLP] is opposed to abortion too.' He went on, 'when the DUP marched into the limelight, liberals saw the chance to attack their biblical literalism and reaffirm that it is they – not the rednecks in the pews – who define what is and what is not acceptable in 21st-century Britain. I am amazed that after the last few days the DUP are willing to help the mainland out. They have been subjected to every violent paddy stereotype going, including from socialists who have a rosy view of the IRA.'[22]

There was indeed something juvenile, at times hysterical, about the way some in Great Britain reacted to the DUP. The similarity of much of the criticism, especially over abortion and gay rights, also suggested the research was based on superficial internet searches. Of course, abortion and marriage equality did not feature in the May/DUP deal – but that seemed hardly to matter to the critics. Some also did not know, or declined to mention, that May was only doing what others had sought, or contemplated. An exception was the *Daily Telegraph*, which revealed that, after the general election of 2015, which David Cameron had won by only a small majority, these Tories had also discussed a 'confidence and supply' deal with the DUP.[23] It also reported that the Tories and the DUP had been 'hand in glove' in parliament for the previous two years.[24]

Moreover, the *Irish News* later reported that, following the general election of 2010, the Labour Party had contemplated the same dance with the same partner. Newly released emails to Hillary Clinton when she was US secretary of state provided the evidence. In a previously confidential briefing paper, US officials reported on the endeavours of Shaun Woodward, Gordon Brown's outgoing Northern Ireland secretary: 'Shaun, for his part, is working on an economic package for Northern Ireland to win support from the DUP and other parties for Labour – a package to be proposed in the Queen's Speech.'[25]

In the end nothing came of this, but the intent was there – as indeed it had been in 1977–79, when the Labour government headed by James Callaghan made a parliamentary pact with the Official Unionists, who had governed Northern Ireland for fifty years after Ireland's partition with intolerance and discrimination. Callaghan had run out of allies in the House of Commons, so he agreed to increase the number of Northern Ireland MPs in return for Unionist support in parliament. May was only following in Labour's footsteps.

There were other double standards. It was only when the DUP signed its deal with the Conservative Party that the opponents of that party – and even, as we have seen, members of that party itself – became agitated. Yet the DUP had been the lead partner in governing Northern Ireland for over ten years. That power-sharing government had recently collapsed, leaving a potentially serious situation, but this had attracted only minimal interest, and little serious inquiry in the mainstream or indeed the left-wing British media. It was only when the DUP was asked to interfere in the politics of Great Britain that fingers were pointed in England. They could behave as they liked in Ireland, but when they transferred their influence to Great Britain? Shock, horror, indignation! Go home, you crazy Irish!

Just how crazy were they? In November 2013 the DUP produced a 'Mid-Term Report' on its 'Top Seven Priorities', which it had laid down two years earlier. It recalled, 'Supporting more jobs was our first priority', and claimed,

> Despite the global recession we have made Northern Ireland an excellent place for business investment. Northern Ireland is on the road to recovery. At the mid-point of the Assembly term we are now ahead of our target of 20,000 new jobs and have already attracted almost £1 billion of Foreign Direct Investment. Unemployment in Northern Ireland is lower than the UK average and in November the claimant count fell for the ninth consecutive month.

The second priority in 2011 had been 'LOW RATES. The DUP has always been a low tax party.' Again, two years later, the party boasted: 'We have delivered on our pledge not to introduce water charges and to freeze the Regional Rates in real terms. As a result of our policies Northern Ireland has the lowest local taxes in the UK with average household taxes less than 50% of the English average and less than 60% of Scottish and Welsh average.'

The third priority had been 'Tougher [prison] Sentences'; the fourth was 'Fix Education'; the fifth was 'Better Health'; and the sixth was 'Work Together'. Here, the significant claim concerned reconciliation: 'On the issues that affect people's everyday lives [the power-sharing] Executive has worked together well in a number of key areas. We delivered a highly successful International Investment Conference and published the first local community relations strategy "Together: Building a United Community".'

So, there it was: the DUP, at least according to itself, was a modern party concerning itself with the everyday issues common to many political parties throughout the UK and Europe – even attempting, with others, to cross community divides. The seventh and last priority had been, it was true, more traditional. This was 'STRENGTHEN UNIONISM'. Here again there was self-congratulation:

Northern Ireland's place within the United Kingdom has never been more secure. Survey after survey shows support for the Union at an all-time high with more Catholics supporting staying with the UK than opting for a united Ireland. The choice of Northern Ireland to host the UK's G8 Presidency and HM The Queen's public visit to Stormont are further signs of our established place within the UK.

For the DUP, the deal with May was meant to cement this unionism. For some Conservatives and their supporters, it offered better times ahead. A *Daily Telegraph* editorial headlined 'A DUP Deal May Lead to Brexit Consensus', argued: 'The DUP deal may offer a modicum of stability at a time of great political uncertainty.' It dismissed John Major's warning of the consequence for the Irish peace: 'Although Mrs May appeared determined to plough ahead with the same Brexit policy she had before the election, there is growing pressure for a cross-party consensus. The deal with the DUP may be the beginning of one.'[26] That, it was to turn out, was an over-rosy prognosis, but several months after the implementation deal it seemed the *Telegraph* might have been right. Even the *Guardian* mellowed. A page-long profile of Arlene Foster offered reassurances:

Her leadership of the DUP since 2015 has ... cemented its transition into unionism's big tent. It had emerged in the early 1970s from Paisley's Christian Free Presbyterian church which regarded the Pope as anti-Christ and used its influence to lock up playgrounds on Sundays.

But Foster came from the mainstream Anglican Church of Ireland tradition and while the DUP has blocked gay marriage in Northern Ireland, Rev Chris Hudson of Belfast's All Souls church, the spiritual home of LGBT Christians believes: 'Arlene has many gay friends ... she is no homophobe.'[27]

While this may have been a much needed 'Don't Panic' call to fellow journalists, it is worth pointing out that it also displayed an ignorance of Irish matters. First, the locking of swings had been initiated long before the DUP was in power anywhere in Northern Ireland. Second, the Church of Ireland, while part of the Anglican Church, was the epitome of unionism and the Protestant ascendency throughout its history. As the established church in all of Ireland for most of the nineteenth century, it had received the payment of tithes from the country's Catholics, and indeed Presbyterians, thus becoming a grateful recipient of English colonialism and Protestant sectarianism.

Meanwhile, with the ink barely dry on the May/DUP deal, there occurred in Belfast a dispute within the wider unionist community that cast doubt on claims of normality and modernity. This concerned the traditional practice of the building and lighting of bonfires in celebration of the victory of King William III over King James II at the Battle of the Boyne in 1690. For many Protestants in Northern Ireland, these bonfires, then as today, had a significance way beyond the heat they produced. In July 2017, the building of four of them in East Belfast attracted the interest of Belfast City Council, which took out an injunction to stop them being built any higher than they already were. A council spokesperson said this was prompted by concerns for public safety, citing the Grenfell fire, which had occurred in a London residential tower block the previous month and had resulted in seventy-two deaths.[28]

The largest party in Belfast Council was Sinn Féin, but the injunction was, according to Naomi Long of the moderate Alliance Party, an initiative of council staff, and was supported by some unionist councillors, as well as those from Alliance and Sinn Féin.[29] For some, though, this represented a conspiracy. Belfast councillors from the DUP and the Progressive Unionist Party, both of which had roots in Protestant paramilitarism, issued a joint statement saying that what was really afoot was a 'cultural war' started by Sinn Féin. 'We must not let our unity of purpose be disrupted or harmed by actions of those who want to devalue and demean us', they insisted, urging the community 'to ensure our celebrations continue to be bigger, better and more successful than ever before'.[30] It was then reported that '[men] wearing balaclavas and scarves over their faces could be seen using a cherry picker to stack pallets on top of one of the four pyres'. Election posters of Alliance and Sinn Féin were also used as combustible material.[31]

One of the bonfires subjected to injunction was in the car park of Avoniel Leisure Centre in East Belfast. On top of it was placed a banner referring to footballer Scott Sinclair, who played for Glasgow Celtic – the team with roots and support in the Irish Catholic community in Glasgow and Ireland. Scott Sinclair was also a person of colour. The banner read: 'Scott Sinclair loves bananas'.[32]

Four months later, at the November 2017 party conference of the DUP, Arlene Foster displayed the different, more diplomatic and reputable image she had projected since signing her deal with May. She proclaimed: 'It is an honour underpinned with a solemn responsibility to be able to help bring stability to our United Kingdom in these challenging times and we do it seized with an abiding sense of duty to the national interest. We will avail of every opportunity now and in the future to advance the Union as a whole and Northern Ireland's place within it.' Her deputy, Nigel Dodds, boasted extravagantly:

Today, it is the DUP that stands in the heart of government, not in Northern Ireland, but across the United Kingdom. Our position at Westminster has never been stronger, our support in the country has never been greater. Our political opponents have either been defeated or have walked off the pitch altogether … In 1985 we were powerless to stop the Anglo-Irish Agreement, in 1998 we were powerless to block the Belfast Agreement, but today our future lies in our own hands.[33]

As it turned out, neither the grip of the DUP nor of May's government proved secure. One casualty was the commitment in the May/DUP deal over power-sharing. Northern Ireland's power-sharing executive had collapsed in January 2017 over allegations of mismanagement and corruption by the DUP relating to the Renewable Heat Incentive and the role played in it by Foster, who was the minister responsible for this policy before she had become first minister. When it had quit the executive, Sinn Féin had said that Foster should step down as first minister while an inquiry was held. But it then focused on broader issues around the non-implementation of aspects of the GFBA. A major complaint was the failure to legislate on the Irish language. Others included the need for investigations into past deeds of the British and Northern Ireland security forces.

The DUP made counter-accusations against Sinn Féin; both parties were warned to resolve their differences by the June elections or suffer the imposition of formal direct rule, but, for whatever reasons, under the May government the deadlines came and went. Eventually, in February 2019 it seemed a deal had been made. Sinn Féin agreed that Foster should remain first minister and dropped its demands for funding for legacy inquests and inquiries into cold-case killings. In return, the DUP leadership agreed to Irish-language legislation. But there was then a revolt against this concession from within the unionist community. From the Orange Order lodge – LOL 1845 at Queen's University Belfast – came a public statement:

When the pages of history are written there are two ways in which the events of the coming days may be remembered. Either it will be remembered as the occasion unionism stood firm and defeated an Act which paved the way for a republican state in all but name. Or, alternatively, it will see the current crop of DUP politicians, and grassroots members, remembered as the people who failed Ulster in her hour of need; the people who chose political expediency and self-preservation over the needs of the people they were elected to represent.[34]

With this warning in her ears, Foster withdrew her support for the package. There was great significance in the fact that it was a branch of the Orange Order that had led the revolt – an organisation that, as we shall see, has always had an influential role in unionism in the north-east of Ireland. This was the self-same Orange Order that the cartoonists of the British press had featured as described above when unionists, notably Christopher McGimpsey, had insisted their portrayal of its influence was a caricature. The role of the Order in scuppering the February 2019 deal suggested he might have been protesting too much.

That the establishment of power-sharing failed because of the opposition of the Orange Order was barely reported or commented on by Britain's politicians or media. Maybe it was because the issue of Brexit had by then come to dominate everything in Great Britain. It was the referendum to leave the European Union of June 2016 that had led to May becoming prime minister – a vote supported at the time by the DUP; yet it was differences in implementing that very decision that had led the Tory/DUP alliance to begin to founder. Despite promising to support May over Europe, the DUP sabotaged her proposals for exit from the EU. In November 2018, when she was about to sign a deal that included the prospect of a customs border in the Irish Sea – between all of Ireland, including the north, and Great Britain – Foster telephoned the British prime minister and told her that this threatened the very union to which both were meant to be pledged. May dropped the deal and replaced it with the 'backstop' proposal. This would have kept Northern Ireland in some aspects of the European single market, until an alternative arrangement was agreed between the EU and the UK. The proposal also provided for the UK as a whole to share a common customs territory with the EU. It would only come into operation if a permanent solution to the issues it sought to address – including avoiding a new border in Ireland – were not found.

Most parties in Ireland, south and north, supported the backstop, including the Alliance Party, the SDLP and Sinn Féin. The DUP still shouted betrayal, noting especially that, if the backstop and its special arrangements for Northern Ireland did materialise, there was no time limit on them. The DUP joined enough critics within May's own party and Labour – all of whom had their own objections – to ensure that her proposals were defeated three times in the House of Commons. May announced her resignation on 24 May 2019. The DUP had helped bring her down.

Even before May left, the Brexit mire had produced what the *Spectator* called a 'national catastrophe'.[35] The DUP's part in it had seen the *Sun*, which had initially welcomed the DUP/Conservative deal, denouncing them for not whistling May's tune. 'What flimsy allies they proved', the paper complained.[36] The *Guardian* had already arrived at its conclusion: that this was

> an example of English Toryism's chickens coming home to roost … [Mrs May] ignored warnings that a post-election deal with the DUP – a party fundamentally out of step on Brexit opinion with majority opinion in Northern Ireland and the Republic – would come back to haunt her. Not for the first time in British history the Tory party is again faced with a choice between protecting its narrow interests and what Sir Robert Peel, at the height of the Corn Law crisis, called for the need to 'understand this Irish case' … Peel did. Mrs May doesn't.[37]

Let us not linger on the *Guardian*'s rather selective understanding of Irish history, in this instance causing it to elevate the man who in his own time was once called 'Orange Peel' to the status of an Irish saviour, and instead record that the fortunes of the DUP waned. The signs were there even before the June 2017 post-election deal. As the *Guardian* noted, the referendum had seen Northern Ireland voting by 54 to 46 per cent for 'Remain', against the advice and campaigning of the DUP. Then, in March 2017, an election for the Northern Ireland Assembly saw Sinn Féin increase its vote to 27.9 per cent – an increase from 24 per cent the previous year; the DUP, with 28.2 per cent, just edged them out.

The subsequent European election, on May 2019, saw Sinn Féin top the first-preference vote, winning 126,951 votes to the DUP's 124,991. Sinn Féin was pro-Europe, as was the Alliance Party, which was neutral on the British/Irish Union. The latter secured 105,298 votes at the European election, winning a seat from the UUP. Then, in the May 2019 council elections, the DUP's number of seats fell from 130 to 122, Sinn Féin held steady at 105, and the UUP fell from 88 to 75. The biggest gains were achieved by the Alliance Party, which increased its seat count from 32 to 53; the SDLP's number of seats fell from 66 to 59; and the Greens doubled their representation from 4 seats to 8. These indications of public opinion meant that there were those within the DUP who were quite happy that the power-sharing executive was not up and running, and that semi-direct rule by the Conservative government would operate instead. Indeed, as early as January 2018, Ian Paisley, Jr – citing Sinn Féin's demands on the Irish language, abortion rights and marriage equality – said power-sharing was no longer viable, that 'devolution will soon be a distant memory', and that, instead, 'the British government must demonstrate back bone and determination to make direct rule a working reality'.[38]

This was a return to arguments with unionism concerning whether complete integration into the UK or devolution was preferable. Paisley's father had usually favoured devolution; that the son was now moving in a different direction suggested a growing tactical uncertainty within the DUP. The party's decline in popularity, and the whole related Brexit controversy, also drew attention to the issue of the Irish border. Under the GFBA, the British government was obliged to consider a poll on Irish reunification if a majority of voters indicated support for such a course. Just after May fell, an opinion poll in Northern Ireland conducted by the Conservative peer, Lord Ashcroft, showed 46 per cent for reunification and 45 per cent against. Among Protestants, 5 per cent supported reunification, as did 59 per cent of those who described themselves as having 'no religion'.[39]

This poll and the election results, as well as being a consequence of the DUP's loss of support over Brexit, were also a more general indication of the changing demographics of Northern Ireland. For whatever reason, Irish reunification was back on many agendas. On 11 December 2017, the following letter, from Barney Gadd of Belfast, was published on the unionist *Belfast News-Letter* website:

> I have been a unionist since I was in short trousers and yet the view in our pro-Union household, was always 'there'll be a united Ireland eventually'.
>
> However … I thought constitutional change unlikely to happen within my lifetime. Now, I am not so sure. The day will come when the growing nationalist share of the vote overtakes the shrinking unionist vote and I now believe that this change will happen much sooner than any of us ever thought.
>
> Reponses to the Brexit referendum would indicate that 52%–48% seems to be the acceptable majority by which irrevocable and seismic political changes may be implemented and while the united Ireland lobby may not reach that at the moment, when you realise that more nationalist voters are being added to the electorate each year and more unionists are shuffling off this mortal coil (or moving to 'greener' pastures) I cannot but believe that the inevitable will actually happen and moreover, that I will live to see it.
>
> The choice then for unionists (many of whom are represented by the DUP) is fairly stark. What kind of united Ireland do you want?
> …

What must be equally important for unionists is: what will our role be in the governance of an Ireland in which we are a significant minority?

...

Some unionists may not believe in the certainty of a united Ireland at some stage. They are deluded. Failure to prepare for such an event unfortunately may see them isolated and irrelevant.

The rest of us may just take a deep breath and say 'OK, how can we help?'

My Irish passport application is in the post.

Obviously, one letter writer does not represent a community. But the questions posed by Mr Gadd were undoubtedly more relevant at the end of Mrs May's premiership than they had been when she signed her deal. The popularity of the DUP in Northern Ireland and support for the 'precious Union' were declining. To compound the party's difficulties, there was also defeat on the contentious issues of abortion and marriage equality. In July 2019, a private member's bill in the House of Commons legislated for reform on these in the event that the Northern Ireland Assembly did not reconvene by early October. Marriage equality won by 383 to 73 votes, abortion rights by 333 to 93. The DUP of course voted against both, but the scale of their defeat showed just how isolated they were. As Ian Paisley, Jr, said on the issue of marriage equality, 'We are at different ends of the scale in terms of opinion on this matter.' This was also illustrated by a speech by Jim Shannon, the DUP MP for Strangford:

It will come as no surprise that I cannot support these amendments. I say that with respect to all those who have spoken or will speak afterwards. I ask hon. and right hon. Members to respect my point of view, which might be very different from the views of others in this Committee. The reason is twofold. First, I say unequivocally that, in every word I utter, I do not judge how anyone chooses to live their life. I am a man of faith, as others will know. I believe God almighty will judge every one of us in this Committee, and I will have enough trouble explaining what I have done, never mind anybody else.

I believe the Bible is the inspired word of God, and I do not believe it can or should be altered. I believe what it says is true, and many of my constituents feel and think the same ... These people – my constituents, myself and others – are not homophobic and do not hate others. They treasure the word of God ...[40]

It was as if Shannon lived a different world, and certainly subscribed to different value systems than did most British MPs and their constituents. But did that really apply to Shannon's constituents, as he and other DUP MPs claimed? The 2018 *Northern Ireland Life and Times Survey* asked, 'Is it a woman's right to choose whether or not to have an abortion? Thirty-nine per cent said they 'strongly' agreed, and a further 32 per cent said they agree. The figure for Protestants was 33 and 33 per cent. Only 18 per cent either disagreed or strongly disagreed. In the same survey the question on equal marriage rights was: 'Do you think marriages between same-sex couples should or should not be recognised by the law as valid, with the same rights as traditional marriages?' To this, 68 per cent said it should be recognised as valid, including 53 per cent of Protestants. On both of these issues, the DUP's social conservatism was thus at variance with views in Britain, in their own Protestant community, and in Northern Ireland generally.

Northern Ireland, it appeared, was not inhabited by as many 'crackpots' as the electoral success of the DUP implied. What these figures also showed was that, as in relation to Brexit, the DUP's claim to be speaking for 'Ulster' was not the reality. An obvious question arising from this was whether the DUP was similarly unrepresentative of its voters in other aspects of unionism, including allegiance to the union itself. This book offers an enquiry into that question.

But first, let us note some other indications of the expanding gulf between traditional unionism and the British political class. One was expressed shortly after the debates on abortion and marriage equality in the Commons, when David Cameron, May's predecessor as prime minister, published his memoirs, *For the Record*. He recounted his first experience of watching an Orange Order march: 'Their traditions and fervour seemed alien to me and the UK I knew.'[41] Cameron's estrangement was not unique in his party, or among its voters. In October 2018 the Centre for Constitutional Change released findings of in-depth research conducted by the universities of Edinburgh and Cardiff concerning Brexit and Northern Ireland. The results showed that 75 per cent of English Conservatives would support the collapse of the peace process as the price of Brexit.[42]

The period from the emergence of the May/DUP deal to the fall of May shattered the optimism the DUP had shown in the aftermath of the deal about being 'at the heart of government' and 'enhancing the union'. Instead, it raised controversies concerning what the DUP and its electorate stood for politically and culturally, and whether a leading British political party would feel comfortable entering an alliance with the party. More broadly, these two years also shone a critical light on the union between Britain and Northern Ireland itself.

2

The Precious Union

What exactly was the 'precious union' that Theresa May referred to so frequently during the calamitous Brexit debate? This is not as simple a question as it might appear. Was it the union of Great Britain and Northern Ireland as set out in the Good Friday/Belfast Agreement (GFBA), which allowed the people of Northern Ireland to leave the union if they so decided? Was it the union as set out by the Labour government of 1945–51, which gave the Belfast parliament the right to veto any constitutional change in Northern Ireland? Was it the union as defined in the Anglo-Irish Treaty of 1921, which not one Ulster or indeed Irish MP voted for in the House of Commons? Or was it located in the Act of Union, which came into effect in 1801, abolishing Ireland's devolved parliament of the time and replacing it with direct British rule?

Let us assume it was the last, for that was the root from which the others grew. The passing of the Act of Union was a shoddy business achieved in part through bribes, and what turned out to be false promises to a devolved Irish parliament. It had been enacted after that parliament had sought greater independence, and then when the United Irishmen had sought freedom in the 1798 Rising. This was inspired by the American and French revolutions, and had sought a complete break from Britain, and the establishment of an Irish republic.

Both the existing Irish parliament and the founding leadership of the United Irishmen were exclusively Protestant, the former because Catholics were prohibited from membership.

The opposition to the Rising in Ireland was also dominated by Protestants and had been bolstered by members of the Orange Order. The Order was founded in 1795 after the Battle of the Diamond in County Armagh – a conflict between rival groups of lower-class tenants, with Protestants organised in the Peep O'Day Boys and Catholics in the Defenders. Thirty Catholics died in this clash. Afterwards, a group of the victors met to form the Order; Orange as in William of Orange, the Dutch king who had secured Britain for Protestantism at the Battle of the Boyne in 1690. The Order's founding principles were the maintenance of Protestant privilege in Ireland and the Protestant religion in Britain and Ireland.

Although the Orange Order was formed by lower-class Protestants who were mostly descendants of the seventeenth-century Ulster Plantation, as it grew it was soon taken over by the gentry and aristocrats. When the Yeomanry, financed by the British colonial regime in Ireland, was formed in 1795 to take on the United Irishmen, 30,000 Orange Order members joined. It was a counter-revolutionary organisation, fighting against Ireland's 'croppies' – a nickname referring to the cropped hair associated with French revolutionaries. One of the most famous Orange songs explained:

> We'll fight to the last in the honest old cause,
> And guard our freedom religion and laws.
> We'll fight for our country, our king and his crown
> And make all the traitors and croppies lie down.

The use of the Orangemen to help defeat the 1798 Rising is the first example of the alliance between that organisation and the British colonial state. Yet, when it came to the Act of Union, the Grand Lodge of the Orange Order was divided. The initial impulse of the leadership was to abstain, citing a fear that 'expressions of opinion could only lead to disunion'.[1] This plea was not heeded, and, while some lodges supported the proposal, others did not. An example of the latter view was a meeting of thirty-one lodges held at the Maze in County Down in March 1799, which passed a resolution saying: 'We consider a legislative union with Britain as the inevitable ruin of the peace, prosperity and happiness of this kingdom.'[2]

These and other Orangemen opposed the proposal for a variety of reasons. Their priority was the defence of Protestant interests in Ireland. Some were concerned that Ireland under the union might be reduced to a province of England and suffer financially; others noted the promise of the prime minister, William Pitt, that Catholic emancipation in Ireland would follow the Act of Union, and they feared that. That was a promise unfulfilled until 1829. What remains an irony is that the 1801 union, in whose defence Orangemen have marched in their tens of thousands throughout the nineteenth, twentieth and twenty-first centuries, was not originally supported by the Order.

During the first half of the nineteenth century, the relationship between the Orange Order and British governments and the establishment fluctuated. For example, for some time the main spokesperson in the House of Commons in the early battle against Catholic emancipation was Robert Peel, the Tory government's chief secretary for Ireland from 1812 to 1818. The ferocity of his policies and statements caused him to be given his nickname of 'Orange Peel' by the Irish nationalist leader Daniel O'Connell. On 9 May 1817, Peel concluded his speech rejecting full rights for Catholics by recalling the 'Glorious Revolution of 1688' – defence of which was the hallmark of Orangeism. His message was in the same mode, linking the supremacy of Protestantism to the glories of the country: 'Let us recollect, that, under the constitution which we have derived from our ancestors, we have enjoyed more liberty, we have acquired more glory, we possess more character and power, than has hitherto fallen to the lot of any other country on the globe.'

Peel was also a fervent defender of the Union, and he undoubtedly spoke both for the British parliament and state at this time, as well as for many generations to come, when he proclaimed in the House of Commons on 8 May 1843:

> I can state to my noble Friend, that her Majesty's Government in this country and Ireland are fully alive to the evils which arise from the existing agitation in the latter country in respect to the Repeal of the Union; and I further state this, that there is no influence, no power, no authority, which the prerogatives of the Crown and the existing law give to the Government, which shall not be exercised for the purpose of maintaining the Union – the dissolution of which would involve, not merely the repeal of an act of Parliament, but the dismemberment of this great empire.

In 1829, Peel had famously changed his mind on Catholic emancipation, earning for himself the fury of King George IV. That enmity was not surprising: the Duke of York, a member of the royal family, became grandmaster of the Orange Order in 1821, and was succeeded by the Duke of Cumberland, the fifth son of George III. On the other hand, the Order was subject to legislation such as the Unlawful Societies Act (Ireland) 1825 and the Party Processions Act (1832), which led to its temporary dissolution or restriction of activities. These measures were due to the frequency with which Orange marches resulted in public disorder, occurrences of which even sympathetic British governments grew tired.

Thus, in the first half of the nineteenth century the relationship between the Orangemen and the British establishment fluctuated. An Orange songbook published in 1848 reflected this:

> Ye loyalists of Ireland,
> Come rally round the throne
> Thro' weal or woe,
> Prepare to go
> Make England's cause your own.

On the other hand, another song observed:

> And though in days not long since past,
> High men on us did frown,
> And Whig and Tory both combined,
> To pull our colours down.[3]

Such was the uneven relationship between the Order and the British establishment that, on rare occasions, some Orangemen even began to question the union. Thus, in 1870, after legislation again restricted Orange activities, an Omagh lodge called for the repeal of the union, and one Orange leader proclaimed: 'If England does not give us justice I would not care if there was repeal of the Union tomorrow.'[4] But by and large they did care, and when the repeal of the union was posed in practice, the relationship between British politicians, Orangemen and unionists in Ireland, especially in the north-east, entered a new and in many ways definitive era.

The trailblazer in this development was Randolph Churchill, who was very far from either innocence or ignorance concerning the politics of Ireland. He was born in 1849 the son of the seventh Duke of Marlborough, who had served in Disraeli's cabinet and on the Privy Council, and was lord-lieutenant of Ireland from 1876 to 1880. This was at the time largely a ceremonial role, but when he did intervene in Irish politics, he gained a reputation as one of the more enlightened British representatives. Randolph was his private secretary, and he too earned a similar early reputation. In a speech in 1877 he accused successive English governments in Ireland of 'years of tyranny, years of oppression, years of general misgovernment'.[5] More generally, after being first elected to Westminster in 1874, he cultivated a reputation as a Tory rebel attacking what he saw as the old-fashioned views of the Tory front bench, while still a vocal opponent of the Liberals, and especially their more radical policies. He also presented himself as an expert on

Ireland, maintaining his attacks on government coercion and championing Catholic education rights, and even local government reform, while denouncing 'foul Ulster Tories'.[6] All of this secured the attention of Parnell's Irish Parliamentary Party. Following promises from Churchill to oppose coercion, Parnell recommended that the Irish in Britain should vote Conservative in the 1885 general election. At the same time, Churchill was always delivering other messages. He was appointed secretary of state for India to Lord Salisbury's government in June 1885, and behaved in traditionally brutal imperialist fashion, culminating in the invasion and annexation of Burma. Prior to his decisive intervention in Ulster, he had also demonstrated his sympathy for what his biographer R. F. Foster called 'unreconstructed Protestantism' and 'hard-line Protestant unionism'.[7]

But the circumstances that promoted his political pilgrimage to Belfast involved not so much what was happening in Ireland but rather the political situation in Britain. This was indicated when Churchill played what he called 'the Orange Card' – a reference discovered by his son Winston when he was researching his father's life. Randolph employed the phrase in a letter dated 16 February 1886, on the eve of a visit to Belfast. As Randolph said in a letter, 'I decided some time ago that if the G.O.M. went for Home Rule, the Orange card would be the one to play. Please God it may turn out the ace of trumps and not the two.'[8] The 'G.O.M' was William Gladstone, the 'Grand Old Man'. In December 1885, he and the Liberal Party returned to power, winning 335 House of Commons seats in Britain and Ireland. The Irish nationalists, or Irish Parliamentary Party (IPP), led by Charles Parnell, secured eighty-five seats, which happened to be the size of the Liberals' majority over the Tories. Gladstone, through both personal conviction and parliamentary arithmetic, was now resolved to legislate for Irish Home Rule – which if not literally the repeal of the union was a step in that direction.

The fate of his government depended on his success, and this spurred Randolph Churchill to try and bring him down on the issue. He decided to do this by stressing and encouraging the opposition to Home Rule in the north-east of Ireland. Accordingly, he was eager to accept an invitation to speak at a February 1886 meeting in Belfast organised by the recently formed Ulster Loyalist Anti-Repeal Union – an organisation in which the Orange Order was well to the fore. He shared the platform with, among others, Colonel Edward Saunderson, a landowner, evangelical preacher for the Church of Ireland, and Tory MP who had joined the Orange Order in 1882 because it was, he said, 'an organisation capable of dealing with this condition of anarchy and rebellion'.[9] At the rally there was a large banner proclaiming 'England Cannot Desert the Protestants of Ulster'. Churchill showed his solidarity with such sentiments and those of Saunderson when he told his audience, 'I am anxious to ascertain how you propose to face and deal with this crisis, that is, the contingency of Home Rule, and the resources you can reckon upon, and to what length your resistance may go.'[10] When some in the audience reportedly shouted, 'To death', he offered a history lesson and a warning:

You will find things greatly changed since the days of 1848, when the Government served out arms to the Orangemen. Now they will have to find arms for themselves. Statements made to the Imperial Parliament as to the strength and numbers of the Orange Party are received with shouts of derision by Radicals and Parnellites. There is a general misbelief in England as to the amount of resistance the Loyalists can offer to Repeal. The process of resistance to this policy meditated by this combination primarily rests with you – upon you lies this most tremendous responsibility, and to you the issue means everything, honour, religion, and liberty … It means possibly not only all that makes life worth having, but it means life itself.

It is only by demonstrations the most imposing, by energy the most striking, and by actions the most resounding, that you can rivet the attention of the Democracy of England … the time is approaching of test and trial for you, a time to say whether all these symbols and forms practised in your Orange Lodges are real living forms, and not idle or meaningless symbols.

As well as this poorly disguised advocacy of physical resistance to Home Rule, Churchill was not shy of echoing the anti-Catholic sectarianism associated with Orangeism. Referring to the National League that worked with Parnell, he said:

There is something very sad in the connection between the local clergy and the local branches of the National League, because from the peculiar practices of the Church of Rome, the most cherished practices, many of the priests who take part in the National League must know beyond a doubt the inseparable connection that exists between crime and the local branches of the League.

The other words that evening that produced excited cheers in his audience have been quoted often, but they bear repetition:

If the struggle should continue ... then I am of the opinion that the struggle is not likely to remain within the limits of what we are accustomed to look upon as constitutional action ... and if it should turn out that the Parliament of the United Kingdom was so recreant from all its high duties ... as to hand the Loyalists of Ireland to the domination of an Assembly in Dublin which must be to them a foreign and an alien assembly ... in that dark hour there will not be wanting to you those of position and influence in England who would be willing to cast in their lot with you ...

While there was always an element of opportunism in this speech, and in Churchill's decision to go to Belfast and make it, it was also calculated and rehearsed. As Foster notes, it may have contradicted previous statements of Churchill's,[11] but it was consistent with his populist pro-imperialism. Thus, one of the key sentences of his speech was when he accused Gladstone and his Home Rule policy of 'plunging the knife into the heart of the British Empire'. Moreover, in his own and his party's terms, his intervention was a success. He later said he had played an ace and not a two. One historian has commented: 'His appeal to the Calvinist instincts of the Orangemen proved an unqualified success from a party point of view.'[12] His message not only won him support from Ulster unionists but also from parts of Britain where anti-Catholicism remained a strong sentiment and, more poisonously, hostility to the growth of Irish immigration to Britain since the Irish Famine or Great Hunger of 1845–52 was common.[13] As Churchill left Belfast that evening, rioting broke out in the city. He was never to return to Ulster or indeed to Ireland, but his legacy was made. He was soon to write in an open letter that 'Ulster will fight and Ulster will be right' – a slogan that was to be repeated endlessly, woven into Orange banners and painted on Belfast walls for the next hundred years and more. He had, said a motion later tabled but not debated in the House of Commons, threatened civil war.

Oddly, in the House of Commons during the parliamentary debates on Home Rule, Churchill was somewhat reticent on Ulster. In the first reading of the Government of Ireland Bill, which commenced in April 1886, he contributed just one paragraph in a long speech to the province, and that was on the somewhat tangential issue of whether an Irish government could survive financially without the northern counties: 'Some people call it Loyal Ulster; some call it Protestant Ulster; but all will call it prosperous and wealthy Ulster.'[14] The other reference was his insistence that, in his Belfast speech, 'I only expressed my belief in Belfast that, under certain circumstances, civil war would break out in Ireland.' He would expand on this theme during a debate on an Arms Bill on 20 May, when he said that if the Government of Ireland Bill was passed, 'the consequences of such legislation would be civil war', and that, 'those who took part in resisting those consequences ... would be right in resorting to arms'.

During the second reading of Gladstone's bill, Churchill chose not to speak at all. Perhaps he thought his point had already been made – or, as some saw it, that the damage had already been done; but his silence was mocked during the debate by Alfred Illingworth, MP for Bradford West:

> The silence of the noble Lord, the Member for South Paddington (Lord Randolph Churchill) was still more remarkable. How was it that he had got nothing to say in this debate – he, the stormy petrel that was ever on the wing, when there were clouds hovering round about and storms were brewing? The other night he gave the incomprehensible reason, forsooth, that he did not wish to take up the time of the House.[15]

The most substantial challenge to Gladstone on Home Rule came from within his own party, in the shape of Joseph Chamberlain, who was to play his own Orange card with persistence, both in and out of parliament. He began his first speech on the Government of Ireland Bill by saying, 'Since I have been in public affairs, I have called myself, I think not altogether without reason, a Radical. But that title has never prevented me from giving great consideration to Imperial interests.'[16] This was indeed the case throughout his political career.

Chamberlain was born in London in 1836, but then moved to Birmingham, where he became a successful businessman, Liberal politician, and ultimately Lord Mayor. Had the Labour Party been in existence then, he would possibly have been attracted to it; but he joined the Liberals and placed himself firmly on their radical wing. Not unlike others before and since, he combined this reformism at home with an enthusiasm for the British Empire, seeing Great Britain as having a moral and cultural superiority over other nations and races.

This is how he approached Ireland during the Home Rule controversies, mostly distinguishing the Protestant, pro-British settlers in the north from the rest of Ireland's population. He wrote in a book published in 1886 that,

> However indefensible may have been the system of English rule in Ireland between the rebellion of 1641 and the year of 1782, it is none the less true that whatever civilisation or political institutions Ireland possesses it owes to England, and that since 1800 English policy towards Ireland, though often unwise, has been guided by the sincerest desire to promote the good of the country.[17]

As to the Protestants of the north, he asked in a speech in June 1886,

> Who are these Ulstermen? They are our flesh and blood. They come of old English and Scottish stock, and they have done more for the prosperity and welfare of Ireland than any other part of the population ... They have created a vast foreign trade and a prosperous shipping trade, and their only fault is, if fault it be in these days, that they are too demonstrative in their loyalty. They are too devoted to the religion they profess ...[18]

He returned to the religious issue in a speech on Home Rule at Cardiff in July 1886:

> The Protestant Church is founded upon the principle of toleration. It admits – I do not think it always practices – toleration. The Catholic Church, by the necessity of the case, is opposed to toleration and repudiates the doctrine of religious equality ... We are told we are reviving religious bigotry when we talk of these things. We do not; but we are not going to blind ourselves to the facts.[19]

In the same speech he said that Ulster Protestants were the 'most industrious, intelligent and loyal in Ireland'. But, more generally, he concluded: 'You might cut Ireland adrift, and a pretty mess she would make of her own affairs then.'[20] He exuded a similar contempt when he wrote: 'Household suffrage, like trial by jury itself, is essentially an English institution, for which Ireland is totally unfit ... there is no such thing as manly and intelligent public opinion in Ireland.'[21] But more usually, especially as the Home Rule crisis continued, he differentiated between Ulster and the rest of Ireland. In a book produced in 1888 by the 'English Radical Union', no less, he wrote: 'Ireland is and always has been wretchedly poor ... It is useless to enquire whether a more enterprising race would have overcome natural difficulties, although the comparative prosperity and industrial development of the North of Ulster proves that these disadvantages, which it shares with other parts of Ireland, are not insuperable by an energetic people.'[22]

Chamberlain's colonial – and what would today be termed today supremacist or even racist – sentiments are clear in these excerpts; and yet his steadfastness on the Ulster question, like Churchill's, may be questioned. He made it clear during the parliamentary debate that this issue was neither his priority nor the one that determined the direction of his vote: 'I have never been opposed to Home Rule ... I have been willing ... to give to Ireland the largest possible extension of local government consistent with the integrity of the Empire and the supremacy of Parliament.' Then, during the second reading, he declared: 'I have never made the question of Ulster a question that should decide my vote on the second reading.'[23]

On Ulster, Gladstone said he might consider special measures during the committee stage of his bill if it passed at second reading, and he invited those who advocated them to spell out what they should be. Chamberlain declined to do so – suggesting again that, at this juncture, his politics were more rhetorical than practical. Indeed, some historians see his whole positioning on Home Rule as being informed by his personal ambition to replace Gladstone as Liberal leader.[24]

Certainly, when Gladstone challenged him and others to spell out in practice what their opposition to Home Rule and Ulster involved, he was exploiting an obvious weakness, illustrated in the result of the 1885 general election in Ireland. In this, in the nine-county province of Ulster, Home Rule candidates won seventeen out of thirty-three seats – a reflection of the fact that, in terms of population, Catholics and Protestants were approximately equal. Thus, if (nine county)Ulster opted out of Home Rule, or had its own federal parliament, as some were beginning to suggest, it would still face a very uncertain future. This explains why no Irish MPs, including Ulster Unionists, suggested a devolved Ulster parliament. What did they say? One reaction reflected the now familiar supremacism. The Tory MP for Londonderry, Charles Lewis, said of nationalist MPs:

> I am prepared to contend that although these 85 Members may represent a very large number of people in Ireland, they do not represent the majority of the people; still less do they represent the majority of the intelligent people of the country. I will venture to ask how were these Members elected? What amount of priestly tyranny was exercised in bringing them here to Parliament; what amount of National League oppression was brought into operation in order to get the voters to the poll; and what amount of actual ignorance was exhibited by large numbers of voters on the Nationalist side?[25]

What then was his answer? Well, it was not an Ulster separate from the rest of Ireland:

> We do not want any tinkering, or exceptional legislation; we do not want to be invited to form for ourselves a separate Parliament, and desert all the Protestants to be found in the other three Provinces of Ireland. We want to walk with them

43

as members of the same community, as subjects of the same
Queen, and by sending Members to the same Parliament ... We
have no alternative to propose but a United Empire; there is no
other alternative.

These protestations are important: they show that in these years
the political representatives of the Protestants of Ulster had no
wish to form their own parliament – indeed, they rejected this
suggestion strongly and repeatedly. Even today, the Orange
Order's own web history records that, in 1886, 'The whole
influence of the Order was to be on the side of continuing union
with Great Britain on the existing pattern.'[26]

It is also the case that, while there were Irish Tory MPs who
undoubtedly did share the view of Chamberlain that the Ulster
Protestants were somehow morally and intellectually superior
to the Catholic Irish, they did not necessarily subscribe to the
view then being expounded by the leader of the Conservatives,
Lord Salisbury, that the Protestants of Ireland were a different
nation from the rest of Ireland. For example, during the debate
another Tory MP for Ulster, Sir James Corry, who represented
Armagh North, rebutted a suggestion that the Protestants of
Ireland had no Irish patriotism. Hansard records that 'all he
could say, knowing his fellow-countrymen in the North, was
that if patriotism was extinct in their breasts he knew not
where to find it ... He had been always proud to call himself
an Irishman.'[27]

The Government of Ireland Bill was defeated in the Commons
on 8 June, and a general election followed that returned to
power the Conservatives and the 'Liberal Unionists', who
had split from Gladstone. Four days before the vote in the
Commons, Protestant workers in Belfast attacked Catholic
workers in the first of a series of events that, if not a 'civil war',
in Churchill's phrase, were certainly serious civil disturbances.
A commission of inquiry into these events was later appointed,
and its report established the context and immediate cause. It

began by noting, 'The month of June 1886, opened in Belfast upon a condition of great excitement.'

It outlined aspects of the social geography of Belfast, in particular that Queen's Island of the Harland and Wolff shipyard employed 3,500 men, 'the vast majority' of whom were Protestant. These, the commission said, were well paid and normally 'well behaved', but also 'in times of excitement' showed 'a strong sectarian spirit'.

Contrasting this was the nearby Alexander Dock, where Catholics were mainly employed; the commission said that the Protestant minority were not subjected to sectarianism from Catholic workers.[28] It was on Alexandra Dock, on 3 June, that a row broke out between a Protestant and two members of a Catholic family, one of whose members seems to have been the instigator. Only insults were exchanged, but the next day Protestants from Queen's Island intervened. The commission reported that large numbers of these, 'armed with sticks and various missiles', rushed to Alexandra Dock and physically assaulted the Catholic workers there: 'some of them were badly beaten by the Island men'. One of the Catholics was drowned.

Attacks on Belfast Catholics and their property by Protestants spread elsewhere in the city, continuing into early June. When the Royal Irish Constabulary (RIC) intervened against the Protestant mobs, they too were attacked. Indeed, this became the next major feature of the 1886 riots, which lasted fitfully until September. This was partly because the RIC were seen as defenders of the Catholics, but also because of a growing paranoia among the Protestant working class in the city. This was registered by the commission, which attested to 'the extraordinary belief which so largely prevailed amongst Belfast Protestants – a belief that the late [Liberal] Government of the Queen was packing the town of Belfast with Catholic policemen'.

Overall, the commission was in little doubt. The vast majority of violence during the Belfast 1886 riots was committed by the Protestants. As to the Catholic community, the commission quoted a Protestant magistrate lauding its 'endurance and patience' as 'simply wonderful' and put this down to the intervention of the Catholic clergy, who 'laboured persistently in the cause of peace'. It then observed that within the Protestant community there were 'certain persons having great influence in Belfast' who were prone to 'indulge in language, written and spoken, well calculated to maintain excitement at a time when all men of influence should have tried to assuage it'.

The commission's report, while concentrating on the immediate causes of the various riots, made few recommendations – though it did say that paving stones in the future should not be so easily transformed into missiles. Others offered a more strategic analysis, most notably during a debate in the House of Commons on the riots in early September 1886, which took place before the commission had even begun its work. This was a short amendment debate, and its principal speaker was Thomas Sexton, the Irish Parliamentary MP in whose constituency many of the Catholic victims of the riots lived. He recounted that many of these had their houses attacked, and that 600 Catholic men and women had been driven from their workplaces. But of greater significance was his accusation that the 'fiendish passions' of the Protestant mobs had been 'excited by politicians for their own ends'.

He named these politicians as Churchill and Chamberlain. He quoted them at length, especially Churchill's Belfast speech, and asserted: 'The advice of the noble Lord was understood to mean that in the event of the passing of a certain law [Home Rule] the Orangemen were to rise in arms against it.' He then compared Churchill and Chamberlain, whom he also quoted concerning their encouragement of Belfast loyalist resistance to Home Rule: 'The noble Lord [Churchill], if strictly construed, meant that they should rise into arms, after the passing of the law. The right hon. Member for West Birmingham [Chamberlain], on the other hand, advised them to rise before.'[29]

46

The linking of Churchill to the riots was also made outside parliament. For example, following the riots the *Pall Mall Gazette* recalled Churchill's Belfast speech, saying it had been 'an incitement to violence', while the *Scotsman* said that Churchill had stirred up 'the passions of a section of the people who have always been ready enough to listen to violent counsels'.[30]

These and Sexton's accusations have merit. Of course, the actual incidents that instigated the riots had their immediate cause, but the way they developed and the sectarian consciousness that inspired them had been fed and fuelled by Churchill and Chamberlain, admittedly among many others, who between them had assured Protestants of both their superiority over Catholics and their right to wage battles outside what then passed as normal legal restraints. This was not the first time such anti-Catholic riots had taken place in nineteenth-century Belfast – but these riots had their own political context, which established a new template.

This was illustrated by Churchill's Belfast meeting and the coming together there of Ulster loyalists, including the Orange Order, and the Conservative Party in an alliance that was to last for another hundred years. For many – including Churchill and Chamberlain – the purpose of all this went beyond Ulster, which was just a convenient peg on which a more fundamental ideology could rest. The politicians' motivations were often tied up with their own ambition; but also present was a deeper ideology, summed up by two editorials in the ultra-imperialist English magazine *John Bull*, one of which appeared just after Churchill's Belfast speech, the other on the eve of the 1886 election:

That the issue at stake is the continued existence of the Empire is the simple fact. If we cannot hold and govern Ireland how … can we hold and govern India, or maintain our supremacy over our Colonies, or retain our commerce throughout the world?[31]

[Gladstone] will represent that the question at stake is simply whether the Irish shall be allowed to manage their own affairs, and will give no indication that the real issue is whether the kingdom is to be split up into fragments and a hostile power established on the other side of the St. George's Channel. He will plead pathetically that the English people shall trust Ireland, and will expect men to be perfectly oblivious of the fact that the Ireland which they are expected to repose a childlike confidence in ... this Ireland of dynamite, of assassination, and of outrage – the Ireland that is simply a treasonable and rebellious conspiracy ... [is] animated by bitter hostility of race and religion to the English Crown.[32]

Such propaganda had its effect. When the Home Rule issue was put to a vote at the 1886 general election, Gladstone and Irish Home Rule lost. The Scottish, the Welsh, and of course the Irish voted for Home Rule parties; the English against. Sir Randolph Churchill's playing of the Orange card had worked.

The now familiar arguments were to be repeated in 1893, when another Gladstone-led government again attempted to pass Home Rule. Then, too, there were violent outbursts on the streets among Ulster loyalists. On this occasion the House of Commons did pass Gladstone's bill, but it was rejected by the House of Lords. But during the run-up to this election, unionism in Ulster again reiterated and further clarified its brand – notably at the Ulster Unionist Convention of 17 June 1892. The *Belfast News-Letter*, a unionist newspaper, previewed this event, explaining: 'The Protestants of Ulster all detest and dread the threatened revolution' of Home Rule. The economic argument was advanced: 'Prosperity in Ulster is an undeniable fact ... under the equal and judicious government of the Imperial parliament there is no reason why this should not continue.' Religious fear and paranoia were also expressed: 'It is a sober statement of an admitted fact to say the present Nationalist Ireland is controlled by the Roman Catholic priesthood. This majority in an Irish parliament [under Home Rule] would govern Ulster.'[33]

The first two objects of the Convention were 'to express the devoted loyalty of Ulster Unionists to the Constitution and the King', and 'to resolve to retain unchanged our present position as an integral portion of the United Kingdom'.[34] In opening the Convention, the Duke of Abercorn highlighted the notion of Ulster Protestant exceptionalism. He told his audience: 'Before Ulster was planted by Scotch and English settlers it was the poorest and most turbulent part of Ireland ... Your energy has given richness and fertility to a sterile soil ... Your ports send vessels laden with manufactures to every land. These are things that can only be achieved by a strong and self-reliant people.'

He went on to speak of the prospect of Ulster unionism's cause being supported in England, but also made clear the Irish nationality of his audience: 'I hope that England will not desert Irishmen who have done so much to increase, who have done nothing to impair, the greatness and glory of the Empire. But above all you have reliance on yourselves.' He did add that Almighty was also on their side: 'Look to God to guard his own. He is watching all your movements. His right arm is around you thrown.'[35]

The final speaker at the rally was the Rev. Dr Kane, the grand-master of the Belfast Orange Order, whose organisation had played a key part in organising the Convention. He spelled out the meaning of its second aim, relating to Ulster as an integral part of the UK:

> To propose that there should be two parliaments in the United Kingdom – one in London and one in Dublin – is certainly in our opinion a foolish and treasonable proposal ... but it is no more foolish and treasonable than to propose that there should be three – one in London, one in Dublin, one in Belfast. Our position is that in one Kingdom there should only be one Parliament.[36]

There was thus a cultivation of Ulster exceptionalism during these crucial Home Rule years: by the Orange Order, by English and Northern Irish unionists, and on the streets and workplaces by the violence of Belfast Protestants. These traditions were to be passed on – but there were also, even within this cultivation, expressions of Irishness, and so too an insistence that the north-eastern unionists did not want their own parliament: 'a treasonable proposal'. Twenty years later, a different variety of treason was being promoted by the same forces that coalesced from 1886 to 1893 – and different Orange cards were being played.

North of Ireland voting, 1918 UK General Election

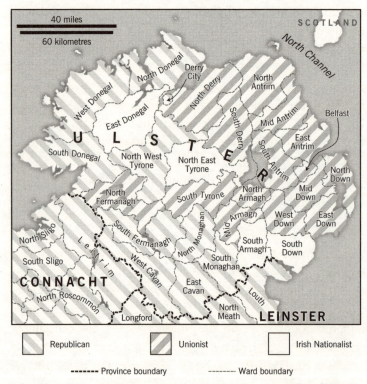

The votes in the historic province of Ulster gave unionists only a marginal majority. "Northern Ireland" was created to give them a working majority of between 65 and 70 per cent.

3

The Appearance of Northern Ireland

The semi-state of Northern Ireland was born of rebellion. It was a rebellion staged by unionists, whose actions weakened the union; and by 'loyalists', whose actions were disloyal to the British government and parliament. It was supported by a Conservative Party that openly backed the rebellion; it involved private armies, gun-running and its leader admitted it was committing treason. The consequences were a six-county Northern Ireland that gave practical effect to the supremacist ideology that had motivated its creation. What follows seeks to explain how and why all of this occurred.

These exceptional times began when the third Irish Home Rule Bill was launched by the Liberal government at Westminster on 11 April 1912. The bill itself was cautious and unambitious. It 'offered only a narrow measure of autonomy', with a 'moderate character', whose actual terms were 'comparatively modest'.[1] Ireland was to have its own parliament and senate, but Westminster would retain ultimate responsibility over relations with the Crown, defence, foreign policy, customs, taxation and, for an initial period, the police. The new Irish parliament was prohibited from favouring any religion, and Ireland would continue to send MPs to the UK parliament, although fewer than before. This was such a restricted vision of Home Rule that 'It required all the persuasive powers of the [Irish] Home Rule Leader, John Redmond, to allay the chagrin of his followers', who had hoped for so much more.[2]

The Liberals' move to legislate for any form of Irish Home Rule, like the Tories' opposition in the 1880s, was influenced by British politics. A substantial majority of the Irish had voted for parties of self-government throughout the nearly twenty years since Gladstone's 1893 second Home Rule Bill, and indeed before then. Even in north-east Ireland, the 1910 religious headcount, which usually reflected political allegiances, showed Protestants (unionists) in the majority in only four of Ulster's nine counties: Antrim, Down, Armagh and (London)Derry – and in the last Catholics were in a majority in Derry City. The Liberals had remained formally committed to Irish Home Rule since Gladstone, and it was part of their programme for the two elections in 1910. They faced the opposition of the House of Lords, but the Parliament Act of 1911 ensured that the Lords could no longer kill a bill that had passed the Commons, only delay it for two years. This legislation had been introduced after the Lords had rejected the Liberals' progressive budget of 1909. Both the budget and the reform of the Lords had been supported by the Irish nationalists in the Commons, the Irish Parliamentary Party (IPP), on whose support the Liberals were dependent to govern. The Home Rule legislation was payback.

For the Conservatives, both the budget and Lords reform were contrary to their own policies and the interests and privileges of the upper class in which they were embedded. Moreover, they were divided by the major issue of tariff reform and needed a unifying cause. After the Lords defeat, as the Irish historian J. C. Beckett put it, 'they would go to almost any lengths for the sake of revenge. Like Lord Randolph Churchill in 1886, they believed that "the Orange card was the one to play".'[3]

By now Irish unionism was becoming more identified with north-east Ireland, outside of which there were two unionist MPs. In 1886 the Ulster Loyal Anti-Repeal Union was formed to press for the special interests of the province. Then, in 1892, the Ulster Unionist Convention League was established. This initiated a process culminating in 1905 with the formation of the Ulster Unionist Council (UUC) – an attempt to bring together all unionists in nine-county Ulster. From the start, the Orange Order was given a quarter of the council seats. Sir Edward Carson, then MP for Trinity College Dublin, who hitherto had little knowledge of Ulster, became leader of the Irish Unionist Party at Westminster in February 1910. On 25 September 1911, 400 delegates of the UUC unanimously agreed that, in the event of Home Rule, they would establish their own government and defend it, if necessary, with an armed force of volunteers. The provisional government, limited to Ulster, was indeed convened, and its first meeting took place in July 1914.

The volunteers were organised by the Ulster Clubs, revived from the previous century. In January 1913 the UUC had announced that these clubs, which by now numbered over 300, would unite with Orange Order lodges and others into a single Ulster Volunteer Force (UVF). By April 1914 the UVF had a membership of 90,000, organised in a military fashion into battalions and regiments, that marched and drilled openly. The organisation bought 20,000 rifles and ammunition in Germany, and in March sailed first to Larne in the north-east of Ireland, where they landed on 24 April, and then proceeded to other north-eastern ports of Belfast, Bangor and Donaghadee.

The intention of the arms-running, the establishment of the provisional government and the military preparations had been spelled out on 28 September 1912, when, in a grand piece of theatre, Carson led the signing of the 'Ulster Solemn League and Covenant' at Belfast's City Hall. In this, the signatories complained that Home Rule 'would be disastrous to the material well-being of Ulster, as well as to the whole of Ireland, subversive of our civil and religious freedom, destructive of our citizenship and perilous to the unity of the Empire'. They promised to use 'all means which may be found necessary to defeat the present conspiracy to set up a Home Rule Parliament in Ireland. And in the event of such a parliament being forced upon us, we further solemnly and mutually pledge ourselves to refuse to recognise its authority.'

Thus, while it was labelled an 'Ulster' cause, and while Ulster was specifically mentioned in the text, the stated intention was to oppose Home Rule for all of Ireland. The Covenant was signed by 237,368 men, and its version for women by 224,046. This was out of a nine-county Ulster population of 1,581,696. The nine counties were the six counties of what later became Northern Ireland – Antrim, Armagh, Down, (London)Derry, Fermanagh and Tyrone – plus the three other counties of historic Ulster – Monaghan, Cavan and Donegal. The six counties had a population of 1,250,531, so while the number of signatures on the Ulster Covenant was impressive, it was a majority of neither six- nor nine-county Ulster. Carson's mandate was therefore limited.

Carson was born in Dublin in 1854 into a Scots Presbyterian family on his father's side and a Galway Anglo-Irish Protestant ascendency family on his mother's. He first gained attention as a crown prosecutor when he won convictions against campaigners and activists of the Irish tenants' rights movement in the late 1880s. This earned him the post of solicitor general in Ireland, and then the same position in England. He was elected to the British parliament in 1892 as a Liberal Unionist – an identity he lost when the party merged with the Conservative Party in 1912. In parliament he adopted the Tory cause, voting against the disestablishment of the Anglican church in Scotland and Wales in 1893, the reduction of miners' hours in 1894, trade union rights in 1900, and various attempts to democratise electoral law in 1893, 1894, 1906 and 1913. In 1895 he won attention for his cross-examination of Oscar Wilde, a one-time college friend, who was suing Lord Queensbury for libel after the latter had accused Wilde of being a 'sodomite'. In the witness box, Carson extracted damaging admissions from Wilde, which eventually led to his being tried and jailed for homosexuality.

Two quotations can be offered as a summation of Carson's general politics. In 1912, when Poor Law reform was being debated, he declared that 'the abled-bodied paupers if well conducted might be placed in labour colonies, if ill-conducted in detention centres'. In 1933, at the Conservative Party conference, when advocating a hard line in India he argued: 'Our friends first, our friends second and our friends third.'[4]

His political lieutenant in Ulster in these years was James Craig, the son of a Belfast whiskey distiller millionaire and a veteran of the Second Boer War. He left the army as a captain, returned to his large mansion and the Craigavon estate on the shore of Belfast Lough, and was elected as an Ulster Unionist MP for East Down in 1906. That election saw the return of the Liberal Party to government for the first time in a decade.

Although the new administration announced no intentions on Irish Home Rule, Craig was quick to warn them against doing so. In February 1907, in a precursory intervention during a debate in the House of Lords, he said that if proposals on Home Rule were forthcoming, 'I would only say that the whole power of the Unionist Party and the Orange organisation would be used to defeat the policy of the Government'.[5] In another early intervention in the Commons, in March 1907, he displayed his Orange credentials in a less threatening question to the prime minister, Henry Campbell-Bannerman. He implored: 'I beg to ask the Prime Minister whether he will recommend that the statue of William III, Prince of Orange, about to be presented by the German Emperor, be erected in Belfast, Lisburn, or Londonderry, where the memory of that king's services in the cause of civil and religious liberty in Ireland is treasured.' The Liberal premier was having none of it: 'My right hon. friend the First Commissioner of Works has decided upon a site which is to be in front of Kensington Palace – in the neighbourhood of the Orangery.'[6]

In parliament Craig showed his interest in matters outside his local concerns. In April 1907 he objected when a government spokesperson announced that 506,368 'aliens' had arrived in the UK in 1906. Craig was perturbed: 'Will the Government take steps to prevent the landing of these aliens to this enormous extent, and thus enable the British workman to find employment in his own country?'[7] As for Craig's 'own country', in these early years in the Commons the subject he returned to almost obsessively was the alleged misdemeanours of some slightly rebellious fellow citizens.

Ireland at that time was on its way to resolving at least the most contentious of the issues on land ownership and the rights of tenant farmers. The Tories' Wyndham Land Act of 1903 had offered landlords a 12 per cent bonus if they sold their estates and provided loans for tenants to purchase. However, tensions between landlords and their tenants and the poor rural communities remained, and between 1906 and 1909 there occurred in parts of central and southern Ireland what has been dubbed the 'Ranch War'. On the one side were large landowners, who had taken to grazing their livestock on their land, and in some cases their wealthier tenants; on the other side were members of the rural working class who had once worked or aspired to farm the land. Weapons in this 'war' included intimidation, boycott and cattle-driving – that is, driving the owners' cattle off the land.

This was not as intense or widespread as the land wars of the last two decades of the nineteenth century, but in the House of Commons James Craig repeatedly rushed to the defence of the landlords, drawing attention to the disobedience of the rural poor. For example, on 22 April 1907 he alleged that 'threatening notices' had been posted in two towns in County Clare and called for police action. For example, from March to July 1907 he raised incidents of cattle-driving, boycotting or intimidation in County Clare (22 April), Roscommon (23 June) and Killarney (31 July). In the spring of 1908, the same was reported in Mayo and Longford (3 March), Queen's County (11 March), Westmeath (13 May) and Galway (17 May). The rest of the year saw similar incidents in Mayo (22 July), Galway (20 October), Mayo again (26 November) and East Kerry (18 December).[8] Craig was to continue to raise cattle-driving and similar issues in parliament for the next two years.

What is significant about this record, which is often ignored by historians, is Craig's personal identification with landlords throughout Ireland, and his vendetta against those who mostly constituted the rural poor. Ulster unionism has often been caricatured as a revolt of the industrial interests in north-east Ireland. What Craig's diligence in raising what were minor incidents of rural civil disobedience outside Ulster suggests is that he was also an enthusiastic defender of the landed class throughout Ireland. Also, his parliamentary record in this regard does rather obviously invite accusations of hypocrisy. Here was someone who condemned cattle-driving, the occasional bit of intimidation and minor law-breaking; someone who demanded strong police action against any suspected culprit – and yet someone who, a couple of years later, was openly organising a private army and threatening a coup in part of what was then the King's realm. There is also the following question, which he asked in the House of Commons on 29 October 1908:

> I beg to ask the Prime Minister whether he is aware that it is necessary to be licensed in order to carry arms in England and Scotland, but no such restriction exists in Ireland since the dropping by the Government of the Peace Preservation Act; and whether, in view of the increase of outrages in Ireland in which firearms, including revolvers, are used, the Government will take immediate steps to restrict the free sale of such arms to irresponsible persons in Ireland.

Craig had his facts wrong here. But he did not ask this question again in the House of Commons after the unionists brought the German guns to Ulster. No doubt he did not consider the UVF recruits 'irresponsible persons', even if they did threaten armed revolt against an elected parliament. Carson and Craig made such intentions clear, both in public and private. In a private letter from Carson to Craig of July 1911, Sir Edward wrote, 'I am not for a game of bluff, and unless men are prepared to make great sacrifices which they clearly understand the talk of resistance is no use.'[9]

At a rally at Craigavon on 23 September 1911, Carson promised: 'We will yet defeat the most nefarious conspiracy that has ever been hatched against a free people ... We must be prepared ... the morning home rule is passed, ourselves to become responsible for the government of the Protestant province of Ulster.'[10] At a demonstration at Blenheim, near Oxford, on 27 July 1912 Carson declared:

> I can imagine no lengths of resistance to which Ulster will go in which I will not be ready to support them ... We shall shortly challenge the government to interfere with us ... They may tell us if they like that that is treason; it is not for men who have such stakes as we have at issue to worry about the cost. We are prepared to take the consequences.[11]

In all of this they were encouraged by the Conservative and Unionist Party. Andrew Bonar Law became leader of the Tories on 13 November 1911. He had a personal affinity with the more fundamentalist wing of Ulster Protestantism, having been born into a Scottish/Canadian family whose patriarch was a Presbyterian minister who had once lived in Ulster. He moved to Glasgow in his early youth to live with the merchant banking family of his deceased mother. He had a successful business career before being elected as Conservative MP for a Glasgow seat in 1900. When he secured the leadership of the Conservative Party, he was MP for Bootle.

Among other contenders for the Tory leadership at the time was Carson, although he did not in the end stand in the leadership contest, as well as Walter Long, a former leader of the Ulster Unionists. Another defeated contender was Austen Chamberlain, son of Joseph, who had inherited his father's unionist and Protestant supremacist views. Support for Ulster was thus a way of uniting the various components of the Conservative leadership. Accordingly, on 26 January 1912, at a meeting in London's Albert Hall, Bonar Law said, referring to Ireland, 'We who represent the Unionist Party in England and Scotland have supported and we mean to support to the end the loyal minority.' What that support meant was spelled out by Carson at the same meeting: 'I am here to tell solemnly and honestly that we mean to see this matter through. The cost may be great, the suffering may be terrible.'[12]

Then, at a huge meeting at Belfast's Balmoral showgrounds in April 1912, Bonar Law evoked both history, citing Derry's siege of 1689, and the Parliament Act restricting the power of the House of Lords:

> Once again you hold the pass for the Empire. You are a besieged city ... The timid have left you; your Lundys [traitors] have betrayed you; but you have closed your gates. The Government have erected their Parliament Acts as a boom against you to shut you off from the help of the British people. You will burst that boom ... and you will save the Empire by your example.[13]

Following this, at the meeting at Blenheim Place referred to earlier, the Tory leader declared: 'If any attempt were made to deprive these men of their birth right – as part of a corrupt parliamentary bargain – they would be justified in resisting such an attempt by force ... I can imagine no length of resistance to which Ulster can go which I would not be prepared to support.'[14] As historian Alan Parkinson, who cannot be described as being a pro-nationalist, has commented, 'To describe Bonar Law's choice of words as intemperate and ill-advised is an understatement ... to use the language of sedition, especially in an age of political conformity, was truly remarkable.'[15]

It was not just the individual speeches or rhetoric that informed the unionist cause. Ever since the election of a Liberal government in 1906, Ulster's loyalists and their Conservative allies had been organising. A major vehicle was the Union Defence League (UDL), which had been founded in London by Sir Walter Long, Carson's predecessor as leader of the Irish unionists at Westminster and a former Conservative chief secretary for Ireland. From 1907 onwards, the UDL produced *Irish Facts* as a propaganda tool. Its first edition, in April that year, reproduced the by-now familiar supremacist messages:

> The truth is that no Irishman, except agitators, would dream of stating that 'Ireland' wants Home Rule. They know that although some three million people of Ireland have been persuaded ... to vote for Home Rule there remain one and a half million of Loyalists who are inalterably opposed to it. They know that the Loyalist minority contains the brains and the grit and the money which has done more to keep Ireland's head above water than anything else except the generosities of the British taxpayer ... they know that if the Loyalists of Ireland were to leave their country there is neither the character nor capital nor energy nor education enough among the remaining three million to keep the country from national bankruptcy.
>
> ...
>
> There is little education in Ireland, and the lack of education makes the learning useless. Emotion dominates intellect instead of being governed by it. For instance, they are taught to read history but not to understand it, they scream learnedly about grievance, but seldom suggest an instructive remedy.
>
> ...
>
> The payment of rent ... is not part of the social morality preached by the instructors of this unhappy people, it is regarded rather as an extortionate tribute. From the dissemination of this pernicious doctrine, which is subversive of the fundamental

principles of civilisation, springs the crimes and outrage and misery associated with the history of land agitation.

...

> Observe the average cottager, as he sprawls lazily before his cabin door on a fine summer afternoon, smoking his pipe; look at the way he keeps his patch or his bit of garden. It is usually a wilderness of weeds.[16]

Five years later, the message from *Irish Facts* was the same:

> It may at once be admitted that there is a majority in Ireland in favour of Home Rule. But the demand for Home Rule must be measured by the quality of those who make it, as well as by the quantity. Measured by such a standard a majority diminishes in importance. The north-eastern counties, which contain almost all that makes for industrial progress, are against Home Rule.[17]

The Tory/Ulster unionist alliance attracted significant support. Most spectacular was backing from the officer class of the British army, highlighted in March 1914 when fifty-eight out of sixty officers at the Curragh barracks declared they would resign their commission rather than move against any resistance in Ulster to Irish Home Rule. The leader of what in effect became a mutiny was Hugh Gough, who in October 1913 had written to the king's private secretary forecasting that between 40 and 60 per cent of British army officers would refuse to fight against Ulster unionists.[18] The government was reluctant to move against the mutineers, and the affair eventually petered out; but its aftermath was a belief in unionist circles that, in the event that the crisis escalated, the British government would be unlikely to move against them.

Among those supporting the Curragh officers were the *Daily Mail*, *The Times*, the *Pall Mall Gazette* and the *Moring Post*. More general support for 'Ulster' came from the *Daily Express*, the *Observer* and the *Spectator*. Parkinson has further listed those *Friends in High Places* who supported the Tory/Unionist resistance to Home Rule. These included cultural celebrities, including Edward Elgar and Rudyard Kipling; wealthy figures such as William Waldorf Astor, Lord Rothschild and the Duke of Bedford; and eccentric aristocrats – most notably Lord Willoughby de Broke, who was later to be famously described by George Dangerfield as 'a genial and sporting young peer, whose face bore a pleasing resemblance to the horse'.[19]

More seriously, there is no doubt that the various campaigns in Britain to support Ulster resistance attracted impressive mass support. A total of more than 5,000 meetings were held by Ulster unionists and Conservatives between September 1911 and July 1914.[20] The largest was on 4 April 1914, when a huge crowd – estimated at between 100,000 and 500,000 – gathered at Hyde Park in a meeting called by the British League for the Support of Ulster, the Union Defence League and the Primrose League. When Carson toured the UK in the winter of 1913–14, his meetings were generally packed and his audiences enthusiastic.

In March 1914 a British version of the Ulster Covenant was launched. It was supported by a new magazine, the *Covenanter*, whose motto was: 'Put Your Trust in God But Keep Your Powder Dry'. The Union Defence League claimed it attracted 2 million signatures.[21] A recent academic study of support in Britain for the Ulster cause has concluded that, 'For no other reason than their opposition to Home Rule, if a general election had been called in 1914 the Unionists [Conservative Party] would have won.' The same writer argued that the Unionists' campaign in Britain had 'demolished … the belief that the British public could stomach Home Rule for Ireland'.[22] The evidence offered for this includes reports of local public opinion, the success of public campaigning, and by-election results showing popular support for the Tories. The sentiments suggested for this support, especially from the middle and working classes, include an identification with the Empire, the contemporary and traditional strength of Protestantism, and antipathy towards the Catholic Irish of both Ireland and in Britain.

The extent and intensity of these sentiments is easy to over-state; but it is also true that the tendency of some historians, especially those on the left, has been to ignore or underplay them. The British labour movement, as this author has recorded, were 'hesitant comrades' when it came to expressing support for Irish self-determination from 1916 to 1921, and there is no evidence to suggest this did not apply to the years 1912–14.[23] Certainly, Carson and his allies were denounced in the labour press and from labour platforms, but there was nothing like the level of public campaigning from the left on behalf of the Irish majority comparable to what unionists conducted for 'Ulster'. The left wing of the British labour movement in 1913 did have a well-supported campaign in solidarity with the Irish trade unionists involved in the Dublin lockout, led by James Larkin and James Connolly; but trade-union struggles were more easy to identify with than the national struggle – especially as there remained some English and Scottish cities and towns where anti-Irish feeling persisted, and green-versus-orange tensions persisted.

The mass campaigning, threats of civil war, supremacist propaganda and support in Britain for Ulster's loyalists pushed the Liberal government, and indeed the IPP, into concessions. What would have happened had world war not broken out will never be known; what did happen was that, on the eve of war, a third Home Rule Bill was passed but its operation suspended through the added proviso that six counties of Ireland would temporarily have the right to opt out. The principle thereby established was cemented when Ireland and Britain returned to consider an Irish settlement after the war.

By then the 1916 Easter Rising and the events it set in train had changed Ireland's political landscape. The results of the 1918 British general election in Ireland had illustrated this, with the eclipse of the moderate IPP, and Sinn Féin sweeping the board – winning 70 per cent of the Irish vote. The election results also saw the return of a Conservative-dominated coalition government, though it was headed by the Liberal Party's David Lloyd George. This government defied the Irish popular vote, went to war with the self-proclaimed Irish Republic, and eventually negotiated the Anglo-Irish Treaty.

Among other things, this made partition permanent, establishing an Ulster Home Rule parliament that was subservient to Westminster. The government promised a border commission, which it hinted might reduce the six-county territory, and the establishment of an all-Ireland council. The border commission was delayed, but when it did finally produce a report, it recommended a marginal expansion beyond the six counties. It then disappeared into oblivion. The Council of Ireland never met.

Thus, contrary to the Ulster Covenant, Ulster did get Home Rule, but the Treaty satisfied the unionists' deepest wishes to be excluded from Irish democracy. As to what 'Ulster' constituted – that is, what it had previously been understood to constitute, namely the six north-eastern counties plus Cavan, Donegal and Monaghan – the 1911 census had shown a 56 per cent Protestant population. That was too close to call for unionists, so they opted for a six-county statelet in which Protestants constituted 65.5 per cent of the population. Carson complained bitterly that, by agreeing the Treaty, the government had sold out all-Ireland unionism. In this he had a point, but the strength of Irish nationalism meant it could no longer be denied the settlement offered, even if that did not represent unconditional self-determination.

Before that came to fruition, Carson had one last Orange card to play. This was in July 1920, when Ireland was engulfed in the War of Independence. Although Sinn Féin had emerged as the political representative of the Irish majority, among Catholics in Belfast the old IPP was still strong. But there was also a challenge to 'Carsonism' from the Belfast Labour Party (BLP), a pro–Home Rule organisation organised by the Independent

Labour Party, the Belfast Trades Council and trade unions. In the Belfast municipal elections, the BLP won twelve seats.

Carson then directed attention to the more traditional enemy. At the annual 12 July Orange Order mass demonstration in Finaghy, on the outskirts of Belfast, and with partition still not secured, Carson turned his now familiar ire on Sinn Féin, saying, 'We in Ulster will not tolerate Sinn Féin', and adding that if government did not act against that party, 'We will take matters into our own hands. We will reorganise our own defence ... and these are not mere words. I hate words without action.'[24]

Tensions were further increased on 17 July by the Irish Republican Army (IRA) shooting of Lt Col G. B. F. Smyth of the RIC, a native of Banbridge in Ulster. Then, on 21 July 1920, a mass meeting in a Belfast shipyard was called by the Belfast Protestant Association, a sectarian and anti-socialist organisation. There, a resolution was passed saying that all workers at the yard had to sign an anti–Sinn Féin declaration – which was in effect an attempt to implement Carson's threats. The most recent research into these events has shown that the Unionist Labour Association, established by Carson to see off the threat of the BLP, played an active role in the expulsions of Catholics from the various workplaces that followed Carson's words.[25]

This mob rule, which spread from the shipyards to other industries, saw the expulsion from the workplaces of approximately 8,000 Catholics and 1,000 'rotton prods' – that is, Protestant workers who were socialist and trade-union activists. Most of the Catholic victims were never to return to their workplaces. Protestant mobs also attacked Catholic homes, shops, public houses, chapels, a monastery and a convent. These riots led to others, and later to armed intervention by the IRA and the British army, as well as attacks on Catholic areas by the exclusively Protestant B Specials, once they were formed by the new unionist government of Northern Ireland in October 1920.

During the violence from 1920 to 1922, 498 people died. A recent breakdown of these figures by Kieran Glennon has concluded that they included 254 Catholic civilians, 181 Protestant civilians, twenty police, four British military personnel, thirteen B Specials, twenty-three members of the IRA and a further six from Na Fianna, a republican youth organisation. Glennon concludes that Catholics suffered disproportionally, and that 'the overwhelming majority of the political violence in Belfast in the pogrom period was perpetrated against Catholics and nationalists'.[26] One consequence of the 1920 expulsions of Catholics from the shipyards and elsewhere, and their permanence, was that the Belfast working class became further divided, the Protestant part consolidating its hold on most of the best jobs in industrial Belfast. Protestants had a stake in this twentieth-century version of ascendency, which they had enjoyed for nearly a hundred years.

The Ulster rebellion is central in understanding the politics of Ireland for the rest of the twentieth century. First, the partnership between the Conservatives and Ulster unionism, formally established in 1886, was consolidated and hardened into an alliance prepared to use force to take on both parliamentary majorities in the UK and popular democracy in Ireland. Second, the establishment of the UVF was followed in the rest of Ireland by the establishment of the National Volunteers, determined to advance the cause of all-Ireland Home Rule. Out of that context emerged the Irish Volunteers and the Irish Republican Army. Third, the more radical wing of Irish nationalism drew lessons on the use of force to establish the possibility of partition and determined to count this as part of its own armed struggle – hence the 1916 Easter Rising and, following the refusal of the British state to accept the 1918 election results, the War of Independence.

There have been those historians who insist the Rising and the War of Independence increased Ulster intransigence, leading to partition. But partition had been agreed in 1914, albeit on a temporary basis, but it was predicted by many at the time that it would stay – notably the socialist and leader of 1916

James Connolly. This partition had been informed both in Ulster and Britain by a supremacist unionism which argued that Protestants in north-east Ireland were superior to the native Irish, and therefore warranted protection by Britain – either by remaining fully integrated in the UK or through the establishment of a subservient state defended by Britain.

At the end of it all, Ulster unionism had its own mini-state, even though this contradicted what most of its leaders had stood for since the 1880s. Many had said they were Irish. Most also said they did not want an Ulster parliament. They had, for the most part, believed their special interest would be most secure through continued integration in the British state. A popular slogan in the Carson years was 'Ulster Will Not Have Home Rule'. In the end, however, 'Ulster' did have it, or at least a version of it, whether it liked it or not.

One of the reasons the Ulster unionists were persuaded to accept this was that they believed, as Beckett said, that 'they need no longer fear, as they feared in the past, that their interests would be sacrificed by a British government seeking to conciliate Irish nationalist opinion'.[27] As it turned out, that fear would be reborn half a century later.

What should be asked is why most of the Protestant working class supported a movement led by upper-class and anti–trade union Carson and the millionaire Craig, and strongly supported by the most privileged in England. Debate over this identification still produces much heat, just as it did in these crucial years – especially within sections of the Irish and British working-class movements. One interpretation was that this allegiance of the Protestant working class was superficial and would soon pass. For example, on 13 August 1913 *Labour Leader*, the newspaper of the British-based Independent Labour Party (ILP) insisted:

Labour propaganda is gripping Belfast. It is to 'Black North' that I look for the economic driving force in the new [Home

Rule] Parliament and it is to the 'Black North' that Labour
must largely look for its first recruits. Once these hard-headed
Scots-Irish find out they have been cajoled by the Carsons and
Craigs – fooled by the Ulster landlords and sweaters of the
past two generations – taught that the Catholic was the enemy
instead of the profit-monger – once they find this out, and they
are finding this out under the Labour stimulus, then it will be a
case of curtains for Carson and Craig.

Despite the occasional success of the BLP that followed, the
optimism evident here is misplaced – though, in fairness, the
prediction does assume an all-Ireland parliament. Even at the
time, more sober and rational views were being expressed.
One neglected example is an article in the *New Statesman* – a
publication that during this period and for the next several
years was exceptional among the British progressive press in
covering Ireland seriously.[28]

This article, by C. H. Walsh, appeared in a July 1913 'Irish
Supplement', and discussed 'industrial Ulster'. It began by
arguing that this was divided into three parts. The first was
Belfast, whose class society and economics, marked by the
combination of a specialised and a skilled working class with
great inequalities, Walsh compared to Liverpool and Glasgow.
The second part consisted of the smaller manufacturing towns
that included Derry, Ballymena and Portadown, where a single
industry dominated, and where women were more likely to be
employed. The remainder was rural Ulster, whose economic
problems, according to Walsh, resembled those of the rest of
Ireland.

Walsh then went on to discuss trade unionism in Belfast,
which he correctly observed was 'very strong in membership'
but 'practically negligible in parliamentary affairs'. He argued
that this was down to 'politico-religious antagonism':

The Belfast Orangeman who is a trade unionist is more often afraid of the Church of Rome than he is of the most extreme Protestant Tory, Irish or English ... Even when a strike is on the ultra-Protestant working man of Belfast feels a bond of agreement with the ultra-Protestant employer ... and he feels a barrier between himself and his Catholic mate ... It is beyond question that creed and party differences split the Labour vote vertically.

Walsh continued by noting that the working class was split 'horizontally', by which he meant that Protestant working-class men occupied the more skilled trades and were better paid than the often unskilled Catholic workers. He defined the Protestants as an 'aristocracy of labour'.[29]

This sort of materialist explanation was also available at the time in the writings of James Connolly, who a couple of years earlier had debated with William Walker of the Belfast ILP in the pages of *Forward* – the newspaper of the Scottish ILP. This was on the topic of 'Socialist Unity in Ireland', and it was concerned with whether Irish workers should join an all-Ireland labour organisation or a British one. More essentially, it centred on whether Ireland should even seek self-government. Walker asked: 'What do you want an Irish Labour Party for? ... Everything that the people of Ireland want can be safeguarded much better under the protection of the United Democracies than if we were isolated.'

Walker argued against an Irish socialist party, insisting he was an internationalist, but in a specific British context: 'I speak the same tongue as the Englishman: I study the same literature: I am oppressed by the same financial power: and, to me, only a combined and united attack, without geographical consideration, can assure to Ireland an equal measure of social advancement as that which the larger and more advanced democracy of Great Britain are pressing for.'[30]

The assertion here that Britain had an 'advanced democracy' compared to Ireland can be interpreted as reflecting other examples of unionism's insistence on British and Protestant superiority and was not out of character for Walker. Connolly reminded his readers that Walker had once promised to 'resist every attack upon the legislative enactments provided by our forefathers as necessary safeguards against the political encroachments of the papacy'; and that he had also proclaimed: 'Protestantism means protesting against superstition; hence true Protestantism is synonymous with Labour.'[31] In reply to his general arguments, Connolly quoted Marx's support for Irish independence, and similar sentiments from other international socialists. The essence of his position for an Irish as opposed to a British-based socialist party was that the latter represented 'the merging of subjugated peoples in the political system of their conquerors'.[32]

For Walker, the Protestant working class was right to support unionism, but he also argued that it would at the same time be possible to maintain an independent progressive and influential voice. This, then and later, proved largely illusory. When Carson's unionist party was faced with challenges from the BLP, he established his own Unionist Labour Association in 1918 to stand in a few Belfast seats; this, for the most part, saw off any independent labour challenges.

After partition, it was Connolly's warnings that would be remembered. He said in 1914 that, if partition was enacted, 'All hope of uniting the workers, irrespective of religion or old political battles will be shattered, and through North and South the issue of Home Rule will still be used to cover the iniquities of the capitalist and landlord class.'[33] In 1911 Walker said, 'I affirm that it has now become impossible in Belfast to have a religious riot, and this is due to the good work done by that much despised body, the ILP.' Well, not quite. In July 1912 Protestant workers expelled approximately 3,000 Catholic workers from shipyards and engineering works – a foretaste of 1920.

Much of Walker's analysis was apparent in the opposition to Home Rule among the north-east Irish Protestant working class. On 29 April 1914, a packed meeting of Protestant trade unionists took place in Belfast's Ulster Hall to express opposition to Home Rule and explicitly support the leadership of Carson. One resolution said that Home Rule 'would be destructive of the peace and prosperity of Ireland and injurious of the industrial interests of [Belfast]'. Another attacked the British Labour Party, the ILP and the Belfast Trades Council for supporting Home Rule.

One speaker, James Cunningham of the Amalgamated Society of Engineers (ASE), complained that while the British labour press and the Labour Party said the Belfast working class was being manipulated by the Tory press, and backing disloyalty, in reality: 'There were no more loyal subject in the United Kingdom than the working men of Belfast.' He insisted that 'the working classes of Belfast were as independent as could be found in the United Kingdom'; rather contradictorily, though, he went on to say, 'The employers and working class of Belfast were on the best of terms.'

Another speaker, John Wilson of the Sheetmetal Workers, evoked the 1689 Siege of Derry, and declared that 'Ulster men were called upon once more to stand up for their birthright and liberties'. He said that Home Rule was no more than an attempt by Catholics to dominate Protestants – a remark greeted by a shout from the audience: 'It is all Popery.'

Another speaker, George Crothers of the ASE, said Belfast Protestants were determined 'never to submit' what he called 'the most thriftless class in the country' and 'the lawlessness and sluggishness of the South' – in other words, the Irish majority. He said that 'Nationalists had never done anything to leave their mark on history as being capable of anything in the shape of a large industry: in fact, their only industry had been conspiracy and their only manufacture had been crime.'

Another speaker, George Stephen, explained how, having been born and raised in Portsmouth, he was not a Belfast Orangeman but was 'a Protestant, a trade unionist and a

Volunteer', by which he meant a member of the UVF. He said that Home Rule 'would not only be disastrous to them as trade unionists, but it would be disastrous to the British Empire'.

Towards the end of the meeting, speaking to the resolution expressing confidence in Carson, Mr A. Nobel of the Amalgamated Society of Carpenters, quoted 'as appropriate' some poetry:

> Statesman, yet friend to Truth;
> Of soul sincere
> In action faithful, and in honour clear
> Who broke no promise; served no private end;
> Who gained no title, and who lost no friend.[34]

This snapshot of Protestant working-class opposition to Irish self-rule, and of the faith in the Tory leadership that directed this opposition, can be taken as representative. Identification with the British Empire was not manufactured. It was shared, of course, by many in the British working class, although the Ulster Protestants had their own reason to be particularly 'loyal' to a British state, since they relied on it to protect them from the Irish majority. The belief that the industry established in Belfast was best protected by staying in the UK is also expressed here, but so too is the sentiment that this economic condition was due to something intrinsic in Ulster Protestantism, contrasted with the 'thriftless' or 'sluggish' or 'criminal' Catholic south.

A determination to put first the interest, as they saw it, of the Protestant working class, yet to surrender their political leadership to the British Tories and Carson, was part of the all-class alliance that had existed since the 1880s at least and was to remain for a long time to come. Consequently, the enemy were not employers, with whom they were 'on good terms', but 'Nationalists' or 'Popery' – or, in effect and close-at-hand the Belfast Catholic working class, who were shown where to go in both the 1912 riots and the 1920–22 pogrom.

The sentiments expressed in the 1914 Ulster Hall meeting were also expressed in the Northern Ireland state that appeared after partition. A general history of that statelet is not the subject of this book, although various details will be provided throughout. What is noteworthy is that the all-class alliance in the form of the Ulster Unionists – or the Ulster Unionist and Conservative Party, as they were also known – was in power in the Northern Ireland government and parliament until it was suspended in 1972. There were tensions within that government – for instance, over whether or not to pursue what Paul Bew, Peter Gibbon and Henry Patterson have called 'populist' policies designed to ensure the continuing allegiance to the government of the Protestant working class.

These policies required the maintenance of Protestant privileges. As these authors explain, the 'object of Ulster politics', that is unionist politics, was 'the continued split between the Protestant and Catholic working class.'[35] From a different perspective, Robbie McVeigh and Bill Rolston have recently written that partition 'enabled the state under unionist control to revert to the default [British] position on controlling Catholics – repression and hyper-sectarianism', while 'ruling class exploitation and encouragement of sectarian division' was 'an everyday element in the operation of the state'.[36] McVeigh and Rolston offer as evidence a quote from a report of a famous speech by Basil Brooke, later Northern Ireland prime minister, speaking at a 12 July rally in 1933, which remains very telling. The 'he' in the report is Brooke:

> There was a great number of Protestants and Orangemen who employed Roman Catholics. He felt he could speak freely in this subject as had not a Roman Catholic about his own place. He appreciated the great difficulty ... in procuring suitable Protestant labour, but he would point out that Roman Catholics were endeavouring to get in everywhere and were out with all force and might to destroy the power and constitution of

Ulster ... He would appeal to loyalists, therefore, wherever possible to employ good Protestant lads and lasses.[37]

Thus, the unionist leaders continued to practise and preach the sectarianism that had been a central part of their politics since their political organisation had emerged in the 1880s. Anti-Catholic riots also continued to feature in Northern Ireland, especially Belfast – most notably in the riots of 1935, when Catholics were once again expelled from their workplaces, and more than two thousand were forced out of their homes by Protestant mobs. As for the British state, although its troops were deployed in Belfast during these riots, the Tory government at Westminster refused even to hold an inquiry into the disturbances, insisting: 'the matter is entirely within the discretion and responsibility of the government of Northern Ireland'.[38]

By the same logic, discussion of Northern Ireland was prohibited in the British parliament until the Troubles. The colonial overseers in Northern Ireland were allowed to do as they wanted. Eventually this state of affairs could no longer hold, and the British army was dispatched to the province in August 1969. It is perhaps only fair that a judgement of what they found there should be offered here. This is how Northern Ireland was described in the official, post-Troubles review by the British army of 'Operation Banner', as their deployment in Northern Ireland was named, and of what they found when they first went onto its streets. It was a legacy of much that had gone before:

Scottish Presbyterians began to settle in Ulster in the 16th and 17th centuries ... The two communities of native catholics and immigrant protestants remained largely separate, attending different churches and being brought up in different cultural traditions. The protestants were generally the more affluent; they tended to have larger farms, built mills, and dominated the professions ...

One of Stormont's [the Northern Ireland government] early acts was to remove the safeguards for the catholic minority. All important posts were held by protestants, and local elections were manipulated to ensure a protestant advantage ...

By the early 1960s discrimination had become institutionalised. It was not that legislation was discriminatory in itself, but rather that the way it was applied in practice discriminated against the catholic minority. In 1969 Londonderry was the most deprived city in the United Kingdom. 33,000 of the 36,000 catholics were crowded into the Victorian slums of the Creggan and the Bogside. Unemployment in Londonderry was the highest in the UK. A similar pattern applied in Belfast (with a population of 385,000) and many of the other towns throughout Northern Ireland. ... By the late 1960s poverty and social deprivation in the catholic enclaves of Londonderry and Belfast was appalling. In some cases families of 14 lived in four rooms, with children aged five woken at 2 a.m. every night to roam the streets, in order to allow sleeping in shifts. This deprivation and discrimination was well known in Stormont.[39]

4

Betrayals

For many Northern Irish unionists, the prevailing story of Northern Ireland's 'Troubles', from 1968 onwards, is one of betrayal. Often this betrayal came from across the Irish Sea: from the very British state to which Ulster Protestants had for so long pledged loyalty. Moreover, the treacheries were usually committed by their old allies, the Conservative and Unionist Party – and not only during the Troubles, but after they had officially ended. Here is the story of the worst of false friends.

Take, for example, the extent of the 2019 betrayal by Conservative prime minister Boris Johnson. This emerged in the early afternoon of 21 October when Stephen Barclay, the Brexit minister, was answering questions from a committee of the House of Lords. Asked if the proposed new deal for the UK to quit the European Union might require Northern Ireland businesses to fill in custom forms if they wanted to send goods to Great Britain, Barclay offered reassurances that this would not be the case. A few minutes later he corrected himself, saying that this would indeed be the procedure. For Northern Irish unionists, it was difficult to tell which was the bigger shock: that the government minister did not know the details of the deal he was advocating, or that, when he did know, those details revealed the extent of the separation between Great Britain and Northern Ireland he was now proposing.

Even before this revelation there had been howls of bitterness in Northern Ireland. The front page of the unionist *Belfast New-Letter* of 18 October had denounced 'A Great Betrayal', and featured a photograph of Boris Johnson, Irish premier Leo Varadkar and German chancellor Angela Merkel sharing a joke. A similar photograph, although this time without Merkel, appeared on the front page of the Northern Ireland edition of the *Daily Mirror*, with the headline, 'WE'VE BEEN DUPED', and reporting 'Arlene's Brexit Deal Fury'.

The criticisms poured in. The *News-Letter* quoted the UUP and its outgoing leader Robin Swan saying the deal 'annexe[d] Northern Ireland from the rest of the UK' and placed it 'on the window ledge of the Union'. There was a quote from Jim Allister of the self-explanatory Traditional Unionist Voice party, declaring that Johnson's proposals 'put us in the waiting room for Irish unity'. When Johnson explained his 'Get Brexit Done' plan to the House of Commons, the DUP MP Jim Shannon heckled: 'Sell-out! Treachery! Betrayal'.[1]

Jeremy Corbyn, for whom unionism had never been an obvious political affiliation, complained in parliament that Johnson 'threw Northern Ireland under the bus' – although, if he was throwing anyone under the said vehicle, it was not so much Northern Ireland but its unionism.[2] Corbyn even cited criticism of Johnson by the DUP's Sammy Wilson – someone who, as we shall see, had a history of sectarian intolerance. Labour's official spokesperson on Northern Ireland, Tony Lloyd, said that the 'Unionist community' had 'frankly been betrayed by the decisions of Conservative MPs who once were Unionists and who have now abandoned their erstwhile friends'.[3] More predictably, in the *Belfast Telegraph* of 22 October the leading and well-informed unionist columnist Alex Kane reported: 'There is an anger in unionism I haven't seen since the Anglo-Irish Agreement in 1985. There is an anger that spreads right across unionism. They feel betrayed. Even those who voted Remain and worried about the consequences of Leave at the time.'

The *Irish News* reported that there was extra-parliamentary resistance afoot. The story was that 'Loyalists – including the alleged leaders of a number of rival paramilitary factions – met last night in an unprecedented show of unity following what they have claimed is a betrayal by the British government over Brexit'. Those reported present included the Ulster Defence Association (UDA), the Ulster Volunteer Force (UVF), and former members of the Red Hand Commando, all of whom had a long record of sectarian assassinations and other crimes, as well as 'leading members of the Orange Order', including its grand secretary.[4]

The anger behind such shenanigans was unsurprising. In proposing what amounted to a border in the Irish Sea, Johnson had in effect reinstated the outlines of the deal Theresa May had been forced to drop in early December 2017 following protest from the DUP.[5] Moreover, speaking of the EU withdrawal agreement, Johnson himself had told the DUP conference in November 2017 that it would be 'damaging to the Union' to have 'regulatory checks and even customs controls between GB and NI … No British government could or should sign up to anything of the kind.'[6] In December 2017, the joint report agreed by the UK and the EU as they began Brexit negotiations stated: 'In all circumstances, the United Kingdom will continue to ensure the same unfettered access for Northern Ireland's business to the whole of the United Kingdom internal market.'

Nevertheless, there were those, especially from Northern Ireland's Irish nationalist community, who were not over-sympathetic to the unionists' complaints. *Irish News* columnist Allison Morris said the DUP had 'badly overplayed their hand' with the Conservative government. She asserted that it was always likely that an 'English nationalist' prime minister would 'spare no-one' in his pursuit of Brexit. The DUP had 'learned the hard way that the posh Tory old boys' club at Westminster is about self-preservation at all costs and the DUP have been deemed, like many who came before them, expendable'.[7]

The more knowledgeable figures in unionism probably knew all this. In the Alex Kane article quoted above, he recalled previous occasions of alleged sell-outs, observing: 'And yet, time after time, we return to the same anger, the same sense of betrayal and the same clarion call for protest.' That was true; throughout the Troubles, British politicians and their schemes had been denounced from within the Protestant community.

As early as 1972, a song included in *Orange Loyalist Songs*, produced by the 'Red Hand Brigade', had featured then Northern Ireland secretary William Whitelaw. 'Outlaw Whitelaw' began:

> The Enemies of Ulster are winning day-by-day,
> It is time we said to Whitelaw
> Pack your bags and move away.

In 1973, another loyalist poet had written in *Orange Cross*:

Mother England
Oh England, mother England, why have you let us down,
We Protestants of Ulster, who stood the test of time
They fought in France and Flanders and by the thousands fell,
Those loyalists of Ulster who fought for England's crown.

Such was the disillusionment that the last verse threatened rebellion:

So let Ulster be our watchword, 'No surrender' be our cry,
If Britain does desert us, let no tears drop from our eyes
We'll fight for God and Ulster, we'll fight to keep her free,
The Ulster flag with red and white will fly across our land.

The implication in the last two lines was that, by their actions, British politicians were driving Ulster Protestants to consider breaking from Britain and establishing an independent state. This was a move considered by some in 1972 after the Heath government suspended the Stormont government and parliament, then headed by the Unionist Party's Brian Faulkner, and imposed direct rule. This was when the accusations of betrayal began in earnest.

Direct rule was the political aftermath of Bloody Sunday, when, in January 1972, thirteen protesters against internment in Northern Ireland were killed by British soldiers in Derry, with another later dying of his wounds. In imposing direct rule, the Westminster Tories were telling their then Northern Irish counterparts they could not be relied on to run their polity properly, even though the Bloody Sunday killings were the responsibility of the British army, and ultimately the UK government. The transfer of power began with a suggestion by Heath that all law-and-order responsibilities should reside at Westminster. Faulkner's reaction was hostile. He said that this 'would be widely construed as an acceptance of totally base-less criticism of our stewardship'. When Heath then proceeded to full suspension, Faulkner complained: 'I thought by our actions and our attitudes we had earned the right to the con-fidence and support of the United Kingdom Government.'[8] In Westminster the Unionist MPs were divided. The more liberal Robin Chichester-Clark favoured the complete integration of Northern Ireland into the UK, but fellow MP Captain Lawrence Orr was more intent on the theme of betrayal:

> I must tell this House that we shall be unrealistic if we do not realise that what has happened will be looked upon by the major-ity in Ulster as a victory for the IRA. We would be unrealistic if we did not realise that was the case, that whatever be the merits or demerits of a local Parliament, whatever be the merits or demerits of direct rule, about which people can argue, the bring-ing about of a constitutional crisis and the imposition of direct rule against the wishes of the majority can only be described as an act of folly.[9]

The most militant mass opposition to direct rule came from the recently formed Ulster Vanguard, a semi-paramilitary organisation, and later a political party, set up in February of that year by William Craig, a former Unionist government hard-line home secretary, who organised military-style parades of supporters. Vanguard complained of British 'Jack-boot Government'. It said there was now a Conservative party 'converted to a belief in a United Ireland as the best long-term solution of the old Irish problem'. Accordingly,

> The minimum condition for safeguarding the loyalist cause is plain. The power to damage it, in what Westminster conceives to be British interest, must be removed from Westminster's hands. This entails that Ulster must have control over her own internal security and be able to deploy whatever forces she considers necessary to meet any challenge coming from any source in Ireland. It also entails that Ulster must have her own Parliament with such enlarged powers as are consistent with these minimum conditions for her security.[10]

Vanguard was relatively short-lived. However, the most spectacular example of resistance by the unionist community against British plans for their 'province' was from late 1973 to May 1974. The controversy this time was over the Sunningdale Agreement, which had been drafted by Heath and then, following the February 1974 general election, overseen by the Labour government of Harold Wilson. This promoted power-sharing, in effect between the Unionist Party and their then chief opposition in the Northern Ireland parliament, the Irish nationalist–inclined Social Democratic and Labour Party (SDLP), and the establishment of a consultative Council of Ireland between the two parts of Ireland. Ian Paisley, at this stage in the running for most popular politician in Northern Ireland preached a sermon:

> Where did 1973 leave us here in Ulster? It left us in a state of calamity. Our cities, towns and villages have been bombed. Our beloved Province has been burned. Our Parliament has been

over-thrown by the capitulation of Westminster to Republican agitation and violence. Almost 1,000 lives have been taken and to crown it all former IRA men and fellow travellers have been set over us in an autocratic regime with as much semblance of democracy as Hitler's government in Fascist Germany. While the bombs go off a lying press, lying parsons, lying politicians and a lying premier tell us glibly that this road of gore is in reality the road of peace ... Is it any wonder that Ulster people are outraged and frustrated? Is it any wonder they turn from such leaders with the utmost of contempt? While even ungodly people are utterly disillusioned and despair the people of God need not suffer any such disillusionment or despair.[11]

Certainly, most in the unionist community opposed Sunning-dale. Even though it had originally been agreed by the Unionist Party, then led by Brian Faulkner, it divided his party; the majority who opposed him subsequently became the Official Unionists. In the UK general election of February 1974, the three main anti-Sunningdale unionist parties – the Official Unionists, led by Harry West, the DUP and Vanguard joined forces in the United Ulster Unionist Coalition (UUUC). They won eleven out of the twelve seats, with just 51.2 per cent of the votes cast.

In May 1974, a general strike organised by the Ulster Workers' Council brought down the short-lived power-sharing executive, and its chief executive Faulkner. By now the Labour Party was in power at Westminster, attempting to carry out the Tories' Sunningdale Agreement. But the UWC strike brought an end to that. Again, the loyalists sang, mocking the British prime minster this time with a rewrite based on the Second World War anthem of the UK's Home Guard: 'Who do you think you are kidding Mr Wilson, If you think old Ulster's done?'

The thoroughly proletarian UWC emerged out of Belfast's shipbuilding, engineering and power industries. Its first pub-lication produced after its strike showed off its working-class credentials and traditional unionism: 'We regained our dignity as Loyalists after years of double-dealing and appeasement ... we reminded Harold Wilson and his colleagues in government, the Ulster workers (just like their fellow workers in Britain) could not be pushed around ... we reminded Britain that Ulster loyalty could not be taken for granted, it must be earned.'[12]

By this time an English politician had been elected to serve in a Northern Ireland Westminster constituency, so perhaps these words were relevant to him. He was none other than former Tory cabinet member Enoch Powell, whose populist racism had captured headlines in April 1968. By the early 1970s, he had fallen out with the leadership of the Conservative Party, and successfully won the South Down seat for the Ulster Unionists in October 1974. Powell had been making speeches about Northern Ireland for some time, and he too had detected British government failings. For example, at a Unionist Party rally in Ballymena in September 1972, he said: 'The troubles in this province are about whether this province is to be part of the United Kingdom. They are about nothing else. They are not about civil rights or discrimination or franchises or constitutions.'

Elsewhere, Powell said of successive British governments since 1968: 'Policies could not have been better designed if the purpose had been to inspire and maintain doubt and uncertainty about the future of the Union and to convey the message that the British government was emotionally and politically uncommitted, if not averse to it.'[13] But despite his track record, the level of distrust at the time against those outside the six counties meant that not all unionists were ready to hail him as a messiah. The right-wing and viciously anti-Catholic *Loyalist News* declared: 'We cannot trust Englishmen ... Enoch is no fool and like all Englishmen, when he gets what he wants who is to say that his loyalty would be to Ulster ... Enoch if you want the leadership of Great Britain, fight in your "own country".'[14] Powell was no doubt under the impression that

Northern Ireland, as part of his own United Kingdom, was his 'own country'; he remained an MP until he lost his seat at the general election of 1987. Throughout this time, he advocated complete integration of Northern Ireland into the Union.

Nevertheless, the most vocal unionist critic of British policy in Northern Ireland throughout the Troubles remained Ian Paisley – who, whenever British politicians suggested power-sharing or the reform of Northern Ireland, waved placards declaring: 'Ulster Says No'. In June 1982, his DUP launched a new journal. The very first edition of *The Voice of Ulster* set the tone for much of what was to follow. Jim Allister, who was later to split from the DUP and form Traditional Unionist Voice, asked in a headline, 'Could Ulster Men Have Done Any Worse?' and then listed Britain's crimes. These included the loss of the Northern Ireland parliament, the 'evacuation of industries', and 'unchecked IRA terrorism'. He concluded: 'Such are the fruits of Direct Rule by Westminster politicians who are sent to Northern Ireland, whether they want to or not, to preside over the Province in which they have no real interest.'[15]

There were British politicians who did show an interest; but when one did, there occurred what, for many unionists, was the greatest betrayal. This was the Anglo-Irish Agreement of 1985 (AIA), signed by Margaret Thatcher on behalf of the UK and Garret FitzGerald for the Irish Republic. Its central feature was that the two governments would regularly and formally consult on Northern Ireland. It established the Anglo-Irish Intergovernmental Conference, under which regular meetings would take place between the Irish minister for foreign affairs and the secretary of state for Northern Ireland. To service this arrangement, there was to be a small secretariat of British and Irish civil servants based near Belfast, where the issues to be discussed included cross-border cooperation on security and legal and political issues of mutual interest. Both Britain and Ireland agreed that that there would be no united Ireland unless the people of Northern Ireland voted for one.

Despite this reassurance, for Northern Ireland unionists of all varieties the AIA was calamitous, allowing the Irish government a right to interfere in their 'Ulster'. Accordingly, it was denounced not only by all of the unionist parties and the Orange Order, but also by the main Protestant churches. A protest rally was attended by 200,000 people in Belfast. A one-day strike was organised, all unionist MPs resigned from the Westminster parliament, and, with one exception, were subsequently re-elected in by-elections. Their election slogan was 'Ulster Says No'. Just before this, the Northern Ireland unionists voiced their sentiments in the House of Commons in dramatic language. Peter Robinson of the DUP told the Commons: 'When the Prime Minister signed the agreement in Hillsborough Castle, she was in reality drafting the obituary of Ulster as we know it in the United Kingdom.' He went on to compare Thatcher signing the AIA with FitzGerald to Neville Chamberlain signing the Munich Agreement of 1938 with Adolf Hitler:

> I was born a free citizen of the United Kingdom. I was brought up to respect the Union flag ... We cheered with this country during the Falklands campaign. Ulster suffered its losses just as many did on this side of the Irish Sea. During the second world war, we made sacrifices, just as many people in this part of the United Kingdom, and we did it without conscription. During the first world war, Ulster gave of its best for Britain ... on the Somme when 5,000 Ulstermen lost their lives at the enemy's hands ... That has been the way of loyal Ulster. I never believed that I would see a British Government who were prepared to damage Ulster's position in the United Kingdom.[16]

Much more was to follow. Harald McCusker of the UUP recalled how he had taught his children to honour the British flag, but now: 'It would have been better if they had never looked at the Union flag or thought that they were British or put their trust in the House of Commons.'[17] The Rev. William

McCrea, a DUP MP for Mid-Ulster, attacked Thatcher in Biblical fashion: 'Why did she do it?' That solemn question will be answered in the Prime Minister's conscience not just tonight but in the years to come. It is a matter that is solemn before God. She will answer to the betrayed people of Ulster.[18]

The passion and sincerity in these comments were not manufactured. Nor is there any doubt that the two days of debate displayed another of those huge gulfs between Northern Ireland's unionists and those English parliamentarians who claimed an adherence to the same principles. Among the English was William, now Viscount, Whitelaw. Speaking in the House of Lords, he sought to conciliate, but sounded more like a patronising former colonial administrator explaining the foibles of the natives:

> Contrary to the unfortunate impression given by some politicians in the Province, there are many people there who only want to live in peace with their neighbours and to carry on a normal life in the beautiful country which is their home. Amidst all the trouble and difficulties no one should forget these friendly and warm-hearted people to whom we in the rest of the United Kingdom owe our understanding.[19]

Heath himself was not so understanding. There may have been an expectation that he might take the opportunity to attack Thatcher, not just given the animosity he had towards her, but also because, between 1971 and 1972 in talks as prime minister with the Irish government, he had been very wary about entering into negotiations on anything touching on constitutional issues.[20] This was not a hesitancy he evoked now. Rather, he offered an admission that included not just the Protestants but the Northern Irish Catholics, and indeed the southern Irish as well: 'I confess that I have always found the Irish, all of them, extremely difficult to understand.'[21]

Such comments did little to help Thatcher sell her deal to

Northern Irish unionists. The same was true of the attitude of the Labour Party, whose spokesperson, Peter Archer, told the Commons:

> We have been honest and open with the unionist people about our view of the future. We believe that the future of Ireland should be as one country. We do not delude ourselves that the unionist people agree with us, but disagreeing is better than misleading people ... Having given the unionist people the bad news in plain English, I shall set it in context. We have no intention of imposing unity at gunpoint. If Ireland is one day to enjoy the peace and security which history has always denied it, it must be on the basis of a settlement achieved by consensus ... I believe that the Opposition will be able to persuade the people of Northern Ireland to choose the option in which we believe. It is in that sense that I see [the Anglo-Irish Agreement] as the first step.[22]

There were those who, on hearing such words offered sympathy to unionists. Mary Robinson, a future president of Ireland, resigned from the Irish Labour Party over its support for the AIA. Tomás Mac Giolla, the leader of the Workers' Party, which had roots in the Official IRA, called on the Irish government to suspend the operation of the intergovernmental conference to take account of unionist sensitivities.[23] There were also those in academic circles who detected grand conspiracies at work. For example, a then lecturer at the University of Ulster, Arthur Aughey, wrote a book *Under Siege: Ulster Unionism and the Anglo-Irish Agreement*, in which he insisted: 'the British government has been prepared to indulge in the morally dubious exercise of power to humiliate and demoralise unionism.'[24]

Others went even further. Ian Paisley, a few months after the AIA was announced, preached a sermon in which he detected a conspiracy that had consisted not just of Thatcher's AIA, but also of an attempt by her to liberalise Sunday trading laws:

The Loyalists of Ulster have been sold like cattle on the hoof to their enemies. Neither the ballot box, neither the voices raised emphasising that democracy has been destroyed and the democratic principles have been violated will stop this woman on her tracks. With a stubborn arrogancy, with a determination filled with her own egotism and pride she is determined to destroy the Ulster Protestant people. With a rush of blood to her head and madness in her heart she thinks as she conquered the miners, and as she conquered the dictators of Argentina she will conquer the most law-abiding Loyalist section of Her majesty's subjects. She reckons without God whose day she has decided, through legislation, to destroy and make it like any other day. But that God is in the heavens, and He that sitteth in the heavens shall laugh, the Lord shall have them in derision.[25]

Bringing God into the debate was of course not new for Paisley; but the venom displayed here, as in Aughey's conspiracy theory and the criticisms in the House of Commons, was at times beyond rationality, and certainly misjudged Thatcher's motivation. Explaining the Agreement to the House of Commons, she said its purpose was to 'stamp out terrorism' and not 'give a single inch' to terrorists. She also praised the unionist community for its loyalty and argued that the Agreement enhanced the union.[26]

For Northern Irish unionists, Thatcher's use of the phrase 'not a single inch' must have been particularly galling, because the phrase 'Not an inch' was part of their traditional repertoire of slogans. Moreover, her assertion that she was not conceding even this to the 'terrorist' – if by terrorists she meant the IRA – was not true. By recognising that the North of Ireland had an all-island context, she was giving ground to all those, including the IRA, who insisted this was and always had been the reality.

What Thatcher was concerned about was the rise of Sinn Féin and the successes of the IRA. She saw the AIA as combating both. By offering the Irish government a consultative role in Northern Ireland, she hoped to appeal to the more moderate

elements within the Northern nationalist community. By securing the promise of closer security cooperation with the southern
state, she hoped the IRA would be, if not defeated, then at least
damaged. In other words, in the grand scheme of things, the
intent of the Anglo-Irish Agreement coincided with the Ulster
unionists' wish to weaken Irish republicanism. What was at
stake in the argument was a difference about priorities and
tactics, not principles.

Similarly, when Thatcher was later to have doubts about the
AIA, this was principally because it did not work to the extent
she had hoped in making life difficult for Irish republicanism.
As the above quote suggests, Thatcher was as strong a unionist as any British politician – at least as far as she understood
unionism. There were some in the Commons who opposed
the AIA for that very reason. Jeremy Corbyn, then a Labour
backbencher, said in the Commons debate: 'the agreement
strengthens rather than weakens the border between the six
and the 26 counties, and those of us who wish to see a United
Ireland oppose the agreement for that reason.'[27]

Here, Corbyn shared Thatcher's view that she was seeking to
strengthen the union. In her memoirs, she would place herself
again in the camp of traditional unionism, insisting: 'I could
never understand why leading Unionists ... suggested that in my
dealings with the South and above all the Anglo-Irish Agreement
... I was contemplating selling them out to the Republic.'[28] But
she also admitted the strength of unionist hostility surprised her:
'It was worse than anyone had predicted to me.'[29] Once again,
a British politician had failed to read Irish minds.

All this led some within unionist and loyalist circles to question their core beliefs. One was the Rev. Hugh Ross, who began
to advocate for Ulster independence. In 1990 he wrote: 'Ulster
is treated as a colony of the London/Dublin administration ...
We are a land and people for whom no-one seems to care ... no
Westminster government has ever resigned due to its failures to
stop atrocities in Ulster.'[30]

The disaffection was shared by old and young. In 1991 the Young Unionist Council, the youth wing of the Unionist Party, began an article in its publication with the headline, 'What Price the Union?'. It quoted 'an elderly gentleman' at a Unionist Party meeting asserting: 'Sure the English don't want us anyway and the first opportunity they get they will push us into a united Ireland.' The article commented: 'This is a view which is shared by some Unionist activists ... How Britain responded to the Falklands and more recently, the Gulf, stands in very stark contrast to the dithering and blundering which we have had to suffer since 1972.'[31] Four years later, the paramilitary Ulster Volunteer Force was complaining: 'We have had our rights as British subjects ripped from us in the Governments [sic] efforts to appease the minority Republican community and the Dublin Government.'[32]

Apart from Paisley, perhaps the most sustained criticism of British politicians came from the Orange Oder. The year 1991 can be taken as an example – the year after Margaret Thatcher was driven from office by her own party, and when anger within Northern Irish unionism about her 'betrayal' of the Anglo-Irish Agreement might perhaps have been expected to subside. Not so. The December 1990–January 1991 edition of the Order's *Orange Standard* set the tone for the new year with the headline, 'English Politicians Out of Touch'. The complaint was twofold: 'First we had the cheap gibe of Tory Edwina Curry about Ulster MPs, then we had Kevin McNamara [Labour] in an incredible outburst of political arrogance making it clear that [the Northern Irish] had no hope of enrolling in the British Labour Party.' Detailing this, The *Standard* reported Curry as saying Unionist MPs 'should contribute more to national debates and alleg[ing] that they rarely move outside the realm of Ulster matters'.

The *Standard*'s defence was that unionist MPs were rightly preoccupied with defeating the IRA. It criticised McNamara for refusing membership of the Labour Party to the Northern

Irish, drawing a contrast with the post–Second World Labour government, the 'true friends of Northern Ireland ... committed to the unity of the Empire and Commonwealth and protecting British people and their interests in every land where the Union Jack flew'.

The reason the Orange Order had a soft spot for the Labour government of 1945–51 was that, in 1949, it had passed the Ireland Act, which had strengthened partition by giving the Northern Ireland parliament the right to veto Irish reunification – but that was not detailed in the *Orange Standard* during these years.[33] Instead, its emphasis was on the Order's consistent suspicions and criticisms of British politicians in the 1990s. In the February 1991 issue of the magazine, the front-page headline said the government was giving the IRA 'a free rein'. In April it demanded internment. In May it recalled the suspension of the Northern Ireland parliament in 1972 and criticised that. The following month, the AIA was again cited as an example of British folly – 'an act of incredible insensitivity and stupidity'. In July 1991 it levelled a more general condemnation: 'British politicians find it difficult in placing Northern Ireland in the United Kingdom context'. When a government initiative, the Brooke Talks, floundered after unionist opposition to what was in many ways a dress rehearsal for the GFBA, the explanation offered in the August *Orange Standard* was that the British and Irish governments had not listened to unionists – and to this was added a general condemnation of English Tories. In September it was again time to call for 'Internment North and South', and the following month a speech was quoted by one Sir Samuel Foster, a local unionist councillor and Imperial Grand Lecturer of the Orange Order, in which he said unionists no longer trusted the British government. As the year ended, the hostility towards British politicians of all tribes re-emerged when, in November, there were condemnations of 'the double-talk of the Tories and Labour on Ulster'; the following month, a speech by Hugh Ross, East Londonderry Unionist MP, was reported, describing as 'pathetic' the whole period of direct rule. He accused successive governments of 'mouthing pious platitudes and letting Ulster bleed', while they 'bend with every howl of outrage from the lovers of Irish Republicanism and their friends'.

These were the protestations of the Orange Order in just one year of the Troubles. The sentiments expressed came from an organisation that was at the heart of Ulster unionism and Protestant culture and was representative of many in that community. The repeated sense of betrayal by British politicians in these years bordered on the obsessional, but it does illustrate the deepening gulf between British and Northern Irish unionists. There may be some who can explain all this away as a case of collective paranoia. But could paranoia really have engulfed the military-style ranks of Vanguard, the workers of the UWC, religious zealots like Paisley, the more respectable and establishment church leaders who attacked the AIA, the Orange Order, academics and the masses of all classes who attended marches, rallied, and kept voting for the most obdurate critic of British policy on Northern Ireland they could find?

Invocation of some sort of tribal psychosis as an explanation will not do. A better explanation is that, by the closing decades of the twentieth century it was obvious that the British–Irish union was not working. As we will see, the reaction to this fact of most of the union's traditional supporters in Northern Ireland was to ditch the alliance between the Conservative Party and the Ulster Unionists that had been the bedrock of unionism for nearly a century. The Rev. Dr Ian Paisley waited in the wings.

5

Tories Out, DUP In

In April 1960 the Conservative and Unionist Party welcomed a delegation from the Ulster Unionist Council to a dinner. It was held in the luxurious premises of the Junior Carlton Club in Pall Mall, London. It was an event for the like-minded. The guests were members of Northern Ireland's Unionist Party whose MPs and Lords took the Conservative whip at Westminster and had done so since Ireland was partitioned. These were the standard-bearers of the Conservative Party in Northern Ireland; while having a separate organisation and leadership, they also had representation on the Conservative Executive Committee of the National Unionist Associations. They were ideologically, but also organisationally Tory. But there was another perceived aspect of the relationship – a colonial one. This was alluded to when Tory MP Colonel Sir Douglas Glover proposed a toast to the guests: 'Ulster holds a very special place in our hearts. When so many Commonwealth countries are rushing towards independence, becoming republics and even opting out of the Commonwealth, it is a wonderful feeling to know that Ulster's loyalty to the Crown and the British connection gets tighter as years go by.'[1]

The patronising self-satisfaction evident here seems distant. Eight years after this speech, the modern 'Troubles' began, in which more than 3,800 people were killed. They were killed by the Irish Republican Army; the British army, including its Ulster Defence Regiment; the Royal Ulster Constabulary; the B Specials; the Ulster Volunteer Force (which had adopted the name of the old UVF); the Ulster Defence Association; and various other paramilitary groupings. The dead included members of these organisations, but also demonstrators and political activists, killed because of their religion or because they just happened to be in the wrong place at the wrong time. Others were killed when Irish republicans exported the 'war' to England and elsewhere. Many businesses and homes were destroyed in Northern Ireland. And there was another, rather less mourned casualty: the Northern Irish wing of the British Conservative and Unionist Party.

In the UK general election of 1964, the twelve parliamentary constituencies then in Northern Ireland returned twelve Unionist (and Conservative) Party MPs, fighting under the manifesto of the UK Conservatives. They received 63 per cent of the vote. By contrast, in the British general election of 2019, the Northern Ireland Conservatives, fighting on behalf of Boris Johnson's party, secured none of the eighteen seats and received 0.7 per cent of the total vote. The question posed here is whether this collapse of British Toryism in Northern Ireland reflected deeper political changes within Northern Irish politics, threatening the 'Precious Union' itself, or whether Northern Ireland unionism had successfully rebooted and reconfigured itself to meet the new challenges it faced? But first, what was lost?

Most of the twelve Ulster Unionists and Conservatives elected in 1964 had the establishment credentials that made them suitable Tories. Five had attended Cambridge University: Henry Clark, Samuel Knox Cunningham, Stratton Mills, Rafton Pounder and Robin Chichester-Clark. Three more – Stanley McMaster, Patricia McLaughlin and George Currie – went to Trinity College Dublin, the Irish equivalent of Oxbridge. All of these had been to public schools or leading grammar schools. Another, the Duke of Abercorn, attended Eton, and then the Royal Agricultural College.

Some also had uniquely Northern Irish qualifications. Lawrence Orr was an imperial grand master of the Orange

Order and head of the Orange Order in England and had revived the Orange Order at Westminster. He also served in the elite Life Guards regiment. Patricia McLaughlin was a founding member of the Westminster Women's Orange Lodge. Others had a more traditional English Conservative background. Henry Clark served as a colonial officer in Tanganyika. When the UK government granted this country independence in 1961, while Clark welcomed this, he also said, 'I cannot help feeling regret that Tanganyika has not been able to move towards independence at a slightly slower pace.'[2] Such opinions made Clark a natural choice to chair the Conservative MPs' East African Committee between 1963 and 1965 – a position that illustrated the extent to which Ulster unionists were integrated in the Tory party.

This was even more true of Robin Chichester-Clark. He could trace his family origins back to Robert Peel, while his brother James became Northern Ireland prime minister from 1969 to 1971. Chichester-Clark enjoyed a long period at the heart of the Conservative Party at Westminster. He was a front bench spokesperson for the government of Harold Macmillan, and later for that of Edward Heath; he served in the Whip's office, in the Treasury, and as opposition spokesperson on the arts. He was even a spokesperson on Northern Ireland. In 1972, he was minister of state at the Department of Employment. He was also a member of the Orange Order, which was all but obligatory for a successful career in Northern Irish unionism – although in 1969 he was briefly suspended from the Order for attending the requiem mass for an Irish Guards officer and Catholic convert.

George Forrest was also on the more liberal wing of union-ism; indeed, he was originally elected in 1956 as an Independent Unionist. Although he later joined the Unionist Party, his liberal-ism persisted. As a result of it, on 12 July 1967 he was hauled off an Orange Order platform and kicked unconscious by fellow Orangemen.

On the other wing of unionism was Sir Knox Cunningham, who also served in Harold Macmillan's government as his private parliamentary secretary. Although born and raised in an upper-class Ulster family with both land and business interests, he began his political career as a Conservative councillor in Orpington. He was later to serve on the National Executive of the Conservative and Unionist Party. In parliament his political credentials included constant criticism of Harold Wilson in his battles with the racist regime of Ian Smith in Rhodesia – including, on one occasion, accusing Wilson of 'bullying behaviour' towards Smith, and the suggestion that Wilson 'ought to be ashamed of himself'.[3] Wilson had other parliamentary exchanges with Cunningham, including one when the Ulster MP questioned whether the European Court could interfere with the rights of the Appeal Court. Wilson's answer was facetious: 'I always take very great care in all these matters of human rights that are so dear to the hon. Gentleman.'[4]

Whenever MPs sought to raise in parliament the rather sorry state of human rights in Northern Ireland, Knox Cunningham and others were quick to protest to the Speaker that discussion on these matters was beyond the remit of the British House of Commons.[5] Rafton Pounder MP did likewise, but he was also quick to talk up his community. In July 1964, when the high level of unemployment in Northern Ireland was mentioned in the Commons, Pounder offered a reassurance based on watching the annual march of the Orange Order: 'Anyone present in Northern Ireland yesterday, on the occasion of the annual 12th July demonstration, could not have failed to be impressed by the very considerable sense of prosperity, contentment and general economic well-being which existed wherever one went. This is surely something which even the most casual bystander could not fail to have been impressed by.'[6]

Another unionist MP, James Hamilton, the Fifth Duke of Abercorn, was the embodiment of 'prosperity'. He served in the British army, later in life became chancellor of the Order of the Garter, lord steward to the Queen, lord lieutenant of Tyrone, and a member of the House of Lords. He was the first cousin of the 8th Earl of Spencer, the father of Diana, Princess of Wales, and served in the Ulster Defence Regiment. Most of his contributions in the House of Commons were on agricultural issues – not surprising, since he was the beneficiary of a 15,000-acre estate in County Tyrone. Other unionist MPs were less privileged: John Maginnnis had a farming background and George Forrest was an auctioneer.

And then, they were gone. Forrest died in 1968, and in a by-election his former seat was won by civil rights leader and socialist Bernadette Devlin. McLaughlin resigned in October 1968; Knox Cunningham did likewise in 1970. He was replaced by James Molyneaux, also of the Ulster Unionist Party. Clark lost his seat in the 1970 general election to Ian Paisley. Robin Chichester-Clarke declined to stand in the 1974 election, and was replaced by William Ross, who, although a candidate for the Ulster Unionist Party in 1973, opposed the power-sharing Sunningdale Agreement. Maginnis stood down at the 1974 February general election and was replaced by fellow Unionist Party member Harold McCusker.

And on it went. McMaster was defeated at the February 1974 election by William Craig, then the leader of the hardline loyalist Vanguard. Stratton Mills joined the Alliance Party in 1973, stood down before the 1974 election, and was succeeded by John Carson of the United Ulster Unionist Coalition – a label then being adopted by an alliance of anti-Sunningdale unionists. Pounder was defeated in the 1974 general election by Robert Bradford of the UUUC. Orr retired before the October 1974 election, and was succeed by Enoch Powell, who stood as a candidate of the Ulster Unionist Party – which had broken with the Conservative Party by the time Powell was elected. The Duke of Abercorn was defeated in the 1970 election by the Irish nationalist candidate Frank McManus. Currie retired before the 1970 election, and was replaced by James Kilfedder, then standing as a Unionist Party candidate but later as a candidate for the UUUC, before sitting as an 'Independent Ulster Unionist', and then for his own Ulster Popular Peoples Unionist Party.

While the various party labels showed the extent to which unionism was beginning to fragment, what all these successful unionist candidates had in common was their opposition both to the Sunningdale Agreement and, later, for those still active, the Anglo-Irish Agreement. These were enacted by UK Conservative governments and were rejected by most unionist voters in Northern Ireland, who, as we have seen, regarded them as acts of betrayal. But the ending of the partnership between Ulster unionism and the Conservative Party can be backdated to March 1972, when Edward Heath prorogued the Stormont parliament and government – a move that, as we have seen, was also strongly resented by Ulster unionists. That was when the UUP broke formal ties with the British Conservatives – though it did not disaffiliate from the National Unionist Association until 1986, in protest at the Anglo-Irish Agreement.

Was the early 1970s breakup of the long alliance between British Conservative and Ulster unionists caused by a weakening Tory commitment to the union? No. In fact, the Tories remained pro-unionist, in some cases excessively so, both just before and after the Northern Irish unionists declared their organisational independence. One early example of this was a briefing produced by the Conservative Research Department in March 1971 which implied that, if there were problems in Northern Ireland, that was because of 'the existence of a substantial minority in the population unwilling to acknowledge the authority of the Northern Ireland Government or cooperate to any meaningful extent with its administration … for 50 years' – namely, the Catholics.[7]

Others in the Conservative Party during this period were expressing more robust opinions. These were grouped around the right-wing Monday Club and the Conservative Party Northern Ireland Committee (CPNIC), and included MPs such as Jerry Wiggin, Philip Goodhart, Airey Neave, Julian Amery, Julian Critchley, John Biggs-Davison and Edward du Cann. As early as December 1969, Biggs-Davison set the tone by writing in a Monday Club pamphlet: 'The demand for Civil Rights in America, as in Ulster, the cry for one man, one vote in Ulster, as in Africa have been used as a front by ruthless men, not concerned with justice but for social revolution. The grievances of Negros or Roman Catholics are exploited to spread anarchy and bloodshed.'[8]

Critchley also identified with the Orange tradition. After a party of five MPs had visited Northern Ireland to watch the Orange Order demonstrations of 12 July 1974, he told the Conservative Party Northern Ireland Committee that it had been 'an impressive and sobering experience which should be an obligation for all British politicians in Irish affairs'.[9] The following year, Wiggin told fellow members of the CPNIC that 'the problem of security is central, some of the people suffering from violence would find it hard to understand why the Conservative Party should even talk to the SDLP' – that is, the moderate and entirely constitutional party then supported by the majority of Catholics in Northern Ireland. Wiggin's own prescription was that 'martial law should be introduced. No political progress is possible until the security problem has been firmly tackled.'[10]

In the same vein, Neave referred to the exclusively Protestant Ulster Special Constabulary – or B Specials – which had been disbanded after the Hunt Report of 1969 found them incompatible with modern ideas of law and order. Neave's contrary view in 1976, was that 'the Specials ha[d] been the only effective anti-terrorist force in rural areas of Ulster'.[11] Around the same time, du Cann, then chairman of the Conservatives' backbench 1922 Committee, offered a more global context: 'If the forces of violence, revolution and terror were to prevail in [Ulster], the outlook for democracy in the world might be darkened.'[12] Darker still was the analysis of Biggs-Davison, then an official Conservative spokesperson on Northern Ireland, available in a paper produced for the Foreign Affairs Institute in September 1976:

> Like other nationalist and irredentist movements those in Ireland receive money, arms and propaganda support from appropriate ethnic communities in the Free World, as well as from the Communist powers ... Outside assistance for Irish revolutionaries is nothing new: 'England's danger is Ireland's opportunity'. For centuries [Irish] separatists allied themselves with continental empires that were England's enemies.[13]

This thinking was not uncommon. The fear that an independent Ireland might become an enemy base had been a prime reason for the Act of Union in the first place. Biggs-Davison's version of this was also an example of Cold War paranoia with a particular Irish twist. Perhaps the most appropriate comment on it was in a somewhat deadpan memo produced by civil servants at the Northern Ireland Office and signed by a J. H. G. Leahy. He reported the views of the Northern Ireland Office: 'They do not consider that Mr Biggs-Davison's evidence amounts to very much ... It is fair to say we have little to suggest that communist governments are actively involving themselves in Northern Ireland. Indeed, there is some reason to think that they are deliberately keeping their distance.'[14]

It is easy to assume that the above examples are little more than politically illiterate reactions from fringe Conservatives, but that would be too dismissive. Many held influential positions, with Airey Neave set to become Margaret Thatcher's secretary of state for Northern Ireland, before he was assassinated in a car bomb planted by the Irish National Liberation Army at Westminster in 1979. Moreover, the leaders of the party expressed similar views to those just quoted, especially on 'security'. The Saville Inquiry into Bloody Sunday was told by Lord Carver, the British army chief of staff, that just before these killings of January 1972 he had had a discussion with prime minister Edward Heath on Northern Ireland, and that Heath 'was very good to deal with. He ... was influenced by his military background and wanted to solve problems by the use of military means.'[15]

The same inquiry heard that the attorney-general, Lord Hailsham, had suggested at a meeting of a cabinet subcommittee in the summer of 1971 that British soldiers in Northern Ireland 'could shoot anyone who obstructed them or got in their way'.[16] Carver had testified, Lord Hailsham said, that 'under some medieval statute, anybody who obstructed the servants of the king, acting in the course of their duty, was *ipso facto* one of the king's enemies and therefore liable to be shot by the king's soldiers'.[17] As for Heath himself, he told Saville that he agreed at the time with Northern Ireland prime minister Brian Faulkner that the marchers on what had become Bloody Sunday were 'not genuine civil righters but civil disobedients' and 'lawbreakers'.[18]

Nevertheless, from the early 1970s onwards British politicians were steadfast in the view that there could be no return to the old ways, when Northern Ireland was ruled as the Ulster Unionists pleased. Even Airey Neave agreed there was no going back to that. For example, when he 'clarified the meaning of [Tory–Labour] bipartisanship' during a meeting of the CPNIC in October 1975, he noted that it 'existed on basic principles, that is, the Union, the Army presence and power-sharing'.[19] On the other hand, for most Northern Ireland unionists, unconditional support of power-sharing was often the deal-breaker.

Accordingly, despite their sharing a common unionist ideology, the rift between the British and Irish unionists never healed. Eventually, a campaign that originated in Northern Ireland, through a strange partnership between integrationist unionists favouring permanent direct rule and the British and Irish Communist Organisation, secured a victory at the 1989 Conservative Party conference when the party was mandated to stand for elections in Northern Ireland. For a short while this attracted support from some affluent Northern Irish unionists, but in the end it came to little, suggesting full integration was never a popular solution among the unionist community as a whole.[20]

Instead, nearly twenty years later, on 24 July 2008, David Cameron announced talks with the Ulster Unionist Party (UUP), which had evolved from the old Unionist Party, to establish a 'new electoral force in Northern Ireland'. Cameron explained that politics in Northern Ireland needed to 'become more like politics in the rest of the United Kingdom' – a variation on Margaret Thatcher's old theme that Northern Ireland was or should be just like her own constituency.[21] When the British general election came two years later, the results showed it was not. The Conservatives and UUP stood together as Ulster Conservatives and Unionists. They stood in seventeen out of eighteen Northern Ireland seats, won none of them, and secured just 15.9 per cent of the vote, losing out in the Protestant community to the DUP.

For the UUP wing of the alliance, this represented a decline since the 2005 general election, when it had won one seat and 17.7 per cent of the vote. This signalled the end of the 'new force'. A subsequent attempt by the Conservatives to merge the two parties, effectively a takeover bid, failed. Accordingly, at the 2015 general election, the Conservatives contested sixteen out of the eighteen seats in their own right, securing just 9,055 votes – 1.26 per cent of the votes cast. The people of Northern Ireland had spoken, loudly declaring that the Conservative Party was dead to them. Their brand of unionism had no appeal, either with the Protestant or Catholic communities.

Here was evidence that Ulster was, after all, different from Britain, with a sharply divergent political culture. In short, what the Troubles had illustrated was that the versions of 'unionism' functioning in Britain and in Northern Ireland were no longer as ideologically interchangeable as they had been for most of the preceding hundred years. The UUP, the one-time bedfellow

of British Conservatism, also wilted, and the party representing the majority within Protestant political culture was, by the
twenty-first century, the Democratic Unionist Party.

The DUP was founded in 1971 by Ian Paisley and the lawyer
Desmond Boal, a former member of the UUP who had progressive leanings. Indeed, Boal, the first chairman of the DUP,
explained at the party's foundation that, while the new party
would be right-wing on law and order, it would be radical on
social and economic issues, and was hoping to attract Catholics
because of this.[22] But it was, of course, Paisley who led and
became the epitome of the party. He had first come to prominence through his evangelical Calvinistic preaching, establishing
his own Free Presbyterian Church in 1951.

Like many of strong religious faith, throughout his religious
and political life Paisley claimed divine blessing. He told a
dinner marking the twenty-fifth anniversary of his church:
'The Free Presbyterian Church of Ulster is a tangible proof in
this sceptical, blaspheming age, that there is a God in heaven,
and that that God hears the prayers of His people and answers
them more abundantly than ever we can ask or even think.'[23]
This sense of the fulfilling of God's purpose became Paisley's
religious and political hallmark. He came to prominence politically in the Divis Street Riots of September 1964, when he led
a campaign to remove an Irish national flag from a window of
the Republican Party in Divis Street, Belfast – and, in response,
the RUC, under the authority of the Stormont government,
forced their way into the offices and removed the flag. Local
opposition led to riots. Paisley was widely blamed for his provo-
cation. His version of events presented these events in a different
light:

Protestantism has faced many serious crises in its history. We
are facing a crisis now and the province is heading for an even
greater crisis ... God save the city from the scenes enacted by
the Roman Catholics within it. The real nature of Romanism

has been revealed. Its people who have kicked and cursed the police in the Falls Road were the people who would kick all Protestants tomorrow.[24]

Such exaggeration, prophecies of doom, and targeting of Catholicism and Catholics characterised Paisley's message over the next thirty years. Both before and in the early years of the Troubles, he urged resistance to more liberal unionism, seeing enemies all around him. His *Protestant Telegraph* was unremitting in the messages it delivered.

There were also religious conspiracy theories. When, in the winter of 1967–68, foot-and-mouth disease spread among cattle in England, the *Protestant Telegraph* declared: 'This is the finger of God', explaining that God had 'a controversy with England'. He blamed 'covetousness … luxury of living and love of pleasure … negligence of the Lord's Day … scepticism and infidelity' – and, inevitably, 'looking favourably on the Roman Catholic Church'. And he asked: 'when the hand of God is stretched out against us … are we not all over England living too fast?'[25]

The *Protestant Telegraph* had a distinctive world-view, illustrated by this, on the assassination of Martin Luther King:

> The heinous crime of assassination has robbed the American Negro population of its leader – Dr Martin Luther King. He had the name of the Protestant champion, but the Negro leader, also, had not the same gospel to proclaim. He laid great emphasis upon the brotherhood of man rather than the Kingship of Christ. He chose liberal theology rather than fundamentalism. He chose ecumenism rather than separation, he chose pacifism, looking to Gandhi as his 'guru', and to the Pope as his 'friend', but his pacifism could not adequately be transmitted to his followers.
>
> The people that he led have now taken to riot, arson, looting and murder. The smouldering racial tensions have now again been re-kindled. The Communist agitators have whipped up

grief and emotion, into xenophobia and uncontrolled rioting; and America is on the brink of civil war.

There can be no integration or equality of the races, no peaceful coexistence, no international harmony, until and when nations and men submit to Christ – the Prince of Peace.[26]

This was the type of message that Paisley was to deliver over the next thirty years. During the same period, he became the most popular politician in Northern Ireland, and the political party he led eventually attracted more voters than any other party. Was this because of or despite the sort of messages quoted here? To answer that, first it is important to remember that the DUP did not become the most electorally successful unionist party in Northern Ireland parliamentary or Assembly elections until after the Good Friday/Belfast Agreement (GFBA). The reasons it did so then will be examined below (see chapter 7); but one consistent factor in Paisley's rise to political popularity among Protestants was that his warnings of 'betrayal' – from the civil rights' first reforms to the GFBA – were, his followers believed, part of a pattern of prophecies fulfilled. This is illustrated by this statement, made four years into the Troubles, reproduced in the *Protestant Telegraph*:

> The Rev Ian Paisley has been the focal point of abuse both from Republicans and Unionists alike … It was Paisley who awakened Ulster to the betrayals of [Terence] O'Neill's so-called bridge-building policies, Paisley who forced O'Neill out of office, who spoke of no-go areas as far as back as 1969, who exposed the incompetence of Chichester-Clarke, who warned the B. Specials would be disbanded while [Brian] Faulkner said they would stay. It was Paisley who told that direct rule was on the way while press and politicians scorned such a suggestion. NO MAN IN OR OUT OF ULSTER CAN POINT THE FINGER AT IAN PAISLEY'S POLITICAL CONSISTENCY. Paisley has given the lead to Ulster loyalists all down the line. He has always been one step ahead of Ulster's political field.[27]

Such thinking led Paisley to be elected to both the Northern Ireland and Westminster parliaments in 1970, before the DUP was formed. A string of other election victories followed. In 1979, he topped the Northern Ireland European election with 29.8 per cent of the vote, the other main unionist candidate receiving just 11.9 per cent. In other words, he became the politician of choice for a substantial majority of voting Protestants in Northern Ireland. He was charismatic, clever and, for most of his career, maintained astute political judgement. That he was also a bigot and a conspiracy theorist, and claimed he had God on his side, did of course lose him votes among the liberals in the Protestant population; but his voting figures suggest he knew that community better, and indeed often reflected it more, than did liberals, or even the more tolerant unionists.

This raises the issue of the influence of religion in Northern Ireland politics. There are those who see the entire Troubles as essentially a conflict informed by religion. One does not have to agree to this rather reductionist interpretation to recognise that, for some within the Protestant community, religion and politics did indeed inform each other. This was explained by Paisley when he preached in the summer of 1973: 'Northern Ireland, as we know it, owes its existence to the great Protestant Reformation of the sixteenth century. Without Protestantism there would be no Ulster. This is the bedrock of the whole Ulster position. Smash the bedrock, corrode the foundation, break up the fundamentals, and Ulster will crumble, decay, perish and die.' He went on to justify himself in the same terms:

> I am standing in this pulpit and I have had a very stormy career. I have been twice behind prison bars. I am not a loyalist for any self-interest. It would suit me well to be out of politics. It would suit me well to shed all my responsibility and just run this church, but I would be a traitor to God if I did it. There is no discharge from this war.[28]

This was a message that fitted into the type of Calvinism not just preached by Paisley, but followed by many outside the Free Presbyterians, who had never constituted more than 1 per cent of Northern Ireland's population. The extent of this more fundamentalist wing of Christianity was illustrated in a *Life and Times Survey* in 2004, reporting that 23 per cent of Protestants considered themselves to be 'born again', 21 per cent said they were 'evangelical', and 38 per cent said they believed in the literal truth of the Bible.

What these figures suggest is that, while Paisley's religious view might boost his political support, they were not substantial enough to explain it: it was his politics that secured his most impressive victories, and ultimately it was political misjudgement that led to his downfall. Both of these factors will be examined below in relation to the GFBA.[29]

Paisley died in September 2014. But five years later the eight DUP MPs elected in the December 2019 UK general election reflected Paisley-ism in both its religious and political components. To appreciate the social and political nature of the DUP, it helps to delve into the lives and opinions of these individuals.

The incoming Westminster leader was Jeffrey Donaldson, who was born in Kilkeel, County Down, where he attended Kilkeel High School and later Castlereagh College. His political background was one of old unionism; his father was a member of the old Unionist Party, and, as already noted, Donaldson started his political life working as an agent for Enoch Powell. He is a member of the Orange Order and was in the British army's Ulster Defence Regiment. He was first elected to the Northern Ireland Assembly at the age of just twenty-two, in 1985, and then in 1997 to Westminster; both times he stood for the UUP. However, on 18 December 2003, along with future DUP leader Arlene Foster and Norah Beale, he left the UUP over its support for the GFBA, and joined the DUP. Even before joining Paisley, in his maiden speech in the UK parliament on 20 May 1997, he quoted the Old Testament while also asserting 'the rights of the people of Northern Ireland to determine their own political future, free from the threat of terrorist violence and political interference.'

Paisley's son, Ian Paisley Jr, was born in 1966, and inherited his father's Westminster seat – though not his charisma. Like Donaldson, he too became a professional politician early in his life, after obtaining a BA (Hons) in modern history and a Master's in Irish politics from Queen's University Belfast. He had lived in relative prosperity with his parents and siblings in Cyprus Avenue – made immortal by Van Morrison – in East Belfast, and attended Shaftsbury House College, a fee-paying school, and then the sixth-form wing of Methodist College, an interdenominational grammar school. He then became a researcher for his father, before being elected to the Northern Ireland Assembly, and then Westminster.

There, his chief claim to fame – apart from being his father's son – was his involvement in financial scandals. In 2018 he received an unprecedented thirty-day suspension from the House of Commons after failing to declare two luxury family holidays in Sri Lanka in 2013, paid for by its government. In 2014 he wrote to the British prime minister to lobby against a UN resolution on Sri Lanka over its alleged human rights abuses. His parliamentary suspension led to both a temporary suspension from the DUP and an attempted recall petition in his constituency, which failed by just 444 votes to spark a by-election. In September 2020, he was found guilty by a parliamentary standards commission of not having declared an interest over a complimentary holiday he and his family had received in the Maldives in 2016, some months after advocating on behalf of the government there. He was cleared of being paid to advocate on behalf of the Maldives, but the parliamentary commissioner did complain that, during her investigations, Paisley's responses had 'not always been helpful'.[30]

Another DUP MP to come under scrutiny over financial ethics was Strangford MP Jim Shannon. In May 2016 the Independent

Parliamentary Standards Authority questioned his expenses claims. It found that he 'accounted for 26.1 per cent of all staff constituency mileage claimed by the entire House of Commons', and that this 'level of commitment of staff time to driving appears to be neither practical nor plausible'. Shannon agreed to repay £13,926.[31] The committee did note that Shannon took up a range of issues, and indeed in January 2018 the *Belfast Telegraph* reported that he 'is well known among Westminster watchers for his frequent interventions', and that he had contributed to 213 debates and question sessions in the House of Commons in the previous seven months, ranging in subject matter from school funding in North Northumberland and Cornwall's dark-sky status to job losses in Cardiff.[32] On 28 September 2020, Shannon tabled a motion in the Commons offering a somewhat exceptional stand on Covid-19, calling on the prime minister 'to initiate a National Day of Prayer to enable those for whom this is important to seek God for strength, peace, comfort, hope, wisdom, forgiveness and even joy at this difficult time'.

This reflected Shannon's Baptist faith. Along with this common evangelical characteristic among DUP MPs, Shannon shared others: he served in the UDR, and is a member of the Orange Order and Apprentice Boys. He was educated at local primary and grammar schools and has a family farm.

Sammy Wilson, the DUP MP for East Antrim, shared Shannon's Baptist faith. He was born in 1953 and, like Ian Paisley Jnr, educated at the interdenominational Methodist College and then Queen's University Belfast, and Stranmillis College. Wilson became press officer for the DUP. Before that, as assistant press officer, he wrote in the *Voice of Ulster*, in June 1986, an article entitled, 'The Tragedy of Those Unemployment Figurers', where he argued that the government 'should recognise that its present deflationary policy has caused untold misery and waste of resources'. Indeed, even before this the government's Northern Ireland Office had met with Wilson early in his political career, and decided he was, in the words of S. G. Hewitt of the Political Affairs Division, 'worth cultivating', because of his apparent differences with Paisley. In one 1982 meeting with Wilson and fellow DUP member John Foster, they reported: 'expressed some frustration at the way [Paisley] dominates the party policy and strategy. They would like to see more emphasis placed on social issues – housing, employment, etc – and less on the more traditional and conservative issues.'[33]

However, as his political career developed – he became Belfast lord mayor in 1986 – Wilson swung behind the 'traditional'. For example, in September 1989 he described the Gaelic Athletic Association as 'the sporting wing of the IRA'; in September 1991 he said those who voted Sinn Féin in a council election were '5,000 sub-human animals'; in 1992 he said of a gay group who had applied to use Belfast City Hall, 'They are poofs. I don't care if they are ratepayers. As far as I am concerned, they are perverts'; and in 2000 he said, 'Taigs [a pejorative for Catholics] don't pay rates.'[34]

While he became more careful with his words after he was elected to Westminster in a 2005 by-election, he retained the ability to make headlines. In March 2017 he was recorded by the BBC appearing to agree with a member of the public who declared: 'Get the ethnics out'. Wilson's apparent endorsement was, he said, 'taken out of context'.[35] More openly, in December 2008 he described climate change as 'a con'.[36]

Another DUP MP not exactly known for his tolerant views is Gregory Campbell, the MP for East Londonderry, first elected to Westminster in 2001. Like others, Campbell has authentic working-class credentials. He was born in the economically deprived Protestant area of Waterside in Derry in 1953, the son of a navy serviceman. He claimed he had entered politics because of the civil rights movement of the late 1960s and early 1970s, objecting to the view that Protestants were privileged. In the same interview, he said he took his political guidance from reading the Bible, citing his view that homosexuality was 'an evil, wicked, abhorrent practice'.[37] As a member of the Free Presbyterian Church, in the 1980s he helped with the management of a Christian bookshop. In a 2012 story in the *Belfast Telegraph*, he was listed as a Facebook 'friend' of the fundamental creationist group Caleb, and commented that he did indeed support the organisation that believed in the literalist teaching of the Bible in schools.[38] He was suspended from his membership of the Northern Ireland Assembly for a day for mocking the Irish Language in 2014.

Paul Girvan has been the DUP MP for South Antrim since 2017. According to his Facebook profile, he is a 'committed Christian' who 'plays an active role in his local church'. He was born and raised in Ballyclare, went to his local secondary school, and then to the University of Ulster. He worked as an electronic engineer and established his own business. He was first elected to Westminster in 2017, to represent South Antrim in 2017. Before that he was a member of the Northern Ireland Assembly. It was there, in December 2015 he said that scrap-metal dealers should be provided with guns to protects themselves from 'gypsies'.[39] In the Commons he often specialised in interventions reflecting his background and faith – for example, calling for no criminal prosecution of British soldiers who served in Northern Ireland, and deploring the persecution of Christians in Africa. In July 2019 he told the House of Commons that his sister was a missionary in the Democratic Republic of Congo.

After the December 2019 general election, Gavin Robinson was the only DUP MP representing a Belfast constituency – in his case East Belfast, where he was born. While, like all DUP MPs, he voted against abortion rights and marriage equality in Northern Ireland, he did suggest that a way out of the controversy might be to hold referenda on the issue.[40] In parliament he reflected the policies of the DUP on such issues as non-prosecution of ex-soldiers accused of crimes. He was also a regular member of the House of Commons Defence Committee, and the parliamentary Ecclesiastic Committee.

His own religion went through what was, in the context of Northern Ireland, an interesting change: he moved from being a Presbyterian to enter the less Calvinistic but more establishment Church of Ireland. He also championed the occasional progressive issue. In July 1920, for example, he tabled an Early Day Motion calling for the government to extend maternity leave by three months during the Covid-19 lockdown.

That leaves Carla Lockhart, the MP for Upper Ban, elected in 2019. Born in 1985 in Aughnacloy, County Tyrone, to a working-class family, she attended the local high school before studying at Armagh Technical College, and then obtaining a business degree from the University of Ulster. She joined the youth wing of the DUP, and remains a member of the Free Presbyterian Church. She chose to make her maiden speech in parliament on the familiar DUP theme of attacking abortion – but she also indicated her own social background and other interests:

> I had the privilege of growing up right in the very heart of Ulster in a working-class family, and I am proud of the roots and the grounding that I have. Growing up near the border with the Republic of Ireland and knowing many families who had loved ones murdered, I was always very aware of the troubles in Northern Ireland and why we had such a love for the Union and our British way of life.
>
> To that end, I will endeavour to use this position to achieve just that. I want to see changes to our special educational needs provision, and I want to tackle the escalating mental health crisis that exists within our society. Our suicide figures are still among the highest within the United Kingdom. This needs to be tackled urgently, and I along with colleagues will work with the Secretary of State.[41]

Three of these MPs – Lockhart, Campbell and Shannon – were working class; three – Paisley, Lockhart and Campbell – were

Free Presbyterians; and two were Baptists, while the other three all expressed strong Christian views. In contrast to the Tories who represented Northern Ireland in 1966, none were aristocratic, none had gone to public school, nor to Cambridge or Oxford. All spoke and voted against abortion rights and marriage equality. They were, in this respect, out of step with modern Conservativism, and indeed modern Britain – as were their religious affiliations. Moreover, their views on abortion and marriage equality were not reflective of Northern Irish opinion – and, more importantly, their religion did not proportionally reflect the Protestant community as a whole, where Free Presbyterians constituted just 1 per cent of the population, and Baptists 3 per cent.[42]

Such disproportions were reflected in a survey conducted by Jonathan Tonge for the 2014 book *The Democratic Unionist Party: From Protest to Power*. This showed that 30.5 per cent of DUP members identified as Free Presbyterians, 29.1 per cent as Presbyterians, and 17.7 per cent members of the Church of Ireland. For the Free Presbyterians, in particular, this was an astonishing overrepresentation. In class terms, 41 per cent identified themselves as working class, and 34 per cent as middle class. One notable contrast is that, while 19 per cent were trade unionists, 34.6 per cent were members of the Orange Order.[43]

More generally, the DUP was and remains a party that for most if its life had been angry with and contemptuous of most British politicians – especially Tories. In that respect, it was hardly surprising that their effort to rebuild the old alliance with Theresa May's Tories ended so badly. Some of their MPs elected in 2019 did express occasional progressive views, but others showed a penchant for anti-Catholic sectarianism. They all insisted on being British, but it is difficult to see how they fitted in with twenty-first century Britain. They were, at least in class terms, certainly more representative of the community that had elected them than the Tory Northern Ireland MPs of the 1960s, as was the party generally. And yet they were unable to attract such broad support from within the Protestant community as the pre-Troubles unionists. They lived in a society that was evolving away from its majority traditional unionist roots, and one with a growing Irish nationalist population; but they and their party were hostages to these changes rather than informed and influenced by them.

6

What About the Workers?

A number of conflicts within the Northern Ireland Troubles erupted in 1968. One was the conflict between the Catholic and Protestant communities; another was that between Irish republicanism and the British state. A third flash-point emerged in the battle for the political leadership between moderate and traditionalist unionism; and a fourth could be seen in the contest for leadership of the Catholic community between moderate nationalism and Irish republicanism. Many of these contests were intertwined, and they all affected each other.

There is one narrative, one contest, that appeared absent, however: the conflict between classes – between the Catholic and Protestant poor and state forces or employers. There was, of course, the Ulster Workers' Council strike of May 1974, which was successful in bringing down the Faulkner-led power-sharing unionist government; but that was not the Northern Irish working class acting together. Indeed, one of its consequences was increased tension between Protestant and Catholic workers. Moreover, throughout the Troubles, those on the ground who fought hardest against each other were generally from a proletarian background, whether that was the IRA, the loyalist paramilitaries or British soldiers.

The reasons for the non-emergence of inter-class battles produced another conflict – one of interpretations, which has often focused on the Northern Irish Protestant working class. Why have Protestant workers long resisted what has been wished on them by many political activists and commentators within and beyond Ireland – that is to break away from the political leadership of the unionist upper class and/or the right-wing parties? Why have they appeared to be, on the contrary, the most sectarian and violent in the Protestant community?

At the start of the Troubles in 1968, the politics of Northern Ireland were, to say the least, somewhat idiosyncratic. A third of the population was liable to be discriminated against in terms of employment, housing, voting rights and civil liberties. Discrimination is common enough and is usually directed against those of a particular skin colour, class, ethnic background or gender. In Northern Ireland the basis for discrimination was religion – albeit within the same broad Christian religion shared by those in power. Broadly speaking, Catholics were discriminated against by Protestants. This was detailed in 1969 by British judge Lord Cameron, who, along with two others, compiled a sober and restrained government-commissioned report on this situation. He reported a 'rising sense of continuing injustice and grievance among large sections of the Catholic population in Northern Ireland'. Local government election boundaries had been fixed by and in favour of unionists. Unionist local authorities discriminated against Catholics when allocating both public housing and jobs. There was 'resentment, particularly among Catholics, as to the existence of the Ulster Special Constabulary ("B" Specials) as a partisan and paramilitary force recruited exclusively from Protestants'; and that there was 'widespread resentment among Catholics in particular at the continuance in force of the regulations made under the Special Powers Act'.

To combat the discrimination and coercion, the Northern Ireland Civil Rights Association (NICRA) was formed in January 1967. It included members of the Northern Ireland Labour Party (NILP), the Communist Party, trade unionists and the Irish republican movement, which was itself then under the influence of the Communist Party. Lord Cameron described NICRA as modelled on the National Council for Civil Liberties in Britain, and noted it was concerned with combating anti-Catholic discrimination in local authority housing and employment, and promoting one person, one vote in local government elections, instead of giving extra votes for multiple property owners. Crucially, Cameron recorded that NICRA was not challenging partition, but rather seeking to reform Northern Ireland.

The first headline-capturing action of NICRA was a march from Coalisland to Dungannon in County Tyrone in August 1968, over inequalities in public housing allocation. The demonstration was a success, with 4,000 people participating, and was peaceful. Cameron commented: 'There was hope by many participants that something new was taking place in Northern Ireland, in that here was a non-violent demonstration by people of many differing political antecedents ... united on a common platform of reform.' Then came the Derry civil rights march of 5 October 1968. The impetus for this came from those who had been involved in agitation over housing and unemployment and/or who were members of the Derry Labour Party (formally a branch of the NILP) or the local Republican Club. The route of the march, chosen by the local organisers, was outside Catholic areas. This was partly to emphasise the non-sectarian nature of the protest. In the same spirit, Derry Labour Party activist Eamonn McCann has described how, in the run-up to the march, publicity had been built around such slogans as 'Class War, not Creed War'.

The unionist government banned the march, but it went ahead and was attacked by the Royal Ulster Constabulary (RUC). Such was the viciousness of the assault, with television cameras present, that Northern Ireland and its 'Orange State' became world news. As McCann has admitted, there was nobody on the march from the local Protestant working class, despite efforts to enlist support from members of that community. 'We had real hope', he was to write six years later, 'that the socialist movement we were going to build after, and partly as a result of the march would engage Protestant support.'[1]

After the RUC attack, thousands of students, Catholics and Protestants from Queen's University, took to the streets in Belfast to protest, and then established People's Democracy (PD), which organised mass discussions with no structure, no rules, and supposedly no leaders. This was based on the May revolt of 1968 in Paris; PD saw its roots in the international protests of 1968 rather than in Irish nationalism.

Similarly, its most dramatic intervention was the 'Long March' of January 1969, deliberately modelled on the Selma-to-Montgomery march of the black civil rights campaign in Alabama in 1965; it Northern Irish equivalent had already borrowed 'We Shall Overcome' as its anthem. The march was harassed by the RUC and unionist mobs throughout its course – no more so than at Burntollet Bridge, just outside Derry, when the 500 marchers were showered with large stones and bottles, and then attacked by loyalist ambushers, some of whom were wielding nail-studded cudgels. The ambushers included out-of-uniform B Specials. When PD finally reached Derry, they were attacked again. That night the police invaded Derry's Bogside, a Catholic ghetto, smashing windows, banging on doors and shouting sectarian abuse. All of this was later confirmed by the Cameron Commission.

What these early months of what is now designated as the 'Troubles' show is that PD and the Derry activists not only shaped events, but in doing so introduced the new form of politics being developed internationally in this period: young people taking direct action, challenging traditional leaderships and showing they were prepared to challenge the state itself. But that, in many ways, was the easy part. Even in these early days the civil rights left wing was confronted not just by the state forces but by their fellow, often poor citizens from the Protestant population. The protesters might have carried 'Class not Creed' placards, but it became apparent early on that their demands antagonised many working-class 'loyalists', who appeared to identify with the Protestant-dominated state and support the status quo.

Such realities surfaced in an interview in the *New Left Review* in May–June 1969, conducted three days after the election of the PD's Bernadette Devlin as MP for Mid-Ulster as a 'Unity' candidate in a Westminster by-election. The four main interview interviewees were McCann, and, from PD, Michael Farrell, Devlin and Cyril Toman. Farrell noted, 'We have radicalised the Catholic working class to quite a considerable extent and to some degree got across to them the necessity of non-sectarianism.' For McCann this assessment was 'very wrong'; he insisted the left had failed to raise issues outside of civil rights, and that, accordingly, the Catholic working class remained 'sectarian and bigoted'.

While all concerned insisted that they needed to win over sections of the Protestant working class, nobody in the interview seemed to know how this was to be achieved. Devlin maintained that she had won some Protestant votes in her election – as indeed a unionist MP admitted she had. She was the most optimistic when she remarked, 'I think that the Protestants may be the best of our supporters because they are more radical people, and their socialism is more radical.'[2]

The streets told a different story, in which the growing, mainly proletarian 'Protestant backlash' was becoming daily more evident. This culminated in Derry on 12 August 1969 with the annual march of protestant Apprentice Boys – an organisation similar to the Orange Order. As they marched, stones were thrown in the city centre, and then some Catholic marchers and their supporters retreated to the Catholic working-class district of Bogside. The police attempted to follow them, but after some initial success they were driven back. The barricades went up, and for three days the 'Battle of Bogside' raged. This was a straight fight between the state security forces and mainly Catholic Bogsiders, with a few students thrown in. The RUC and the B Specials were soon exhausted, and the unionist government asked its Westminster overlord for assistance. The Labour government sent in the British army.

By now the drama was shifting to Belfast. On the night of 14 August the RUC entered the Falls Road, a Catholic area of Belfast, to confront rioters expressing their solidarity with Bogside. The police came with submachine guns mounted on armoured vehicles and shot four people dead. Protestant mobs followed, burning Catholic homes. The next night Catholic homes were again burned down by Protestant mobs in Bombay Street in the Falls Road area, and in Brookfield Street in the Crumlin Road. Another government-commissioned enquiry, headed by Lord Scarman, later said that these attacks had been largely spontaneous. The just-arrived British army was unable to prevent them, as indeed had the more traditional defenders of the Catholic community, the IRA.

Afterwards, the barricades did go up in Catholic working-class areas, designed chiefly to keep out Protestant mobs, but also the army. The IRA then split, and what became known as the Provisional IRA vowed to do what the old IRA leadership had failed to do: defend its community. For the unionists and then the British army, both the barricades and the Provos were an affront to their authority. As for the hopes of workers' unity, the divisions within the working-class, which were always there, were now consolidating and growing.

By August 1970, *Free Citizen*, the newspaper of PD, was reporting that, in Belfast's Catholic ghettos, the short honeymoon between the army and Catholics was over: 'The troops returned day after day to provocative occupying strength and night after night, pumping in canisters of CS gas, breaking down doors and windows and terrorising people ... the result was inevitable and predictable. Six nights of continuous rioting in almost all the Catholic ghettos of Belfast.' Then came the warning: 'Even now the Unionist right-wingers are not satisfied. Now they want internment.'[3]

Among these unionist organisations named by *Free Citizen* was the Loyalist Association of Workers (LAW), led by Bill Hull, a shop stewards' convenor in Belfast's shipyards and former member of the NILP. His organisation was drawn entirely from the Protestant working class in the shipyards and the engineering industry. As well as marching for internment, it organised to drive out socialists, communists and Catholics from their workplaces. In 1973, PD was to produce a pamphlet describing LAW and similar loyalist working-class organisations as 'fascist'.[4]

As late as July 1970, the *Free Citizen* was still insisting: 'The PD believes that Protestant and Catholic workers must recognise their common identity as workers. As workers they must fight the system that exploits and uses them.' The use of the word 'must' suggested a mood of despair. The reality was that many of the attacks, on both the civil rights marchers and Catholic ghettos, from Burntollet to Bombay Street, had come from sections of the Protestant working class, often acting spontaneously. In voting terms, over the next decades that community increasingly moved not towards liberalism, even liberal unionism – never mind workers unity – but towards the sectarian right led by Ian Paisley. Writing twenty years later, Farrell admitted: 'the loyalist paramilitary groups have drawn their strongest support from working-class Protestants. Uniting the working class proved a lot harder than we had imagined in 1968.'[5] This was undoubtedly true and was being recognised even at the time. Bernadette Devlin, writing in *The Price of My Soul*, spoke of 'the almost insurmountable problem of enlisting the Protestant working class'.[6]

Why did the Protestant working class react in this way? The favouritism they enjoyed under the status quo as outlined by Cameron is one explanation, but there were deeper motivations. As with much else in Ireland, a sense of history is indispensable. We have already seen that socialists of the early twentieth century also pointed to the Protestant labour aristocracy as a material reason for that community's politics. Around this time, another explanation appeared for the divisions in Ireland. This was offered by the Ulster-born unionist and Ireland correspondent for *The Times*, W. F. Monypenny, in his book, *The Two Nations: An Essay on Home Rule*. This was to establish an important and lasting ideological tradition that would resurface in the Troubles.

Monypenny was writing in 1913, during the Liberal government's attempt to legislate for Home Rule, which he opposed. His reasoning was that the divisions in Ireland were so deep that Home Rule would only exacerbate them. He argued: 'the Home Rule Struggle is a struggle between two nations', not the English and the Irish, but the Protestant and Roman Catholic, or more precisely the Unionist and the Nationalist.[7] Thus, he defined the divisions in Ireland on religious grounds, but not entirely. He wrote of 'two nations with separate religions, separate ideals, separate traditions, and separate affinities'. The two nations were not, however, geographically separate: 'The two nations in Ireland live side by side in all parts of the island, and, though the presence of a concentrated democracy in the North is a notable feature of the situation, there is no real geographic line of division.' Also, although he used religion as a 'demarcation' of the divisions in Ireland, he did acknowledge there was also a British factor: 'Antipathies that had their source in the long conflict between English and Irish have deepened and intensified the religious division.' He added: 'The struggle between landlords and tenants that has raged for more than two centuries, often breaking into open war, has also contributed to the capital of the feud, adding to the animosities of race and creed the still more deadly animosities of caste.'[8]

Monypenny's account of these 'animosities' was at times sympathetic to the Irish majority. He wrote of the 'evils of [English landlord] absenteeism, the vices of the land system, the monopoly of patronage of the party of the Ascendency'. He registered the 'terrible calamity' of the famine of 1845–47, and how badly it had been handled by the British Whig government: a 'monument of English folly'.[9] His concern was that such events led Catholics to demand reform, even the end of the union, and that this 're-awoke fanaticism in the Protestant camp in Ireland, and gave a great stimulus to the growth of the Orange body'. He testified to the separate interests and culture of Irish Protestants, and that challenges to the status quo from Catholics made them 'forget their internal divisions'.[10]

Clearly, for Monypenny, the major divisions in Ireland were defined by religion; but he recognised that, for Protestants, an important factor was defence of the traditional Protestant ascendency, which had economic and political determinates as well as religious ones. The difficulty with Catholics demanding change, and even more so acting to bring about change, was not so much the merits of their demands, but that they provoked the Protestants, and that caused even more trouble. This version of the blame-game was to re-emerge during the Troubles.

A case can be made that, had Monypenny been writing today, he might not have used the word 'nations' when describing the divisions within Ireland; perhaps 'communities' would have been more apt, given his observation that there was no geographical boundary between Protestants and Catholics, who shared a common Irish identity. Nevertheless, his 'two nations' analysis, even if it was misunderstood, did establish an ideological tradition that was updated and amended by adherents from the 1970s onwards. Those involved in this project included such writers and academics as Ivan Gibbon, Conor Cruise O'Brien, Brendan Clifford of the British and Irish Communist Organisation (BICO), Tom Nairn, Paul Bew and Henry Patterson.

Less respectably, variations on the same theme were to be taken up by the unionist right, such as Vanguard and the loyalist paramilitary organisations, including the Ulster Defence Association (UDA). While it would be incorrect to say there was a detailed analysis shared by all these, their positions had common features. One of these centred on the argument that not only did the Protestant working class have material reasons to support unionism, but that they were right to do so in the face of a politically backward Irish nationalism whose adherents, it was claimed, often initiated conflict.

The faction that set the pace in this respect was BICO – an organisation that took Stalin's side in the Communist controversies following's Khrushchev's denunciation of him in 1956. From 1969 onwards, it began working on and refining *The Economics of Partition*, which was first issued as a pamphlet in 1969, then revised as a book in 1972, and finally revised again and issued under the authorship of Brendan Clifford in 1992. It summarised its arguments as follows:

> The economic basis of Partition is the two distinctive developments which occurred in Ireland, at widely different separate periods. The first development took place in Ulster in the latter half of the 18th century and culminated in the development of heavy industrial capitalism in the 19th century. The second took place in the South in the second half of the 19th and early 20th centuries and fell short of the development of heavy industry …
>
> Since the early 17th century Ireland has been inhabited by two different communities whose social structures are very different. These two communities have not been prevented from merging over the intervening three and a half centuries mainly by religious or third party manipulation of a third party, but by the different lives of economic development.[11]

By 'third party', Clifford meant Britain, which he thus exonerated from responsibility for the nineteenth- and twentieth-century divisions in Ireland. Thus, it was 'the different stages of capitalist development in the North and South' that were 'the foundations on which the border was erected'. As was true of many of those who claimed Marxist or left-wing ideologies in the 1970s, Clifford was not short of polemical anger against others on the left. In developing his arguments he criticised the Communist Party of Ireland, Michael Farrell and People's Democracy, Eamonn McCann, and Irish nationalism in general.

Their shared sin was that they got the Protestant working class all wrong:

> The section of the 'left' which came under the influence of the Catholic bourgeois nationalist left, propounded a theory elaborated on the notion that the Protestant masses were stupid bigots. The intense energy which they [the Protestant masses] displayed to the Union cause was put down to stupidity ... Some [on the nationalist left] tried to conjure up an appropriate material interest for the masses in the form of imperialist bribery. The 'stupid dupes' of the Orange Order were said to be a labour aristocracy defending their bribes ... you need to be very much lost to the world to be able to feel in the Shankill and the environs that you were in the stronghold of an entrenched labour aristocracy.[12]

To clarify, nowhere in *The Economics of Partition* did Clifford make reference to any left-wing writer, or indeed anyone, who claimed that the Protestant working class were 'stupid bigots'. Similarly, although alleged that they had been called 'stupid dupes', enclosing the phrase in inverted commas, neither did he give a reference for this. It is true that James Connolly more than once referred to the Protestant working class of Belfast as 'dupes', but most of Connolly's writings on this topic were much more sophisticated than this.[13]

There were those, especially British socialists, who did not grasp the reasons why Protestant workers supported unionism – but certainly the 1970s writings of Farrell, McCann, and my own in *The Protestants of Ulster*, are free of any such references to 'stupid dupes'. Instead, they explain how the Ulster Protestants had material reasons to support the status quo. As to the aristocracy of labour, it is beyond dispute that the Protestant working class of Belfast were generally in better jobs, and had a higher level of employment, than Belfast Catholics in the nineteenth and early twentieth centuries. Indeed, the example Clifford gave of the all-Protestant Shankill district of Belfast when he decried the notion that they could possibly be a 'labour aristocracy' was also referred to in 1975 by Peter Gibbon, who was part of the two-nations school. Discussing the Protestants in the Shankill Road in the late nineteenth century, Gibbon wrote: 'Just as the shipyards came to represent the town's industrial success, so the shipyards' men became the symbols of its Protestant manhood, its "labour aristocracy". Their good housing, health, appearance, high wages, and above all their *numbers* served as a living notice of their importance.'[14]

Gibbon did make common cause with Clifford in the conclusion to his study when he noted, 'Ulster Unionism emerged as the product neither of a conspiracy of landed notables and industrialists to "dupe the people" nor from the spontaneous convergence of a set of forces without prior political relations.'[15] Again, there is no reference or explanation in any part of Gibbon's book to where the phrase 'dupe the people' is supposed to have originated.

The two-nations theory as articulated by Clifford, Gibbon and others is that these ideas had significant political consequences, suggesting as it did that British colonialism played little or no part in originating and sustaining the divisions of Ireland. These consequences were illustrated in another book of the early 1970s, *The States of Ireland*, written by the historian and Irish Labour Party politician Conor Cruise O'Brien. His general view, he claimed, was: 'I am not "against [Irish] unity" ... but there is no meaningful sense in which it is possible now while the two communities are so bitterly antagonistic ... it is not merely futile but actually mischievous to talk about uniting.'[16] On the other hand, he talked of a unilateral Ulster declaration of independence which, he claimed, 'was to become increasingly attractive' to 'growing sections of Ulster unionists'.[17] This he blamed both on the left of the civil rights movement, such as PD, and on the two IRAs that had started to emerge by the early 1970s. For O'Brien, they pressed too hard for reform, or went one step further by asking if the northern state was reformable:

The final solution of the problem depends on whether Irish Catholics come to accept the truth ... As long as Catholics generally think of unity as 'the solution', 'the only solution', 'the only thinkable solution', so long will the Provisional IRA draw comfort from this general view ... So long will the Protestants generally feel that the slightest concession to Catholics opens the way to Catholic power over Protestants. And so long will some Protestants feel that Protestant murder-gangs are the only answer to Catholic murder gangs. So long, in fact, will we have all the conditions of sectarian civil war.[18]

First, it is worth noting that 'murder-gang' is exactly what the British called the Irish Volunteers and the IRA during the Irish War of Independence, as the historian in O'Brien would surely have known; accordingly, he repeats this anti-Irish terminology. Second, the new Ulster Volunteer Force (UVF), the first Protestant paramilitary organisation to emerge during the Troubles, was formed and began killing innocent Catholics in 1966, before the arrival of the Provisional IRA, and even before the civil rights movement. But what stands out is O'Brien's demand that Irish Catholics should stop even thinking about Irish unity – and his implied warning that, if they did not, the Protestant 'murder-gangs' were their own fault.

O'Brien mused about what lay ahead. If, he said, the IRA ended its 'offensive', then Britain could end internment, discussions between politicians would take place, and reforms could be agreed. But a precondition for this was the dropping of all pro-Irish unity 'propaganda'. If this path was not followed, then what O'Brien called a 'malignant model' would persist, under which 'the Provisionals offensive will continue and even escalate ... followed by massed Protestant assaults on the Catholic ghettoes'. He warned that the British army would then be attacked by both sides, and British public opinion would force it to withdraw entirely. Civil war would follow, and 'Ireland will be left, once more with two States, but of even more virulent shades of green and Orange. The Orange state will be smaller than before – probably about four counties ... Both states would be under right-wing governments, scruffily militaristic and xenophobic in character.'[19]

O'Brien was eventually to become a leading Irish 'revisionist' historian and a member of the Unionist Party.[20] When his above remarks were published, he was a leading member of the Irish Labour Party and of the Irish coalition government, so he had a significant readership. A different, more left-wing readership attended to Tom Nairn's *The Break-Up of Britain*, which was published in 1977.

Nairn quoted both O'Brien and Peter Gibbon heavily, and with approval; indeed, he said that O'Brien's 'malignant model' was 'nearer realization now than when he wrote it'. Nairn did not subscribe to the two-nations theory as it had been developed by Clifford and BICO. On the contrary, he attacked BICO for its 'uncritical belief in the British state'.[21] Nairn talked instead of 'two nationalities' in Ireland, and of 'two potential communities and states'. He was also more critical of the 'Protestant nationality' – or, as he also called it, the 'Protestant people' or 'Protestant Ulster'[22] – than either O'Brien or BICO. He called the post-partition Unionist Party government 'an odious regime ... of devout spite and discrimination'.[23] He summed up as follows what he called the 'paradox' of the Protestants of Northern Ireland:

A people which has long chosen political retardation to accompany economic advance; a community which has chosen almost to re-live its past, rather than utilize its past to frame an ordinary national consciousness of the present; a society dedicated to the alien – and now collapsing – identity of 'Britishism' rather than to the research and construction of its own distinct character ...'[24]

There is much here with which many on the Irish and British left could agree. But, more controversially, Nairn, echoing Clifford, attacked those in the Irish and British left who said the emerging conflict between sections of the Northern Ireland Catholic community and the British state was an anti-imperialist struggle, or 'Britain's Vietnam'. Obviously, the Catholic communities of Belfast, Derry and elsewhere did not suffer as the people of Vietnam suffered at the hands of the United States – and perhaps the conflict in Northern Ireland was not a classical anti-imperialist struggle in Marxist terms. But in the Catholic ghettos it would have been an uncomfortable exercise to explain to the relatives of those killed on Bloody Sunday, or to the ten Catholics shot on sight in Ballymurphy a few weeks before, or to civil rights activists and Irish nationalists interned without charge and then 'ill-treated' during internment, that, while the perpetrators wore British uniforms, it would be definitionally incorrect to identify them as agents of British imperialism.

That aside, what became the more controversial aspect of Nairn's analysis was his conclusion that 'the only possibility ... of making the miserable best out of an extremely bad job' was 'independence of a Protestant Ulster'.[25] He endorsed O'Brien in foreseeing the withdrawal of Britain and a four-county northern state. He acknowledged 'the very words "Ulster independence"' led to 'a familiar litany: the unviability of such a tiny state, entirely deprived of international or great-power backing; the regressiveness of narrow nationalism; the superiority of a social-revolutionary solution, Irish or "British"; the dreadful human cost of the operation – and so on'. He then commented, 'it is not necessary to pursue these arguments farther',[26] and soon ended the book's chapter on Ireland. This was hardly a satisfactory conclusion.

There was a broader omission, even contradiction in the argument of those who stressed the economic factor in determining partition, and who then went on to advocate independence such as, for instance, that of BICO's *Worker Weekly*.[27] Why would the hard-working, penny-counting, British-benefits-and-NHS-receiving Protestant working class put all of that at risk by marching away from it? Especially when, in 1971 and beyond, Protestants continued to be better off economically than Catholics, and therefore benefited more from the status quo. For example, the census of 1971 and 1981 showed that Catholics were two and a half times more likely to be unemployed than Protestants.[28] As late as 1983, Protestants occupied 88.1 per cent of the highest-level jobs in the civil service.[29] That same year, only 3 per cent of the 7,000 employees at the relatively high-paying aeroplane manufacturers Short Brothers were Catholics.[30] And, between 1983 and 1985, 39 per cent of Protestant men were in non-manual jobs, compared to 30 per cent of Catholic men.[31] Similarly, in 1990, 13 per cent of employed Catholic adults reported earned incomes of £10,000 or more, compared with 21 per cent of Protestants; and 21 per of Catholic households reported a total income from all sources of £10,000 or more, compared with 36 per cent of Protestants.[32]

These discrepancies may not indicate the existence of a comprehensive labour aristocracy, but they remained a distinctive feature of Northern Irish society and represented one reason why the prophecies of doom advanced by O'Brien and Nairn did not materialise. Obviously, the welfarism associated with the British connection was also persuasive. It is therefore hardly surprising that, although independence and even a UDI was advocated from time to time by organisations such as Vanguard and the UDA, it never came even close to receiving majority support within either the Protestant working class or the Protestant population as a whole. The major options that were discussed within unionism were integration – that is, direct rule – or devolution within the UK.

The unpopularity of the independence option brought into question the fundamental premise of Northern Ireland or six-county Ulster as a 'nation', as indeed Nairn acknowledged. The truth was that, historically, the Protestant people of six-county Ulster did not want Home Rule; and during the Troubles, despite all the 'betrayals' by Britain, a majority did not endorse leaving the union and going it alone. That majority had been and remained unionists and were not interested in Ulster nationhood.

Perhaps reflecting this, the latter half of the Troubles and their aftermath saw a search by some commentators and academics for political class differences within unionism, or a left-wing variant of unionism. Often this search concentrated on 'loyalism', which in practice referred to the paramilitaries within unionism. Organisations such as the UDA and the UVF, and their associated political operations, have been examined and written about by such academics as Aaron Edwards, Peter Shirlow, Tony Novesel and Richard Reed.

Certainly, there was a significant pre-Troubles history of radical class politics within the Protestant community – most obviously the United Irishmen, which led the 1798 Rebellion and was originally formed in Belfast by a committee of twenty-three Protestants, twenty-two of whom were Presbyterians. The 1840s saw the emergence of Young Ireland, a radical grouping with many Protestants, including its chief ideologue Thomas Davis, who stressed the common heritage of all those born Irish, rejecting differences of religion or ancestry. The first two leaders of the parliamentary Home Rule Party, Isaac Butt and Charles Parnell, were Protestant.

At the start of the twentieth century the Independent Orange Order (IOO), a breakaway from the Orange Order, was established, and in 1905 issued what became known as the 'Maghermore Manifesto'. This document announced: 'We consider it is high time that Irish Protestants consider their position as Irish citizens ... In an Ireland in which Protestants and Catholics stand sullen and discontented it is not too much to hope that they will recognise their position and in their common trials unite on a basis of nationality.' The IOO was formed by Tom Sloan, an independent unionist of South Belfast who joined up with Lindsey Crawford, from Lisburn. From 1901 to 1906, Crawford edited the *Irish Protestant*, which, while never explicitly supporting Irish Home Rule, came close to doing so, and did support other aspects of Irish nationalism, such as the Irish language.[33] In the end, Sloan reverted to sectarianism and Crawford was sacked from his editorship. But the Maghermore Manifesto remains part of a dissident Protestant tradition.[34]

Also worth mentioning is Jack Beattie, who was one of the leaders of the 1932 Outdoor Relief protests, in which working-class Protestants and Catholics joined forces over unemployment and fought together on the streets against the police. Beattie later became a nationalist MP. The events of 1932 have remained an inspiration for Irish socialists ever since, and two fine books have been written about them.[35]

But did this Protestant radicalism within the working class extend into the Troubles? The obvious candidate for such continuity is the Progressive Unionist Party (PUP), which since its founding in 1979 has declared itself socialist and has been accepted as such by many of the authors cited above, some of whom have interviewed its leading members. However, since its foundation the PUP has been associated with the UVF, which was responsible for the first sectarian killing in Belfast in 1966 and went on to commit many other murders. On the other hand, the PUP's policies have included supporting a woman's right to abortion, opposition to developer-led regeneration, and support for action on climate change. Admittedly, these positions can sometimes appear peripheral.

The PUP's ideological posture is outlined in 'The Principles of Loyalism', adopted in 2002 in the aftermath of the GFBA, which it supported. The text begins by referring to the historical and economic debates discussed above, and quotes with approval pro-union historians such as Paul Bew and Anthony Alcock. It adopts a 'two nations' argument, but also says 'we must seek to develop a multi-cultural and multi-faith society', while insisting, 'Sinn Féin, in spite of its public commitment to non-sectarian politics, is at heart a Catholic Nationalist party', and that the southern Irish state is 'A Catholic nation'. This is conventional unionism; but it contains challenges to what some working-class unionists mocked as 'Big House' unionism – that is upper class led Conservative unionism that ran Northern Ireland from 1921 to 1972:

> Loyalists have a duty to ensure that our people have satisfactory housing that meets the social needs of our people, gainful employment that provides a living wage under satisfactory terms and conditions of employment, adequate health care from the cradle to the grave that is free to all at the point of delivery, efficient public services and utilities that are controlled by elected representatives and accountable to the public, a safe and healthy environment that enhances individual and community.

While hardly representing the most ambitious socialist vision, such aspirations were hopeful signs for those wishing to detect red hues in Orange unionism – but they were not developed in the paper. Instead, and more fundamentally, it outlined a vision at odds with any independent Protestant working-class radicalism, because, for the PUP,

> The fragmentation, rivalries and outbreaks of violent conflict within loyalism [pose] a greater threat to the Union than does the combined threat posed by nationalists and republicans ... Meanwhile both nationalism and republicanism, while divided as to tactics and strategy, maintain a unity of purpose. The warning contained in the slogan, 'United We Stand, Divided We Fall' will go unheeded at our peril.

In other words, rebuilding the all-class alliance was what mattered most. Accordingly, much of 'The Principles of Loyalism' is given over to extolling the Ulster Covenant of 1913 and the movement behind it as the example to follow. This movement, as we have seen, while supported by the majority of the Northern Irish Protestant working class, was led by an upper-class leadership and backed by the British Conservative Party – a real all-class, and indeed cross-national, alliance. What was especially helpful for the PUP and its paramilitary associates was the methodology of 1912–14 – that is, that the unionist leadership 'was quite prepared to set aside the Rule of Law', and that this posture was supported by all those who signed the Covenant.

This example of the 1912–14 UVF was, for the UVF from 1966 onwards, a justification for its own violence. When discussing this, the PUP was almost boastful:

> The UVF has never sought to hide the fact that its campaign was aimed at subjecting the nationalist community to a level of violence that would instil fear and terror in members of that community … It was a harsh and ruthless strategy that was dictated by the nature of the conflict. It dehumanised members of the nationalist community and reduced them to the status of scapegoats who were forced to suffer vicariously for the sins of its 'secret army'. There is no way that that strategy can be dressed up in fancy military terms to make something that was horrible look good. The objective was simple – subject the nationalist community to an oppressive force of violence as retribution for republican violence.[36]

To be clear, nowhere in 'The Principles of Loyalism' are the above tactics criticised, except when admitting they did not really work; but by locating them in the previous unionist illegality of 1912–14, the PUP underlines that they are part of a heritage in which it takes pride.

The reason all of this is important is because there remains an affection for the PUP among some commentators, even in left-wing circles. For example, in July 2021 *Red Pepper*, a British-based radical magazine, published an article praising its imagined virtues. Its author was Sophie Long, who, the magazine explained, had studied working-class loyalism as a PhD student. What it did not say was that Ms Long had been a PUP candidate in the Assembly election of 2016. She had received 1 per cent of the vote – an indication of the fact that, throughout its history, the PUP has garnered miniscule support among the Protestant working class.

Whether this is because of its professed socialism, its association with violence – given that its affiliates, the UVF and Red Hand Commando, continue to racketeer in their community – or because it supported the GFBA, which was to become increasingly unpopular in the Protestant working class, is a matter of conjecture.

In the five constituencies where the PUP fielded candidates in the 2016 Assembly election, it received 4.77 per cent of the vote in East Belfast, 3.38 per cent in North Belfast, 1.17 per cent in South Belfast, 1.54 per cent in Upper Ban and 3.94 per cent in East Londonderry. In the 2017 election, the party stood in just three seats, receiving 6.59 per cent in East Belfast, 4.95 per cent in North Belfast and 4.95 per cent in East Londonderry.

More generally – there is no doubt that various publications and manifestos of both the UVF and the UDA occasionally expressed progressive positions. These included a call for 'social justice' rather than 'traditional policies and religious differences which divided the community', as well as advocacy of 'a democratic state with judicial and social reforms to restore or and guarantee human rights'.[37] Richard Reed uses these quotes and other evidence to argue that the UVF and UDA had 'a strong labourist character' in the 1970s.[38] But there is plenty of evidence around the same time pointing in a contrary direction.

For instance, the UVF's *Combat*, in 1975 reacted to accusations that the East Antrim UVF contained communists as follows: 'Over 95 per cent of East Antrim volunteers are members of the Orange Lodges [and] are firmly attached to the doctrines of our Reformed Faith ... If anything we are Ultra Calvinists.'[39] Then, in a later edition in the same year, *Combat* referred to the 'communist' accusation by stating that the UVF was 'opposed to nationalisations, internationalism, class struggle and atheism ... the UVF repudiates the doctrines of those who are always seeking to level down and has argued that those who make a substantially more important contribution to national prosperity should be paid accordingly'.[40]

Around the same time, the UVF, the UDA and the Loyalist Volunteer Force developed links with the English far right. This included meetings and collaboration between loyalist organisations and the individuals within them and the National Front, as well as the fascist Combat 18.[41] These 'labourist' and far-right associations might seem to convey contradictory messages – and it could be concluded that the paramilitaries were simply politically confused and uncertain. But it is also worth remembering that, historically and internationally, there is a long record of far-right organisations adopting populist social or economic policies. Whatever cloaks were worn by the Northern Ireland paramilitaries, it remains the case that they were killing Catholics because they were Catholics – and that they were and remain a political flop.

By 2021 there were indications that such a lack of progress was driving even the more optimistic academic observers to despair. Thus, Peter Shirlow made a series of pleas at the conclusion of his book *The End of Loyalism?*

He called for 'an expulsion of criminal elements' within a loyalism, that had to 'ditch their regressive elements'. He said there had to be 'a removal of the blank cheque for the bully'. He noted 'the signs of progressive change' in loyalism 'has been submerged', and that 'loyalists must uphold and support the positives with a post-conflict society'. He insisted, 'loyalists must emerge out of a wider sloth like body that has impeded their potential.'[42]

There are a lot of imperatives in these passages, which suggests that not all is well with 'progressive unionism'. There is no doubt that, within the PUP, there have been individuals who have distanced themselves from both the sectarianism and the economic and social conservativism that have directed the unionist family for nearly 150 years. These include people like David Ervine, who founded the PUP, and whose funeral was attended by Gerry Adams, and Dawn Purvis, who succeed him as leader but left over the continuing links with the UVF. As for Sophie Long, she left the PUP, telling Susan McKay for her 2021 book *Northern Protestant: On Shifting Ground* that she was now learning Irish in England.[43] But it remains the case that in the Troubles period and afterwards there has not emerged from the Protestant section of the Northern Ireland working class any substantial indication of resolve to break from the overriding unionist tradition of putting unionist hegemony first.

An example from recent times is the press statement of the PUP 'chairman' Brian Lacey on the eve of the British general election of 2019:

> I am reiterating our call for a Unionist Convention to coalesce the Unionist message. Regardless of whom you hold responsible for creating the uncertainty, it is quite clear that now is the time for Unionism to set aside divisive rivalries and speak with one voice, in promoting the benefits of retaining our place within the United Kingdom and for all concerned to cast their vote in the upcoming Westminster election and return those candidates they believe to be best placed to represent the Unionist cause.[44]

Few within unionism paid much heed to this call; but the fact that it was issued indicates the degree of willingness the PUP had to drop its own 'progressive' identity in the cause of the now vanishing all-class unionist alliance. There are various issues that divide unionism. There are differences in social attitudes, in religion, in how unionism should shape its future. There are differences between the aspirations of rural and Belfast unionism, just as there are generational differences. But the major disputes within unionism have come not over social or economic issues, but when its leaders have been accused of compromising their 'no surrender' traditions: when O'Neil advocated reform; when David Trimble signed the GFBA; when Paisley shared power with Martin McGuinness. And it was usually the Protestant working class that was most intransigent.

Just as the hopes of the civil rights left of 'class not creed' were never realised, and just as the debates around 'two nations' have not pointed a way forward that is acceptable to a Protestant majority, so too has the search for 'progressive' working-class unionism proved illusory. As unionism has been built ideologically on notions of Protestant superiority and ascendency, its incompatibility with progressive politics might simply be what we should expect.

7

The Not-So-Good Friday

On 8 September 2020, in the House of Commons, Brandon Lewis, the secretary of state for Northern Ireland in Boris Johnson's 'Get Brexit Done' government, announced it was about to break international law. This concerned the Northern Ireland protocol in the Withdrawal Act of 2020, which gave effect to agreements Johnson had made with the European Community in 2019. Johnson and Lewis, it emerged, now thought that the protocol part of the international treaty they had negotiated was not such a good idea after all. Accordingly, their government was not going to implement those parts of the protocol that, in effect, imposed a quasi-border between Northern Ireland and the rest of the United Kingdom.

Over the next few months, the Johnson government retreated, advanced, manoeuvred, dithered, and spoke in many tongues on this issue. The House of Commons passed the Internal Markets Bill, which sought to implement the law-breaking. The House of Lords, by a large majority, voted against it. Then, Michael Gove, the cabinet member charged with overseeing Brexit, announced a retreat, suggesting that the protocol would be followed. Next, as the original Brexit legislation came into effect and a border in the Irish Sea was realised, such were the consequences in terms of trade disruption between Britain and Northern Ireland, and political disruption by Northern Ireland's unionists, that the government announced the implementation of the protocol was to be delayed. The European Union then said it would take the UK to court. This one was going to run and run.

When Brandon Lewis launched the controversy, many respectable voices were raised against the UK government's declaration of illegality. Critics included Theresa May, John Major, Tony Blair, Labour leader Keir Starmer, the Irish government, the European Union, many influential voices in the United States – including Joe Biden, soon to be elected president – and other powerful interest groups in the US Congress, who threatened to vote against future trade deals with the British. In Northern Ireland there was also widespread protest. A joint statement from Sinn Féin, the SDLP, the Alliance Party and the Green Party outlined their views in a letter to the British government, which was broadly representative of the wider criticism:

> While we believe that there is no good Brexit, and that the protocol is imperfect, it guarantees that whatever the circumstances, there will be no hard border between Ireland and Northern Ireland and it will protect the Good Friday Agreement 1998 in all its dimensions, North–South cooperation, and the all-island economy … It is entirely unacceptable … that the UK government should seek to abandon these safeguards … the economic and political impact on the island of Ireland … and above all on the people whom we represent would be devastating, long lasting. It would represent a shocking act of bad faith that would critically undermine the Good Friday Agreement political framework and peace process.[1]

The emphasis here on the GFBA was significant, but it was also a reference stressed by those who supported the government's original decision, and who also sought to justify their views as supportive of the GFBA. Thus, when the Internal Markets Bill was introduced in the House of Commons on 14 September, Boris Johnson said he was defending 'the fundamental purpose of … the Belfast Good Friday Agreement', as well as that of the protocol and 'the constitutional position of Northern Ireland'.

In the same debate, however, Sammy Wilson of the DUP told the House of Commons that it was the protocol that was 'a threat' to the GFBA, while, also from the DUP, Sir Jeffrey Donaldson insisted, 'I do not accept the contention that the Bill threatens the Belfast or Good Friday agreement', and that, rather, it was 'the arrangements proposed by the EU which 'threaten the peace'.

The government still insisted it was the GFBA good guy: in the House of Commons on 21 December, its spokesperson Robin Walker defended the proposals, saying 'we cannot allow the gains of the peace process ... to be compromised', adding, in reply to a question from the SDLP's Colum Eastwood, 'We are absolutely committed to the Good Friday agreement.'

All of this suggests a deep reverence for the GFBA. Yet, for many unionists in Northern Ireland and some in Britain this settlement was a questionable achievement in the first place, and of limited worth in its implementation.

The GFBA was agreed in April 1998. The negotiations surrounding it have been outlined by some of the leading participants, as well as by many commentators and academics, and need not be detailed here, but a summary is useful. Especially, the unionist perspective. Barry White, who had a liberal Protestant Northern Irish background, offered one when he wrote in 2000 of the 'peace process' terminology:

> I think Protestants see it as a loaded expression, since it implies that there has been a genuine war, waged with a certain justification by republicans, and that by engaging them, one is trying to reach a compromise which recognises that their objectives can be pursued – and perhaps reached – without violence. As many Protestants refuse to accept any justification for the war, they reject the assumption that republicanism can be bought off in any way, regarding all attempts at peace-making as appeasement.[2]

Barry also pointed out that, 'many Protestants ... already have a constitutional settlement, within the United Kingdom, which suits them ideally'.[3] Even before the negotiations began, there were thus strong misgivings within unionism concerning the road travelled. But the more important player was the British government, first led by John Major and then by Tony Blair; Blair in particular wanted a new Irish settlement. When it was negotiated, its overarching principles were contained in section 1(ii):

> Participants ... recognise that it is for the people of the island of Ireland alone, by agreement between the two parts respectively and without external impediment, to exercise their right of self-determination on the basis of consent, freely and concurrently given, North and South, to bring about a united Ireland, if that is their wish, accepting that this right must be achieved and exercised with and subject to the agreement and consent of a majority of the people of Northern Ireland.

This gave Irish nationalists the principle of Irish self-determination, and unionists the promise that majority support within Northern Ireland would guarantee their existing link with Britain. While not trumpeted at the time, the GFBA also offered assurances that Britain would retain overall sovereignty – for instance, on deciding in the future whether there was sufficient change in public opinion to merit a referendum on Irish reunification.

The agreement was structured around three 'strands'. The first dealt with the internal governance of Northern Ireland, and provided a proportionally elected assembly and an executive reflecting the community balance in that assembly. This meant power-sharing was back. The second strand covered relations between the two parts of Ireland, and provided for the establishment of various North–South bodies including a North–South Ministerial Council, a North–South Parliamentary Forum and a North–South Civic Consultative Forum, which sought to bring together 'representatives of civic society'. This strand provided an all-Ireland dimension and was designed to win over northern nationalists and the Irish government. The third strand promised links between Northern Ireland and the rest of the UK, thereby reassuring Northern Irish unionists. A British–Irish Council was envisaged that would involve the UK government and representatives from Northern Ireland with the other devolved governments of the UK, as well as representatives from the Isle of Man and the Channel Islands.

The GFBA also contained a section on 'Rights, Safeguards and Equality of Opportunity'. This included a promise that the British government would ensure that public authorities in Northern Ireland 'promoted equality' in 'religion, politics, gender, race, marital status, disability and sexual orientation'. To help with this, a new Human Rights Commission was promised that would propose a Bill of Rights for Northern Ireland. Also envisaged was a joint committee of representatives of the two Human Rights Commissions, North and South, which would look at human rights issues in the island of Ireland. There was also agreement in Point 5 of the 'Rights and Equality' section that: 'All participants acknowledge the sensitivity of the use of symbols and emblems for public purposes, and the need in particular in creating the new institutions to ensure that such symbols and emblems are used in a manner which promotes mutual respect rather than division.' The working out of this clause was, in the future, to prove contentious over such issues as the conditions under which Orange Order marches could take place and the flying of the Union Jack.

On another contentious issue, it was promised that the British government, 'where appropriate and where people so desire' it would 'take resolute action to promote' the Irish language, and even 'seek to remove' restrictions on the use of Irish. There was a promise to restructure and reform the police force – the Royal Ulster Constabulary – and that Britain would reduce the numbers of its troops in Northern Ireland to 'levels compatible with a normal peaceful society', as well as oversee-ing 'the removal of emergency powers'. As for home-grown armies, all concerned promised to decommission all weapons held by paramilitaries within two years. Completing the road to pacification, all prisoners involved in the violence of the Troubles would be released early, providing their organisations agreed to permanent ceasefires.

The main signatories to the agreement were the Irish and British governments, the Ulster Unionist Party (UUP), the SDLP, Sinn Féin and the Alliance Party. The Irish government and its civil servants played a significant role in the framing of the agreement; its origins could also be traced to private talks between John Hume of the nationalist SDLP and Gerry Adams of Sinn Féin, which began in 1988 and resumed in 1993. The three strands of the GFBA first emerged from the Hume–Adams talks. On the British side, there had been a growing recognition that the military solutions attempted during two periods – when Roy Mason was Labour secretary for Northern Ireland (1976–79) and the early Thatcher years – were not working, and that a political solution was necessary. A key moment came on 9 November 1990, when the Northern Ireland secretary, Peter Brooke, made a crucial speech in which he said: 'The British government has no selfish strategic or economic interest in Northern Ireland.'

The other signatories to the GFBA were the Progressive Unionist Party, which, as we have seen, had links with the Ulster Volunteer Force and Red Hand Commando; the Ulster Democratic Party, which had links with the Ulster Defence Association; and the Northern Ireland Women's Coalition, which had been formed in 1996, took no position on the border question, and sought to project a feminist voice into considerations of Northern Ireland's future. This organisa-tion was short-lived, as was another GFBA signatory, the 'Labour Coalition', which consisted principally of the Militant tendency, the British and Irish Communist Organisation and the Newtownabbey Labour Party. The Northern Ireland Labour Party had long since dissolved, mainly because of internal differences following its reluctance to embrace the civil rights cause.[4]

There were significant absentees from this list, however – especially from within the unionist community. This was hardly surprising, given that the agreement was based on compromise and concession, and the historic unionist suspicion of such diplomacies. Unsurprisingly, Paisley's DUP came out against the agreement. Its reasons were stated in its manifesto, offered in the election to the new Northern Ireland Assembly of 1998. These included the perceived threat to the RUC; that the cross-border bodies were 'an embryo united Ireland'; the release of 'terrorist' prisoners; and 'terrorists in government' – by which was meant members of Sinn Féin serving on the proposed executive.

Ian Paisley Jr, already a 'Justice Spokesman' for the DUP and emerging as a new voice for the party, wrote a pamphlet, in which he declared: 'There comes a time when the only thing that is appropriate to say is "no". Unionists must reject the Agreement because it will destroy the Union, put terrorists into political office, give Dublin a say in Northern Ireland's affairs, release terrorists from jail and undermine the rule of law.' He complained that the British had proved unable to tackle terrorism, and so had decided to do a deal with those who had used it. He recalled the AIA, saying its legacy had been to 'give the whip hand to IRA/Sinn Féin'. The British government, he said, was not concerned with a 'lasting or just peace', but with finding what would constitute 'enough political concessions to buy the support of IRA/Sinn Féin'.[5]

The Orange Order was also against the agreement. It listed all the complaints cited by the DUP, as well as 'the over-riding role of the Dublin government in the internal affairs of Northern Ireland' and 'the promotion of symbols and culture alien to the great majority of people in Northern Ireland' – among which was the promotion of the Irish language. Its general assertion was that the agreement 'is a very green-tinged document, which has been carefully compiled to placate the pan-Irish front of which Sinn Féin/IRA is an integral component'. The conclusion was that Northern Ireland was now on a 'disaster course'.[6]

There was also opposition from within the UUP itself. This included six out of ten Westminster MPs, most of whom actively campaigned for a 'no' vote in the subsequent referendum. Included here were former party leader James Molyneux and the Rev. Martin Smyth, who had been head of the Orange Order from 1972 to 1996. Another UUP member to come out against was Jeffrey Donaldson – who would later change parties, eventually becoming leader of the DUP. In 1999 Donaldson was to address a meeting of the parliament-based Friends of the Union, where he announced: 'I do not hasten to use the words "peace process", because I am not convinced that the end of the process will be peace. There are times when I think the word "appeasement" is more apt.'[7]

Although the main loyalist paramilitaries supported the GFBA, not all did. The Loyalist Volunteer Force (LVF) insisted, 'The British Government with the help of the Unionist Lundies [traitors] are now prepared to accommodate Republican murderers and give them seats in the Cabinet of a Northern Ireland Assembly.' Like others, it also condemned the release of republican prisoners, and giving 'the Dublin Government a say within the constitutional process and the day to day running of Ulster'. Perhaps most interesting was the LVF's explanation of why the 'act of betrayal' was occurring – namely, the IRA bomb in London's docklands in February 1996, which had caused an estimated £1.8 billion worth of damage. Since then, the LVF argued, the British were only concerned with preventing a reoccurrence of such an attack, and so had acceded to Irish republican demands. The conclusion was that the British had 'lost this war without even fighting it'.[8]

Thus, the old accusation of British betrayal of unionist Ulster re-emerged; even for some who supported the agreement, this was a concern. The UVF argued that such fears were a reason to vote 'Yes' in the referendum, saying, 'A refusal on the agreement will once again leave our future in the hands of British officials at Whitehall who are incessant in their dealings with the Irish government. No one can know what these dealings may lead to in the future, and this could be disastrous to the Union with Great Britain.'[9] For others, the agreement was already such a betrayal that it exceeded everything that had gone before. *Burning Bush*, a newspaper of the Kilskeery Free Presbyterian Church, editorialised as follows:

> The chief source of terror has been the Roman Catholic terrorist organisation the IRA. It was followed closely by loyalist terror groups ... But in truth these deeds of evil have been put in the shade by those engaged in the recent 'peace process'. It must be noted that the participants in this deal signed the agreement on the day Christianity remembered the betrayal and crucifixion of the Lord Jesus Christ. Providence has thus passed its own comment on this event.[10]

Some of these views were on the most traditional wing of unionism, but there are two considerations to bear in mind. The first is the level of a non-acceptance the GFBA received at the time and later. In the subsequent referendum on the GFBA, while 71 per cent of those in Northern Ireland who voted were in favour, estimates of the Protestant 'Yes' vote varied between 50 and 55 per cent. Moreover, in the medium and longer term those opposed to the GFBA secured majority support from their community. In the first election to the new Assembly, the UUP secured 23.3 per cent support, and the DUP 18 per cent. But in the 2003 the DUP was in the ascendency, with 25.7 per cent compared to 22.7 per cent, and by 2007 this had risen to 30.1 per cent against 14.9 per cent.

In Westminster elections, the DUP's share rose from 13.6 per cent in 1997 to 22.5 per cent in 2001, and 33.7 per cent in 2005.

The UUP's share fell from 32.7 per cent to 26.8 per cent and then 17.7 in the same elections.[11] The growing disillusionment with the agreement suggested by these figures was apparent in the *Life and Times Survey* opinion polls conducted in these years. In four successive polls from 1999 to 2005, the share of Protestants who thought that unionists had gained most, or even a little, never rose above 1 per cent. The share who thought both communities had gained equally fell from 32 per cent in 1999 to 2 per cent in 2005. By 2005, 53 per cent of Protestants thought nationalists had gained 'a lot'.

Similarly, from 2000 to 2005 more Protestants always said they would vote 'No' than 'Yes' if a referendum on the GFBA was held again. The 'Yes' vote ranged from 28 to 36 per cent, the 'No' vote from 38 to 41 per cent. The Catholic community was much more positive, with a 'Yes' vote of between 74 and 83 per cent.

A general conclusion of the researchers of the *Life and Times Survey* of 2003 was that Protestant respondents were less confident than Catholics that their rights and traditions were being protected. The conclusion was a troubling one for those who had expected most from the peace process: 'Although the intention of the Good Friday Agreement is to create an inclusive society, the survey findings provide little evidence to suggest that this is the type of environment which is currently perceived by most Protestants.'

The second consideration concerning the rejectionist views expressed by so many unionists at the time of the agreement and the referendum, and afterwards, is that they were endorsed by some influential unionist-minded commentators. Notable here was the opinion of Michael Gove, as expressed in his pamphlet in 2000, noted above. For Gove, like Ian Paisley Jr, the rot set in long before the GFBA. Indeed, Gove went back to the suspension of the Northern Ireland parliament and the imposition of British rule in 1972. These events, he said, had started 'a series of attempts by British Governments to end republican violence by altering the constitutional position of Northern Ireland'. He cited the Sunningdale Agreement of 1973, the AIA and the GFBA as part of this process, arguing that they had the consequence of rendering Northern Ireland 'increasingly detached from the United Kingdom'. It was, he said 'a capitulation to violence'.[12]

The view of Gove, like that of the LVF, that the GFBA was essentially a deal between the British state and the IRA was echoed twelve years later by the academic Henry Patterson, writing in 2012. Patterson said that unionists had 'profound problems with the Peace Process' because of their perception that it was a deal between the British state and the IRA.[13] Patterson was only partially correct. The GFBA negotiations on power-sharing and the other two strands centrally involved the UUP, and would not have come to fruition without their agreement. Jonathan Powell, Tony Blair's chief of staff, has written of the prime minister's initial attitude:

> Our first task was to reassure the unionists. Given the history of the Labour Party they were naturally suspicious about our commitment to the Union ... the unionists were still not convinced we were on their side in the way the Conservatives instinctively were. Tony's first comment on Northern Ireland was scribbled on top of a formal minute ... it said, 'I [Blair] need to do a speech that sets out my view of the unlikely nature of [Irish] unification.' He also proposed that he see David Trimble before he met the then Irish Prime Minister John Burton and we arranged a meeting ... They met in the House of Commons in the Minister's cavernous office behind the Speaker's chair, where Tony reassured Trimble that 'his aim was to sort out the Northern Ireland problem.' He had no predilection whatsoever to a united Ireland.[14]

The truth was that the GFBA was not a settlement dictated to unionists, as the AIA had been. The main representatives of unionism at the time knowingly signed up to the whole package, as did the most prominent paramilitaries – although it is still important to record the views of the dissenters at the time, and to recognise that this opposition did not abate. For instance, the anger towards Sinn Féin for being involved in the executive, expressed in 1998 by all the unionist objectors, was still echoed in 2020 by journalist and academic Dennis Kennedy.[15] William Matchett, a lecturer and former detective inspector in the RUC, also complained: 'The terms of the Belfast Agreement permitted unrepentant ex-PIRA leaders, rebranded peace-makers by political chicanery to enter the government of Northern Ireland.' He also sprang to the defence of the RUC, remarking in hindsight that the inquiry into the police established by the agreement – the Patten Report – 'destroyed the RUC – the law enforcement agency that had the "number" of the PIRA'.[16]

Certainly, the Patten Report was both important and contentious, comparable to the Cameron and Scarman reports of 1969 in its impact. The report was authored by Chris Patten, a former Conservative minister with Irish Catholic heritage. The very title of his report, *A New Beginning*, indicated the direction of travel, as did its opening statement: 'The issue of policing is at the heart of many of the problems that politicians have been unable to resolve in Northern Ireland. As part of any final agreement to establish the customary institutions of democracy in Northern Ireland in a peaceful, civil society, the deeply controversial matters that we address will need to be confronted and settled.' In other words, Northern Ireland had been badly policed. As examples, the report spoke of the importance of 'the protection of human rights and their abuse', of 'the values of liberty, the rule of law and mutual respect, values that have sometimes been casualties of the years of violence', and of the need for 'a police service capable of attracting and sustaining support from the community as a whole'.

This was hardly revolutionary: the proposals sought to establish a police force that was accountable, transparent, politically neutral and capable of attracting recruits from both the Protestant and Catholic communities. This final point was obvious for Patten, as in November 1999 only 7.7 per cent of the RUC was Catholic. The details of how the new vision was to be achieved included a change of name, to the Northern Ireland Police Service (this became the Police Service of Northern Ireland), which meant that 'Royal' was no longer in its title. Neither was the British crown to be on the police badge, and the Union Jack would not be flown from police stations. Other changes included rights training for police members; a police board consisting of Assembly members reflecting the political make-up of the Assembly, but with no party given a majority; a reduction in police numbers; and affirmative action aimed at increasing Catholic recruitment.

Brendan O'Leary's judgement is that Patten was 'a thorough, careful, and imaginative compromise between unionists who maintained that the existing RUC already met the terms of reference of the Agreement, and those nationalists, especially republicans, who maintained that its human-rights record required its disbanding'.[17] The more unionist-minded Dean Godson, on the other hand, says that the report was 'very radical indeed and resulted in the erasure of the symbols of Britishness'. Moreover, 'it offered little in the way of visible recognition of past sacrifices' by RUC officers.[18] This observation was mild compared to that of Ian Paisley, who said the RUC had been 'without defeat', but that now 'it was to be offered as a final sacrificial lamb, to appease the Roman Catholic Republican murderers and their nationalist fellow travellers ... Patten's programme is that Protestants have to be ethnically cleansed.'[19]

Exaggeration aside, Paisley spoke for many. Godson highlighted that the RUC issue, and the Ulster Unionists' support of the GFBA that produced it, cost the UUP heavily in the 2001 Westminster poll – and that, in an opinion poll conducted in February 2000, Protestants ranked the importance of the name and culture of the RUC above that of the Crown, the Union Jack, and even 12 July[20] – the day every year when Orangemen marched in celebration of William III's victory at the Battle of the Boyne in 1690.

It is important to understand these sentiments, and why the RUC was part of the unionists' DNA. For many who followed Irish events outside the unionist community, it was the force that batoned the civil rights demonstrators off the streets of Derry on 5 October 1968, and which went on to show, on many occasions, its sectarian and political bias, to the extent of colluding with loyalist paramilitaries. For unionists, it was *their* RUC, that was from *their* community – the servant and guardian of *their* state which, like the Protestant community from which it was predominantly drawn, was misjudged and misunderstood. But now, as the DUP's Gregory Campbell put it, 'The Patten Commission on policing seeks to establish a policing service that is not identified with the State which that policing service is designed to serve.'[21]

David Trimble, the leader of the UUP, was blamed by many within unionism as responsible for the RUC's destruction. Trimble was born in 1944 into a family who lived in Bangor, County Down, a seaside town thirteen miles from Belfast. The family was lower middle-class, unionist and Presbyterian, though not stridently so. He was the first in the family to join the Orange Order, which he did as a teenager, before the Troubles began. He was also the first in the family to go to university, in his case Queen's University Belfast, which he attended part-time while working in the Northern Ireland civil service. When he graduated, he started a university teaching career. He was the first leader of unionism to go to university, and this, together with his comparatively non-privileged and non-military background, distinguished him from the familiar succession of unionist leaders. His political activism began when he canvassed for a friend, Basil McIvor, who was standing as an Ulster Unionist in the 1969 general election. McIvor was on the more liberal wing of unionism, but Trimble moved in the opposite direction, to the right – some would say towards the more sectarian wing of unionism – when he joined the Vanguard movement in 1972. This evolved into the Vanguard Unionist Progressive Party, for which Trimble stood unsuccessfully as a candidate in 1973, before winning a seat for South Belfast in the Constitutional Convention of 1975–76.

Vanguard was led by William Craig, the former Northern Ireland home secretary who had banned the Derry Civil Rights march of 5 October 1968. Vanguard was a mixture of populism, militarism and occasional anti-Catholicism of the Paisley variety.[22] Vanguard and Trimble were also sympathetic to the two-nations theory; Trimble even assisted the distribution of BICO literature among fellow staff members at Queen's University.[23] He became deputy leader to Craig from 1975 to 1978. However, largely due to Crag's surprising advocacy of a voluntary coalition with the SDLP, which Trimble supported, the party collapsed. Trimble joined the Ulster Unionist Party, and in 1990 was elected to Westminster for the safe unionist seat of Upper Bann.

Before then he had associated with the Ulster Clubs, which had been established in the autumn of 1985 to oppose attempts to reroute loyalist parades away from nationalist areas. With the signing of the Anglo-Irish Agreement (AIA) in November 1985, the Ulster Clubs attempted to expand their role as an umbrella body to coordinate the unionist campaign against the AIA, establishing links with paramilitaries. By the early 1990s the movement had gone into terminal decline. But in 1988 Trimble had written a pamphlet for the Ulster Clubs, *What Choice for Ulster?*, in which he asked whether the best way of 'protecting the interests' of the 'Ulster British community' was 'some form of independence'. Here, he opted for a form of dominion status for Northern Ireland, with 'an orderly transfer of power' from Westminster to a northern Ireland parliament and state in which he said the RUC and the Ulster Defence Regiment (UDR) 'could give security to everyone. The UDR was a regiment of the British army, established by the Labour government in 1970 as a replacement for the 'B specials'. Like the 'Specials' the UDR was recruited entirely in Northern Ireland, became overwhelmingly Protestant, and gained a reputation among the Catholic community for sectarianism. Trimble's support for it and the RUC would have seemed to many Catholics like a threat to return to pre-1968 repression. Trimble also said Britain could continue to oversee foreign affairs, but his central message was that the 'Ulster-British people ... had the right to self-determination'. And what if this right was not granted? The pamphlet indicated an interesting direction of travel on its front cover. This reproduced a unionist postcard from 1914 with a graphic of a young woman standing in front of a Union Jack, holding a rifle and proclaiming: 'I can stand alone.'

On other occasions, Trimble associated himself with the 'modernising' wing of the Unionist Party – although this often amounted to little more than a structural and presentational change. Moreover, he continued to press the traditional right-wing demands – for instance, when he was appointed legal affairs spokesperson for the party in 1989, he advocated the return of internment. His won the leadership of the UUP in September 1995, and this was in no small part due to his participation in the Drumcree protest two months earlier. This was when the Orange Order, backed by the DUP and Trimble as the local MP, objected to a ban on the Order marching in the Garvaghy Road in Portadown, a nationalist area. An eventual compromise saw a 500-strong Orange parade, but without bands. It was led by Paisley and Trimble, who clasped hands and raised them in triumph at the end of the march. The solidarity did not last. In march 1997 Trimble's leader's speech at his party conference mentioned 'aggressive, loudmouth Unionists' – widely understood as a reference to Paisley. Discussing Trimble's leadership around this time, one commentator headlined an article: 'The Trimble Enigma'.[24] A more cynical view was that he was trying to be all things to all – unionist – people. A consistency in his own unionism was that he always opposed the integrationist view, or direct rule from Westminster, of, for example, Enoch Powell, and Trimble's predecessor as UUP leader, James Molyneaux. Like many who had become involved in the 1970s, when Britain's interventions were seen as betrayals, Trimble did not trust the UK government with direct rule. Accordingly, during his career he entertained various degrees of devolution, from the old Stormont variety to independence.

On the other hand, he realised that simply wearing an Orange sash was no longer sufficient for the advancement of either the party's political interests or indeed his own. He did have a wider vision of unionism, than its more traditional adherents, For him, it was both expedient and, in the long term, necessary for unionism to attract voters beyond its traditional base – specifically, among sections of the Catholic community in the north of Ireland. He recognised, as he said in his speech accepting his half of the Nobel Peace Prize, that unionism had 'built a cold house' for Catholics in Northern Ireland. This admission suggested he had finally come down on the side of the 'new unionism' then being articulated by some younger members of the UUP, which stressed the economic and welfare benefits of unionism rather than its tribal heritage.

Indeed, at the time of the GFBA, Trimble had even more extravagant ambitions. His biographer Dean Godson says that Trimble 'genuinely believed that if Sinn Féin were sucked into Stormont, they would be operating British institutions and would thus become "structural" as opposed, obviously, to "ideological" unionists … Trimble believed that republicans could be integrated into existing, albeit reformed, state structures because the traditional ideology that drove them was dead or dying.'[25]

Even after Trimble had been driven out by fellow unionists, this optimism was still preached by some. Henry Patterson argued in 2012 that Trimble's hopes and arguments that a reformed Northern Ireland would integrate republicans into partitionist structures were being realised. He concluded that Sinn Féin's participation in power-sharing represented 'the enthusiastic administration of the 6 County state by those who spent thirty years trying to destroy it'. His optimism was confident: 'the Union appears more secure than at any time since the 1950s' – although he also credited this to the IRA's cessation of violence.[26]

Writing in 2000, the DUP's Gregory Campbell offered a different narrative:

> It is not that the IRA were looking to end their war but that they wanted other means of obtaining more gains, more stepping-stones towards their goal. When seen in this, its proper context, people should neither be surprised nor elated at this so-called Peace Process. It seems as if having been attacked, maligned and misunderstood for over thirty years, the Unionist people are now to be patronised and promised a brighter future, if only we will co-operate in our own demise. As Nationalist demands grow ever more strident, some Unionists seek comfort in withdrawing ever more within themselves, politically, geographically and socially. Is this the dawning of the bright new day we were promised?[27]

At the time, in the aftermath of the GFBA, such scepticism worried the British. Accordingly, and underlining the general importance of Patten's proposed reform of the RUC, the UK government's newly appointed Northern Ireland secretary, Peter Mandelson, sought to row back. He had been told, in Jonathan Powell's words, 'to cultivate the Unionists'; but this, added Powell, 'he rather overdid'.[28] Mandelson was not only a friend of unionism on instruction, he was also one by conviction – or, as he put it in his own account of the peace process, 'I valued the Union'.[29] His narrative of what happened shows his famous ability to 'spin'. He wrote of the police reform: 'This overall was a very sensitive issue for all sides and arriving at a consensus was hard.' So he tried to change the reforms, and admitted that this 'rankled, chiefly, but not only with the SDLP and Sinn Féin, and they were pressing me hard to rewrite some of what I had implemented.'[30]

It was indeed the case that there were objections to Mandelson's Police Bill – but it was not only the SDLP and Sinn Féin that objected. Brendan O'Leary also lists the Women's Coalition; the Catholic Church human rights organisations, such as the Committee of the Administration of Justice; the Irish government; the US House of Representatives; and President Clinton. The reason they objected was not, as Mandelson implies, because he was implementing Patten, but rather because he was not. O'Leary goes on to detail Mandelson's attempt to water down Patten.[31] But eventually, thanks to the impressive opposition, most of Patten won out, and its reforms changed the nature of policing in Northern Ireland. That was important and significant, but so too was the British secretary of state's attempt at sabotage.

It was equally worrying for the GFBA's adherents when, in February 2020, Mandelson proposed and won support in the British parliament for the suspension of the Assembly and executive established under the GFBA. The background to this was continuing arguments over the slowness of weapons decommissioning by the IRA, and the increasing fragility of David Trimble's leadership. But it was also significant that the GFBA did not allow for such a suspension. Indeed, during the negotiations on the agreement, such a power was discussed and rejected. Moreover, any review of the GFBA's arrangements had to secure cross-community support, as well as that of the Irish government.

The British suspension satisfied neither of these requirements. Detailing all this, O'Leary notes, 'The UK government officials knew that suspension, and even acquiring the power to suspend, would breach the treaty incorporating the Agreement.'[32]

Although the right of the secretary of state to suspend the Assembly was later withdrawn, the case was still made that British sovereignty had ultimate authority. If, twenty years later, Boris Johnson and Brandon Lewis were indeed breaking another treaty concerning Ireland when they threatened to opt out of the Irish protocol in the European withdrawal treaty, they were only following precedent.

The GFBA was not the end of the peace process. Over the next twenty years there were a series of agreements that sought to address important issues such as decommissioning, the functioning of cross-border bodies, the Irish-language issue, the all-Ireland civic forum promised by the GFBA, a Bill of Rights, police reforms, paramilitarism, and so-called 'heritage' issues, which included investigations into Troubles-related deaths, pensions for victims, and the establishment of an oral history archive. Perhaps the most significant discussion was around the St Andrews Agreement of 2006, through which the DUP committed itself for the first time to full participation in the power-sharing apparatus of the GFBA.

By this stage, the party was decisively the leading unionist party, having secured 25.7 per cent of the vote, compared with the UUP's 22.7 per cent, in the 2003 Assembly election, and 33.7 per cent against the UUP's 17.7 per cent in the 2005 Westminster election. Two months after the latter, the IRA announced the end of its campaign. This gave Paisley and the DUP the cover to enter the executive – but now as the leader of unionism. In truth, the option of staying outside the tent was made especially difficult for Paisley when the British government implied that, if the DUP did not cooperate, then joint British–Irish governance of Northern Ireland would be 'Plan B'. That would really have been Paisley cutting off his nose to spite his face. He became first minister of the executive in May 2007, sharing power with Martin McGuinness, former Derry commander of the IRA, as deputy first minister.

By then David Trimble was gone. For his unionist critics,

he never distanced himself sufficiently from the features of the GFBA they objected to most strongly. He faced many external and internal party challenges before losing his seat to the DUP in the 2005 Westminster election, when he resigned as UUP party leader. When he was elevated to the House of Lords, he joined the Conservative Party. The world then watched in amazement as McGuinness and Paisley appeared to get along so well that they were famously dubbed 'the chuckle brothers'; but then Paisley met the same fate as Trimble. He had already suffered internal party defections in response to his partnership with McGuinness – notably when his successor as MEP, Jim Allister, quit the DUP to establish Traditional Unionist Voice (TUV), and then when he lost the moderatorship of the Free Presbyterian Church. In March 2008, after a local council election defeat in which he lost votes to both the UUP and the TUV, he announced his resignation as first minister. The man who had found fame denouncing unionist compromises became the victim of his own version. The strains of 'No Surrender!' could still be heard in Protestant Ulster.

The GFBA and power-sharing survived – but perhaps only because they were in effect diminished. In 2018 an Irish High Court judge, Richard Humphreys, produced a scholarly analysis demonstrating this. He listed twenty-five of the bodies whose establishment had been agreed by the GFBA and subsequent agreements. He began with the Assembly and the executive, which he noted were, at the time, 'Not functioning'; he went to assign approximately half of all these bodies to this same category – or the even worse 'Not established'. In the latter category he included the Oral History Archive, the Historical Investigations Unit, the Independent Commission on Information Retrieval and the Implementation and Reconciliation Group. These were all bodies intended to address 'legacy' issues.

Also never established was the all-Ireland Civic Forum. This important part of reconciliation between non–party political bodies and citizens had been agreed by the GFBA, but was downgraded in subsequent agreements to a 'Civic Advisory Panel' – but even this had never met. Similarly, the North–South independent consultative forum, also agreed by the GFBA, had not been established.[33] Humphreys and others also noted the non-fulfilment of other promises, most of which had been instrumental in winning Irish nationalist support for the GFBA process. One of these related to the Irish language. This was covered in the GFBA, and it also featured in the 2006 St Andrews Agreement, which promised that the British government would 'introduce an Irish Language Act reflecting on the experience of Wales and Ireland and work with the incoming Executive to enhance and protect the development of the Irish language'.

This promise was not fulfilled; but it was made again in *New Decade, New Approach*. This came after talks chaired by the British and Irish governments in which all the major parties participated, and which got the Assembly and executive functioning again in 2020. This also included a proposal for a Bill of Rights, another promise of the GFBA that, up to that point, had failed to materialise. Given the comprehensive nature of British and unionist non-compliance with peace-process agreements and treaties by then, it is hardly surprising that a definite sense of disillusionment was detectable in the nationalist community.

In July 2020, Sinn Féin MP Francis Molloy said on Twitter: 'We were sold a pup with the GFA … no commitment from either Dublin or London to deliver for nationalists or republicans. It was just a bluff.' He also remarked to the *Irish News* that it was 'a let-down that people were finding ways of not implementing' the GFA.[34] Six month later, it was the turn of SDLP MP Claire Hanna to tell the House of Commons that the British government had 'an unlimited disregard' for the Good Friday Agreement.[35]

More generally, the GFBA had a chequered career over its first two decades: the agreement itself was signed in April 1998;

a full-scale executive was only appointed over a year later, in July 1999; devolution was suspended by the British government between February and May 2000; further suspensions took place on 11 August 2001 and 22 September 2001; and a longer suspension was imposed between 2002 and 2007, when the UUP refused to share power with Sinn Féin. The second executive was formed in 2007. By then, the DUP was the largest party on the unionist side, and Sinn Féin on the nationalist side. The executive did not meet between 19 June and 20 November 2008, due to a boycott over policing and justice – functions that were devolved in April 2010. After the Assembly elections of May 2011, a third executive was formed, and then a fourth after the May 2016 election – but this collapsed in January 2017. The executive was re-formed in January 2020, following the *New Decade, New Approach* agreement. As we shall see, it was collapsed again in February 2022 by the DUP, in protest, it was claimed, at the Irish protocol in the European withdrawal agreement.

There were thus significant periods when the GFBA proved inoperative. Whatever the reasons, whosesoever the fault, this was hardly political stability, and it certainly reflected unionists' view that the whole exercise was of limited value. The truth was that, for many, it brought into question their core heritage and ideology. This was noted in 2000 by Duncan Morrow. At that time, Morrow was a lecturer at the University of Ulster and a member of Northern Ireland's Community Relations Council. His particular interest was unionism's past and future as redefined by the GBFA, and his analysis was that unionism was 'facing a crisis of predicament'. By this he meant that unionists recognised that, outside their own community, there was no support for the simple majority-rule unionism of the past, and accordingly that some form of power-sharing had to be accepted. But, he wrote, 'to accept this premise is to accept the ultimate failure of the Unionist and Protestant project as it has been conceived since the early Home Rule crises of the

1880s'. It meant the old 'Protestant exclusivism or reliance on the British state' were no longer paramount, and that a new cooperative relationship with Catholicism and Irish nationalism was required by the outside world. It was a problem for unionists that, 'emotionally, government with republicans remains counter-intuitive and undesirable for many'. But, even worse, to participate in what was now being asked of them in the GFBA was 'to acknowledge that the traditional Unionist state has failed'.[36]

This was a dramatic claim. If it was what the GFBA had come to represent, then unionism was indeed in deep trouble even in 2000, according to Morrow – and all the more so during the twenty years that followed, when the unionist leadership changed, new questions were posed and often left unanswered, and the forward march of Sinn Féin continued. Moreover, 'unionism' in this context includes its different varieties – from the traditional sectarian version associated with the pre–St Andrews Paisley and the loyalist paramilitaries to the 'modern' and 'welfare' unionism hesitantly projected by Trimble's UUP up to and after the GFBA. For most of his career Trimble had tried to ride both the Orange and 'welfare' horses. In the end he fell off.

Instead, there emerged a new post-Paisley, post-GFBA DUP, headed by former UUP member Arlene Foster. As we have seen, early in the party's alliance with Theresa May, Foster had tried to project her party's conventional political normality. That, as we have also seen, was mocked by many in Britain; though whether her approach would have been the answer to Ulster unionism's by now apparent identity crisis would become irrelevant, because along came Brexit. But even before then, it was evident for anyone with eyes to see or ears to listen that the GFBA was in trouble.

A *Life and Times Survey* of 2020 found that, in the previous year, only 19 per cent of Protestants questioned agreed that the GFBA was the 'best basis' for governing Northern Ireland; an additional 43 per cent agreed with this, but with the important proviso that it was in need of reform. Another 12 per cent said it was no longer the best basis, while 11 per cent said it never had been. In a 2003 essay, James McAuley had foreseen such dissatisfaction:

> Many unionists believe that the Good Friday Agreement represents a cultural attack, a direct and deliberate attempt to undermine their sense of Britishness. By promoting the agreement, the British government has in fact been asking unionists to sacrifice their British identity ... For many, although Northern Ireland's place within the union might remain guaranteed for the foreseeable future, it is, at best, a different, less 'British' union. The contemporary phase of the peace process has been seen as eroding core elements of unionist identity and key institutions of the Northern Irish state. As one grouping of Protestant church officials recently put it, there is a sense for Unionists of 'everything solid melting into air,' which the Good Friday Agreement is accelerating. The Agreement created a fluidity and malleability about the Northern Ireland State; the whole framework of society is altering.[37]

Both five years after the GFBA, when these words were written, and twenty years after, when the trends it identified had accelerated, it was clear that most unionists were either sceptics or outright disbelievers concerning the peace process. Their objections were not without rationality. The case can be made that the GFBA challenged much that unionism had stood for. It was an acknowledgement of the inadequacies of the Irish partition settlement itself, and a nod of acknowledgement to the civil rights demonstrators of the 1960s and early 1970s. Moreover, encouraging Irish republicanism to sit around the table and then enter government evoked a totally different narrative from the one told by the British when Margaret Thatcher, Merlyn Rees and Roy Mason insisted the IRA were simply criminals who had nothing to say politically, and therefore would not be heard.

The changed British posture meant that, while it is fair to say that many Irish nationalists had substance to their complaints about the non-implementation of aspects of the GFBA in 2021, for most unionists it was the peace process itself that was at fault. They went along with it after a fashion, recognising that there was no other option acceptable to those outside their own world. But it provided the fuel for yet another hunt for traitors within their own ranks, and for yet more accusations of British betrayals. It was not their Good Friday.

The Brexit Vote in Northern Ireland, 2016

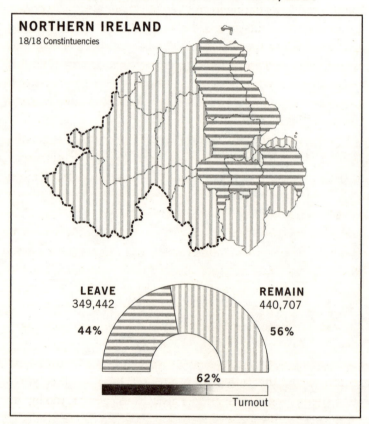

NORTHERN IRELAND
18/18 Constintuencies

LEAVE
349,442

REMAIN
440,707

44%

56%

62%

Turnout

Most of Northern Ireland's people, in most of its territory, voted for the UK staying in Northern Ireland. Northern Ireland was taken out of Europe against the wishes of its majority.

8

The Twilight of British Unionism?

The Tullyglass Hotel is, according to its website, 'an imposing country residence dating from 1890 ... set in beautiful, wooded grounds on the outskirts of Ballymena', and 'was originally built as a highly specified gentleman's residence'. Today, 'the hotel is renowned for its relaxing atmosphere, quality of service and high-quality food using local produce ... The hotel has undergone a £5 million refurbishment and can now boast a banqueting suite fit for a King and Queen.'

The Paisley family is as near as Northern Ireland gets to royalty, so it was appropriate that it was at the Tullyglass that Ian Paisley Jr hosted a political fundraising dinner in September 2017. Tickets were £1,500, payable through the local office of the MP. Those attending were rewarded with a drinks reception, free merchandise promoting the Democratic Unionist Party, and a special after-dinner speaker. It was none other than Michael Gove, then secretary of state for the environment in the Conservative government of Theresa May. Doubtless, this was a happy, maybe even a celebratory occasion, given that three months earlier May had signed up the DUP to the parliamentary pact allowing her to govern and the DUP to be at her elbow.

As we know, that arrangement would eventually turn sour. So too would the Tullyglass fundraiser, because three years later, after a long investigation, Paisley was fined £1,300 by the Electoral Commission for having accepted seat payments at the dinner from two local councils. In addition to the fine, Paisley also paid back a total of £2,600 to these councils. Somewhat obviously, local councils' money was not meant to be spent on fundraising for a political party.

Where Gove led, others followed. On 23 February 2018 at the Galagorm Hotel, also in Ballymena, there was another Paisley DUP constituency dinner, sponsored by Belfast Airport, a private company. The speaker there was Priti Patel, a government colleague of Gove. Later, in December 2018, Patel said the UK should threaten the Irish Republic with food shortages if it did not agree to demands to drop the Brexit 'backstop' agreed by Theresa May. It was a threat, said many, reminiscent of British policy on the Irish famine, and was condemned by May herself and Irish Taoiseach Leo Varadkar.[1]

Next, on 31 January 2019, it was the turn of the Tories' most prominent right-winger, Jacob Rees-Mogg, to avail himself of the delights of the Tullyglass and a Paisley–DUP fundraiser. In one way, his attendance was the most remarkable of all, as he was a fervent Catholic. The chairman of the Northern Ireland Conservatives, Alan Dunlop, was not amused by this support for the DUP for other reasons. He said of Rees-Mogg: 'Sadly on occasions, often in an honest defence of their principal political views, politicians find themselves making odd alliances and standing elements of their own political logic on its head … They make themselves look foolish when they do so.'[2]

That the willingness of Gove, Patel and Rees-Mogg to help raise funds for the DUP seemed contradictory to members of the Northern Ireland Conservatives was unsurprising. It may have represented little more than a show of solidarity with the DUP following the deal with May; but, as we have seen, the Conservative Party had been established anew in Northern Ireland by David Cameron to challenge the alleged identification there with sectarian politics – and the DUP was not only one of the most obvious representatives of this trait, but also an electoral opponent of the Conservatives.

So, did the three Conservative after-dinner speakers represent a return to the old ways of Tories standing shoulder to shoulder with a Protestant Ulster most of the world, rightly or wrongly, viewed as intolerant? After all, Boris Johnson himself had displayed a similar inclination when, as we have seen, he attended the annual conference of the DUP in 2018. Was he too bending a reverential knee to the 'precious union'? More importantly, leaving aside the prejudices and opportunism of individual politicians, were all the embraces of traditional unionism a sign that Britain's finest intended their state to stay in Northern Ireland beyond any perceptible or imagined horizon? On that, there were mixed messages.

The opening year of the Johnson regime – with Gove as his chief lieutenant, Patel his home secretary and Rees-Mogg leader of the House – suggested a degree of inconsistency with their previous DUP flirtations. First, in October 2019, after walking in a Cheshire garden with the leader of the Irish Republic Leo Varadkar as part of his Brexit manoeuvring, Johnson agreed to draw a border across the Irish Sea, through the Irish protocol in the 'Get Brexit Done' treaty – a move which, as we have seen, enraged Ulster unionists. He tried to retreat from this in his Internal Markets Bill of September 2020; but then, in December 2020, he retreated from this retreat amid howls of dissent from the DUP. And who was the cabinet member who announced this particular betrayal? The Tullyglass trailblazer, Michael Gove.

Adding to the confusion, Gove appeared on the *Today* programme on BBC Radio 4 on 10 December, attempting to seek a blessing from the grave for his behaviour by referring to 'the late, great Ian Paisley' – that is, the Reverend, not the son. By now, though, Northern Ireland unionism was not so easily mollified. Columnist Alex Kane wrote for many the following day when he remembered the title of a book on Northern Ireland once written by Dervla Murphy, *A Place Apart*: 'Speaking in the House of Commons on Tuesday Michael Gove confirmed that Northern Ireland would still be governed by EU law in specific circumstances and would come under the jurisdiction of European courts … Northern Ireland is now more than a place apart. His betrayal is unprecedented.'[3]

As tempers flared, there then came Ian Paisley Jr's ultimate humiliation in the House of Commons, on 11 February 2021. The occasion was 'Questions to the Chancellor of the Duchy of Lancaster and Minister for the Cabinet Office' – namely, Michael Gove – on the topic of the 'Strength of the Union'. Paisley intervened to note, 'The Chancellor boasts of his Unionist credentials. Indeed, he even boasted once in my local paper that he could sing "The Sash"'. To which Gove replied, 'The hon. Gentleman is right; I do have a formidable singing repertoire. I can also sing "The Fields of Athenry" and "Flower of Scotland", not to mention "Swing Low, Sweet Chariot"'. He went on to insist, 'I am a convinced Unionist', but added, 'I look forward to working with him and all representatives from Northern Ireland to ensure that our United Kingdom can flourish in the future.'

That Gove should pledge cooperation 'with all representatives from Northern Ireland' – including, presumably, Irish republicans – was bad enough, but the singing boast would have hurt most. 'The Sash' was 'The Sash My Father Wore', the most loved song of Orangeism, which boasted of the great seventeenth-century Protestant victories at Enniskillen, Aughrim and the Boyne. 'The Fields of Athenry' was a glorification of Irish rebellion, narrating how, 'Against the famine and the Crown', a nineteenth-century Irishman 'rebelled', was 'cut down' and deported. In Northern Ireland you just do not sing both songs. This was something Michael Gove, with his knowledge of Orangeism, surely knew. He was adding contempt to the protocol injury.

How did the rupture between those who were the leading exponents of unionism in Britain and Northern Ireland reach this level over the working-out of a Brexit that was meant to unite them? It was not just because of the carelessness of Johnson and the naivety of the DUP in trusting him – although both were important. Another factor was that, during and after the referendum vote on Brexit, most of its protagonists failed to acknowledge the ways in which the UK's departure from Europe would affect Ireland and the GFBA. As Irish novelist Colm Tóibín – never an Irish nationalist – put it when discussing the referendum in Britain, 'No one in the world would claim it was a campaign run with Northern Ireland in mind. It's another example, in case we need one, of how little Northern Ireland matters to anyone in Britain.'[4]

There were exceptions. During the referendum campaign, John Major and Tony Blair flew to Northern Ireland in early June to argue for Remain, arguing that the opposite outcome would damage the Northern Ireland peace process. Foster poo-poohed this strongly, complaining: 'I do find it rather disgraceful for two prime ministers who know full well the importance of the peace process to come over here and suggest that a vote in a certain direction is going to undermine that.'[5] There does seem something incongruous about a unionist leader objecting that two British former prime ministers should 'come over here'; but, perhaps more importantly, subsequent events did rather prove that Major and Blair had a point. The problem was that supporting Brexit meant different things to different people.

The DUP had consistently opposed British and Northern Ireland membership of the European club. Indeed, when announcing the decision to campaign for a 'Leave' vote, Arlene Foster had referred to her party's history, insisting: 'The Democratic Unionist Party has always been Eurosceptic in its outlook.' Similarly, the historic attitude of the DUP was referred to in its general election manifesto of 2017, which stated: 'The DUP's decision to support leaving the European Union was based on principle and practicality. The DUP had opposed joining in the first place, had been consistent in its scepticism throughout our membership and fully supported the question of membership being put to the people of the United Kingdom. This was the demonstration of our commitment to principle.'

What Foster did not detail was the historic attitude she was referencing – but many in Northern Ireland knew what she was talking about – namely, the opinions of her previous party leader, the Rev. Dr Paisley. He had preached during the European referendum campaign of 1975, for example, that the EEC was 'an overwhelming Roman Catholic federation of nations' and 'the kingdom of the anti-Christ'.[6] This strident anti-Catholicism was not repeated when the DUP argued for a 'No' vote in the referendum of 2016, but that did not mean it was not present still in the consciousness of many of the party's followers – especially those who belonged to the Free Presbyterian Church, or more generally held a strongly Calvinistic religious faith.

What is also true is that, by the time of the 2016 referendum, the DUP had other reasons for voting 'No'. One was Sinn Féin's support for a 'Yes' vote: the DUP's reflex on Irish constitutional issues was to put a minus wherever republicanism put a plus. Another was that the EU had brought the two parts of Ireland closer together. A third was what Foster referred to when writing her party's closing campaign article in the *Belfast News-Letter*, where she criticised 'the push for an EU state'. She explained: 'We are now "pooling" the sovereignty we have and will be expected to surrender it.' She ended by insisting: 'Northern Ireland and the United Kingdom as a whole should take back control.'[7]

'Take back control' was of course the main slogan of British Brexiteers, so here Foster may indeed have been making common cause with them – except that, to Foster, 'control' meant 'Northern Ireland and the United Kingdom' working together. That this was not what was meant by the British Brexiteers became obvious when the alliances on Brexit and in parliament between the DUP and the Tories fell apart: 'Control', insisted May, and especially Johnson, meant British control, and from that Northern Ireland was excluded. Moreover, the motivation for the English vote for Brexit was different from that of their counterparts in Northern Ireland. What mattered in England has been well established. Research by the Rowntree Foundation into Brexit sentiment there suggested, in the first place, that there were economic factors at play, those who had voted for Brexit having been more likely than Remain voters to have low skills, live in comparative poverty and suffer from a lack of opportunity. But Rowntree noted that something else was involved:

> The role of values occupied a key position in the referendum campaign, from debates about sovereignty and national identity to the issue of attitudes towards immigration. Unsurprisingly, attitudes on these issues are closely related to the leave vote. Nearly 90% of people who thought immigration was bad for the economy supported leave, compared with just under 10% for those who thought immigration was good for the economy. Similarly, whereas 88% of people who thought that the country should allow fewer immigrants in supported Brexit, the equivalent figure among people who wanted to keep immigration as it is was just 21%. People who feel 'very strongly' English were much more likely to say they would vote leave than anybody else (71 versus 36%) – and it was this narrow conception of national identity – rather than a broader sense of feeling 'very strongly' British that mattered most.[8]

Similar conclusions were drawn elsewhere: as the *Economist* noted on Brexit, 'one of the few interpretations universally accepted is that it was a triumph of English nationalism'.[9] This surely meant that, rather than the shared Leave vote of the DUP and the English majority illustrating a commonality, it was rather that the reverse applied: one was a statement that Ulster Protestants were part of a common UK purpose; the other was an expression of English exceptionalism. It is not surprising that there was a subsequent falling-out. By Easter of 2021, one consequence of this was Protestant rioting in the streets of Belfast and Derry over Johnson's erection of a border in the Irish Sea. The analysis offered by the *Economist* on this was telling. It said that, during the previous five years, the DUP had done more for the cause of Irish unity than Gerry Adams; that its actions had seen a return to street violence; and that, 'drunk with power', it had ditched May to support Johnson's hard Brexit, with the consequence of a border in the Irish Sea. It concluded: 'Now the UK has been symbolically and economically divided', but that 'there is little sympathy now for the DUP's predicament' – by which it meant sympathy in Britain.[10]

The Easter 2021 riots saw other exasperated reactions in Britain. For example, Simon Jenkins wrote in the *Guardian* that Johnson's xenophobia had combined with the GFBA to push Northern Ireland towards the South, and that the logical thing for Johnson to do was to 'carry his Brexit policy to its logical conclusion' – which meant that Northern Ireland 'must abandon its cosily antique relationship with Great Britain, still stuck in 1922, and build a lasting accord with the south'.[11]

What is significant about such comments is not just where they pointed – that is, towards a united Ireland – but the way in which they indicated how little patience the writers retained for Northern Ireland unionism. The crisis of unionism there, rather than, as in the past, producing British expressions of solidarity, was now generating calls to say goodbye. England, especially post-Brexit England, with its assertion of its own renewed nationalism, was going its own way. And perhaps these commentators were tired of trying to accommodate a Northern Irish unionism that always said 'No!' and fomented riots in East Belfast.

While the Brexit controversies fed such opinions, the British public at large had been moving in that direction during all the decades of the Troubles. This, at least, was the story told by opinion polls. A review of such polls conducted by Gallup for the British Social Attitudes Survey showed that, while over 40 per cent of those in Britain were in favour of withdrawal from Northern Ireland between 1971 and 1973, from 1974 to 1996 this figure never dropped below 50 per cent, and usually hovered between 60 and 65 per cent.[12]

Other polls of British public opinion showed the same result. As early as September 1971, an NOP survey for the *Daily Mail* reported 59 per cent favoured British withdrawal from Northern Ireland. In a poll for *New Society* in 1981, 43 per cent thought that the long-term policy should be reunification, while only 30 per cent said Northern Ireland should remain part of the UK. In a 5,000 strong poll for the Channel 4 television documentary *Pack Up the Troubles* in 1991, 31 per cent favoured Northern Ireland remaining in the UK, 25 per cent opted for a united Ireland, and another 25 per cent for an independent Northern Ireland. In the same poll 59 per cent supported British withdrawal. A *Sunday Telegraph* survey found in 1993 that 56 per cent said they no longer wanted Northern Ireland to remain part of the United Kingdom; and an ICM poll for the *Guardian* in 2001 reported that 41 per cent favoured a united Ireland, while only 26 per cent supported Northern Ireland staying in the UK. A survey of English respondents conducted by Lord Ashcroft in 2019 reported that 35 per cent supported the status quo, while 41 per cent said it was up to the people of Northern Ireland to decide.[13]

A fitting summary of British public opinion following Brexit, and of the unionists' threats over the border in the Irish Sea, was published in the *New Statesman* in July 2021. This recorded that only 10 per cent of British people questioned felt 'very connected' with the people of Northern Ireland, while 29 per cent felt 'moderately connected', 27 per cent 'a little connected', and 34 per cent 'not connected at all'. On Irish unification, only 11 per cent opposed it, 21 per cent selected 'don't know', 30 per cent were in favour, and 34 per cent said they neither for or against it. As the *New Statesman* commented, 'Ultimately, the polling suggests that Britain lacks a strong desire for Northern Ireland to remain part of the United Kingdom.'[14]

What both British public opinion and the Brexit rows threw up was a broader question relating both to the Conservatives' and the wider British elite's allegiance to north-east Ulster unionism in the contemporary world. We have seen the history of this backdrop: the passing of the original Act of Union, Randolph Churchill and Joseph Chamberlain's promotion of Ulster exceptionalism, the Tories' support of the UVF's threats of armed revolt in 1912–14, and finally the imposition of partition. We have also seen that, historically, this British unionism had various motivations. There was the military-strategic motivation; the landlords' interests; the incorporation of Belfast and its hinterland into industrial Britain; the familial identification; the fear that a free Ireland would be a radical and dangerous foe on England's doorstep; the belief that the Protestants of Ulster were part of the broader British Protestant faith and cultural edifice. But an often more immediate motivation was the opportunism displayed by both the Conservatives and Labour in forging alliances with Ulster unionists to assist their own political advancement.

By the early twenty-first century most of these motivations were clearly redundant. The absentee landlords had long gone; industrial Belfast with its shipbuilding, mills and large engineering works had been decimated. The worries once nursed by the Tory right about revolutionaries turning the north of Ireland into some sort of mini-Cuba exposed themselves only to ridicule when they were voiced, the more so as time went on. Concerns that an independent Ireland might provide a military base or seas from which the eighteenth- and nineteenth-century French, early-twentieth-century Americans or the twentieth-century Soviet Union might attack England – all fears which were taken seriously by the UK – were now anachronistic.

On top of all these developments came the weakening of the ideological partnership between Ulster unionism and British Conservatism. We have seen how that became strained from the outbreak of the Troubles onwards, and how accusations of betrayal from Ulster unionism were most frequently directed at Conservatives – especially Heath and Thatcher. But then, almost out of the blue, with the signing of the May–DUP deal, the old friendship seemed restored, as if the Ulster Covenant had been recovered from a memory loft. But then Brexit intervened, and the shared value of the 'precious union' revealed itself as mirage.

The upshot of all this, it was not difficult to conclude, was that British unionism and its political leaders were now finally breaking from their pre-1968 history and – echoing the contemporary sensible capitalism of the *Economist*, as well as the more radical sentiments of the *Guardian* – running out of reasons to stay in the six north-eastern counties of Ireland.

To judge whether this is true, it is necessary to consider the broader context. As we saw in chapter 6, Tom Nairn expressed disdain for the idea that the Troubles were at least partly the result of a struggle against British imperialism. By the late twentieth century, few commentators, academic or otherwise, thought that Britain was in Northern Ireland to make money; but a less crude analysis was starting to emerge, or perhaps re-emerge, from traditional Irish radical nationalism.

The publication in 1998 of *Rethinking Northern Ireland*, edited by David Miller, was an important part of this process.[15] Miller's first sentence in his introduction set the tone: 'The standard of academic, media and popular commentary on Northern Ireland remains abysmal.'[16] One of his major criticisms, which he developed in the first essay in the collection, was the failure of such commentary to understand the colonialist aspect of the situation in Northern Ireland, which he further refined as settler colonialism, drawing parallels with Rhodesia, Palestine and French Algeria.[17] He counterposed this analysis to those seeking to explain Northern Ireland by alleging 'backwardness, extremism, myths, tribal conflicts, irrationality, atavism, emotional attachment to self-serving versions of history', and in the process to absolve Britain of any responsibility or blame.[18]

For Miller, and others writing in the same volume, this alleged British neutrality was itself a typical colonialist view, and he argued more generally that 'the dominant explanations of the Northern Ireland conflict are indelibly marked by colonial and neo-colonial ideology. That is, the use of evidence and what counts as evidence is filtered by a model which discounts colonial explanations.'[19] Miller acknowledged that some writers he criticised did agree that colonialism had existed in Ireland, but complained that, even when the they did so, they were vague in specifying if and when it had ended: perhaps at the Act of Union in 1801; perhaps in 1921, with the foundation of the Northern Ireland sub-state; perhaps after 1945, when economic interests clearly diminished; perhaps in 1972, when direct rule was introduced; or perhaps after the end of the Soviet Union, when British strategic interests in Northern Ireland lessened.

For Miller, none of these turning points broke the settler-colonial model. One writer who he did suggest had been imprecise offered an elaboration. In 2019, Brendan O'Leary produced a three-volume *Treatise on Northern Ireland*.[20] This work wholeheartedly expounded the colonial interpretation of Britain in Ireland, and the settler-colonial interpretation of Northern Ireland. For O'Leary, by far Ireland's leading political scientist, the reality was plain to see:

Ireland's colonial treatment by Great Britain, before and after 1801, remains a negative entry in the ledger of the British Empire. In accounting for present passions and argument the 'catastrophic dimensions' of the Irish experience require appropriate emphasis – namely, violent conquest, expropriation, ethnic and religious oppression, and intermittent famine and immiseration. This emphasis is warranted not to provide a brief in courtrooms of public opinion, and not for the joy of savouring ancestral grievances to the neglect of past pleasures. It is required because it is true, because these catastrophic dimensions had long-run consequences, and because they affected and affect the present, by shaping institutions, ethnic and religious boundaries, ideologies, and the arenas of political competition.[21]

Over the next thousand and more pages, O'Leary set out to prove these conclusions. Like Miller, he identified 'settler colonialism' as an explanation of Britain's presence in Ireland, drawing definitions of colonialism from figures ranging from Frantz Fanon and Karl Marx to the *Oxford Dictionary*, all of which, he argued, described England's presence in Ireland. The definition he highlighted was that of the European historian Jürgen Osterhammel, who listed four components of colonialism: control, cultural dominance, an ethos of superiority, and a contrast between 'an indigenous majority and a minority of foreign invaders'.

O'Leary makes a strong case that this is what happened in Ireland, and particularly in the north-east of the island, over hundreds of years. Even the limited evidence presented in the rest of this book suggests examples of these components. The ethos of superiority of the colonial settlers and Protestants in Ireland was illustrated during the Home Rule period; the British control of Northern Ireland is evident in the recent Brexit controversy; the insistence at partition that a minority of unionists had a right to veto Irish majority rule was an example of minority control; and cultural dominance is still present when unionism continues to fight against cultural equality, even in the aftermath of the GFBA.

One aspect of O'Leary's *Treatise* – namely, his dating of the ending of colonialism – needs further interrogation. For the south, he gives a date of 1937, when that state adopted its own constitution without reference to Britain, substituting the recognition of the British monarch with the establishment of an Irish president, and when the last obligations in the Anglo-Irish Treaty concerning British access to Irish ports was abolished. He dates the end of colonialism in Northern Ireland as the period 1998–2007, with the working out of the peace process – which, he suggests, began with the referendum on GFBA on both parts of Ireland, restoring self-determination.

By the third volume of his *Treatise*, O'Leary questions himself on this. 'The 1998 Agreement', he writes, 'appeared to end British political colonialism in Ireland' – the word 'appeared' being significant. He continues, 'The informed Irish nationalist understanding was that Northern Ireland's current status as part of the UK was now a function of Irish choices, not merely the outcome of past British conquest or imposition.'[22] Again, the qualification of the ending of colonialism as a 'nationalist understanding' is important, and O'Leary goes on to detail why this 'understanding' may have turned out to be optimistic. For instance, he cites Peter Mandelson's suspensions of the Northern Ireland Assembly as a reassertion of British sovereignty in Northern Ireland, and he cites the 'truths' in Sinn Féin's accusation that the DUP's increasing use of its veto power in the Assembly on 'legacy' issues, back-tracking on Irish-language equality, and implementation of Tory governments' austerity policies damaged nationalist expectations of how the Assembly was meant to work.[23]

O'Leary finished his highly impressive *Treatise* before the details of Brexit had been finalised; but it is obvious that Brexit – in opposition to majorities in both Northern Ireland and Scotland – was a reassertion of English sovereignty within the UK. It also, of course, increased opposition to that sovereignty in both of these territories. Moreover, the implementation of Brexit, including the inclusion of the Irish protocol in what was meant to be the final settlement for leaving Europe, showed classical colonialist disregard for the interests of the colonial settlers. That disregard, as we have seen, was evident from the imposition of direct rule in 1972, and had been present in Sunningdale and the Anglo-Irish Agreement. The message had always been that Britain ruled; it was the inadequacies of Ulster unionism's own 'Britishness' that failed to give this reality sufficient recognition.

During the opening period of the Johnson premiership, the colonialist model became evident in other ways. His *couldn't care less* attitude to the obligations he had signed up to in the Irish protocol contained in the withdrawal treaty was reminiscent of many other broken British promises concerning Ireland, and indeed other colonies. As we have seen, the British government itself admitted that its Internal Markets Bill broke international law. But even before then the Johnson administration had shown its disregard for previous legalities, and indeed promises made to address them.

One case that highlighted this was that of the murder, subsequently covered up, of Pat Finucane – a lawyer who had often represented Irish republicans, among others. Finucane, aged thirty-nine, was murdered at home in Belfast in February 1989. He was shot fourteen times by two masked gunmen from the UDA in front of his wife, who was wounded, and three children. A fourteen-year inquiry conducted by Metropolitan Police commissioner John Stevens identified the involvement of two agents within the UDA. These were Brian Nelson, a British army agent whose information targeted Finucane, and William Stobie, an RUC informer who provided one of the guns that killed him. Stevens faced obstruction throughout his long investigation, especially from the British and Northern Irish security services, and said further investigation was required.

At the Weston Park political talks in 2001, as part of the peace process, the government agreed to hold a public inquiry. But it showed no appetite for doing so itself, instead appointing a retired Canadian judge, Peter Cory, to look into the case, and other allegations of collusion between loyalist paramilitaries and security forces. Cory reported in 2004, saying there was 'strong evidence' of collusion, and that an inquiry was necessary. After further delays, in 2011 the government asked Sir Desmond de Silva, a former UN war crimes prosecutor, to conduct another non-public review. His report forced UK prime minister David Cameron to apologise for 'frankly shocking levels of collusion', and a public inquiry was promised once again. This, the more optimistic hoped, might even examine British cabinet involvement in the killing: Finucane's wife had said Cory had told her privately of such involvement, and indeed Finucane was shot just weeks after a Home Office minister, Douglas Hogg, had told the House of Commons that there were a number of lawyers in Northern Ireland 'unduly sympathetic to the IRA'.

In 2019, following much further delay, the UK Supreme Court found that there had been no adequate investigation, ruling that it was for the state 'to decide what form of investigation is required'. Again, the British government declined to act. Then, on 30 November 2020, the Northern Ireland secretary, Brandon Lewis, announced that there would be no public inquiry until ongoing investigations by the Northern Ireland police and the police ombudsman had been completed. The following day, both of these bodies said they were not conducting any such investigations.

Even this abbreviated version on the Finucane case offers two conclusions. First, it would be wrong to single out the Johnson administration for the delays and failures to abide by recommendations of various inquiries that successive British governments had appointed to investigate state collusion in the murder of Pat Finucane and others. This was an enduring problem. Second, even when British inaction was in violation of the peace process, the government was willing to countenance the violation. Accordingly, it is difficult not to conclude that British collusion, in the killing not just of Finucane but others as well, went so deep, and was so high up and so generalised, that that British state simply could not allow the truth to be told.

By the time Johnson became premier, the evidence for such widespread collusion, centring on RUC and British army involvement with the UDA, UVF and others, was plentiful. The work of the Pat Finucane Centre, founded after the lawyer's killing, led the way, for example, in helping to research

Anne Cadwallader's book, *Lethal Allies: British Collusion in Ireland*.[24] The text focused on one geographical area in one limited timespan, mid-Ulster from 1972 to 1977. It concluded that 120 people had lost their lives at the hands of the 'Glennane Gang' of loyalist paramilitaries, and that these deaths were 'aided and abetted by state forces'. Only one of the dead was an active republican. The campaign was aimed at the general Catholic community, in an attempt to wear it down and cause it to break with republicanism.

Of course, it had the opposite effect. Cadwallader based her case on hard evidence – government documents, forensic reports, private reports from the Historical Enquiries Teams, and evidence collected on the ground by civil rights activists. She showed government complicity in the collusion. Mark McGovern, a professor at Edge Hill University, added to this analysis in *Counterinsurgency and Collusion in Northern Ireland*, which also focused on specific incidents, locating British army collusion in Northern Ireland in its traditional colonial 'counterinsurgency' practices and methodology.[25] McGovern noted, 'In many ways the story of collusion provides a bridge between campaigns of colonial counterinsurgency in the past and the imperial interventionism of the present. These are concerns that go beyond the conflict in the North.'[26]

One of the cases McGovern raised was that of Billy Wright of the UVF and LVF – one of the most prolific of loyalist sectarian killers. McGovern notes that there were allegations that Wright was a state agent or informer, and that when this accusation surfaced at one inquest in 2013 it was answered with a 'neither confirm nor deny' response from Special Branch witnesses. The issue was raised again at another court case, in 2020, when there was reference to a loyalist interviewed for an oral history project. He too alleged that Wright was a 'paid state agent'.[27] Whatever the truth of this – and if it is true, it is truly shocking: Wright was responsible for up to fifty sectarian murders – it was clear that court cases continued to have the potential to embarrass the authorities. So too did inquests – none more so than a second inquest held into the killing by the British army of ten Ballymurphy residents in August 1971. It eventually reported in May 2021, declaring that all the victims were innocent civilians, and that the army was 'not justified' in firing at them.

By now it was clear that legal proceedings, if not always revealing the exact details of past misdeeds by the army and the RUC, at least allowed issues to be raised. It was at this point that Boris Johnson decided to act: in July 2021 he proposed the abolition of all such legal avenues. This was in defiance of promises repeatedly made by the British during the peace process to investigate historic human rights abuses and general criminality by British forces. This promise – made in the Stormont House Agreement of 2016, and renewed in the *New Decade, New Approach* agreement of January 2020 – committed the British to publishing details of legislation to enact the historical-investigation aspects of Stormont House within a hundred days.

Not only did they not publish details; at the end of the hundred days, they said they did not intend to abide by this promise. Then, on 14 July 2021, came the details of this latest example of British agreement-breaking: there would be no further investigation into any political criminality that took place during the Troubles. There would be no further inquests, court cases, or civil claims arising out of any deaths. While Johnson and Brandon Lewis half-heatedly tried to dress this up as an amnesty for all, there was no doubt who the winners were. The front page of the *Daily Mail* crowed: 'At Last, Justice for Our Troops'; that of the *Daily Express*: 'Witch-hunts of Veterans to End'.[28] The historian and *Irish News* columnist Brian Feeney was not pleased:

Anyone reading yesterday's British government command paper, 'Addressing the Legacy of NI's past', should be warned to keep a suitable receptacle nearby to contain the disgusting product this exercise in hypocrisy, double-think and colonial condescension will induce ... The legislation will be imposed over the heads of the people here as a classic piece of colonialism to protect the behaviours of the colonialists.[29]

Here again – echoing Mark McGovern, Brendan O'Leary and David Miller – the real and present actuality of British colonialism in Ireland is invoked. And how else could it be described when one country tells another they are not even allowed to have inquests for their dead; that the 'mother country' will break agreements; that their armies will not be subject to the law; that the colony will not have control over its borders – that the natives and settlers alike must simply accept that this is the way things are?

The initial proposals of Lewis were broadly confirmed when the legislation enacting them was set out in detail in early 2022. All political parties in Northern Ireland objected, including the unionist ones: here indeed was proof that British colonialism is not a memory, but an everyday, present reality. Furthermore, the Johnson government, for all its carelessness over the border in the Irish Sea, showed it was not so careless of old allegiances. In the forward to *Global Britain in a Competitive Age: The Integrated Review of Security, Defence, Development and Foreign Policy*, published in March 2021, Johnson declared: 'My vision for the UK in 2030 sets high ambitions for what this country can achieve. The Union between England, Scotland, Wales and Northern Ireland has proved its worth time and again, including in this pandemic. It is our greatest source of strength at home and abroad.' He warned of the 'terrorist threat', including a 'Northern Ireland related' one. In the document itself, there was 'at the heart of the Integrated Review ... an increased commitment to security and resilience, so that the British people are protected against threats. This starts at home, by defending our people [and] territory.' By 'British people', Johnson meant UK residents.

Around the same time, the old DUP fundraiser Jacob Rees-Mogg, then leader of the House of Commons, even questioned the famous declaration by the former Northern Ireland secretary, Peter Brooke, that had helped to get the peace process under way: 'Somebody once said the UK had no selfish or strategic interest in Northern Ireland – I dispute that.'[30]

While it is difficult at times to take seriously anything Johnson or Rees-Mogg might say, it remains a dubious assumption that Britain's presence in Northern Ireland will be willingly ended any time soon, with a lowering of the Union Jack and a good old English handshake. While it is the case that the GFBA acknowledged the legitimacy of aspiring to a united Ireland, asserting that it was up to the people of Ireland 'without external impediment' to decide whether this was what they wanted, it left the decision on whether and when there would be a referendum on Irish unity to the British government alone. Under the GFBA, such a poll will be called if it 'appears likely' to the Northern Ireland secretary 'that a majority of those voting would express a wish that Northern Ireland would cease to be part of the United Kingdom and form part of a united Ireland'.

This wording is clearly open to various interpretations; but, more to the point, the record of British governments ignoring and even acting against sections of the GFBA, as described earlier, hardly suggests a dedicated adherence to its provisions or promises. Indeed, the leader of the Labour Party, Keir Starmer, showed where he stood when he visited Northern Ireland in July 2021. When asked about a possible referendum, he said, 'I think a border poll is not in sight. It is not in sight as far as I am concerned.' He went on to say that, if there was such a poll and he was still Labour Party leader, he would go to Ireland and campaign against Irish unification – remarks that *Irish News* columnist Tom Collins described as 'an appalling misjudgement' and 'an affront to the Irish people – north and south'.[31] Collins and others also pointed out that, in such an eventuality, Starmer would be in breach of the Good Friday Agreement under which

Britain had committed itself to neutrality in any future decision on Northern Ireland's constitutional status.

By then, however, Starmer was appearing in public whenever he could with a Union Jack backdrop, in an ongoing effort to prove he was not Jeremy Corbyn. Thus, as so often before – echoing Randolph Churchill's playing of the Orange card – his apparent stance on Ireland was primarily motivated by searching for electoral advantage in Britain, although, as we have seen, the British Labour Party and unionism have not exactly been infrequent bedfellows. Yet Starmer's unionism was exceptional in recent Labour Party history. Not since the government of James Callaghan when Roy Mason was secretary of state in the 1970s had a Labour leader been so explicitly pro-union. The irony was that Starmer was pronouncing his unionism at the very time when it had never been so unpopular in Northern Ireland, as the elections to the Northern Ireland Assembly in May 2022 showed.

Having said all of this, Britain and its political leaders do have a history of leaving their colonies when it suits them. The famous 'Winds of Change' invoked by Conservative premier Harold Macmillan, when he announced the intention to wind up British colonies in Africa in 1960, do seem to be blowing afresh from Ireland, where the most wide-ranging discussion since partition of what a new Ireland might look like began in the aftermath of Brexit.[32] In Britain, the unionist sensibilities of figures like Johnson and Starmer may not be resolute enough to resist the power of common-sense, and even their own state's long-term interests in leaving Ireland. This, despite what short-term diversions might come along.

In the first half of 2022 there was one of these when there was a renewed controversy over the Irish protocol in the European Union withdrawal agreement, with Northern Irish unionists insisting it weakened the British union. As before, Prime Minister Johnson promised to give in to unionist objections, this time by scrapping the protocol, an international agreement he had signed. Again, his intentions appeared to weaken as Europe threatened a trade war and the United States no trade deal with a law-breaking Britain, but in June 2022 Johnson's government did introduce legislation disregarding part of the protocol. This was objected to by Labour, the Liberals, the SDLP, and the Green MP. Even prominent Tories such as May and Simon Hoare, the chair of the Northern Ireland Committee objected, mainly because of the treaty breaking involved. The whole affair had the appearance of game-playing by Johnson, then adding to a reputation for dishonesty and hypocrisy on an almost daily basis. It would be a naïve conclusion to think that principled politics were involved. What certainly was the case was that by now the Tories were divided over Ireland, which was, historically, a comparatively recent phenomenon and one that could only weaken the cause of unionism. When Johnson was overthrown by his own MPs in early July 2022 Northern Ireland did not feature in any resignation letter of those in government who deserted him, but his lack of integrity did: and this was as much a feature of his Irish policies as any other. Certainly, he left office with the union more precarious than ever. He was also one more example of how unwise it is for Irish nationalists, republicans, unionists, or loyalists to place their futures or fates in the hands of English politicians.

So, no confident predictions of British withdrawal will be made here. Instead, two final observations are offered. The first is that, if a reunited Ireland comes within reality's grasp, there will be no return to the Britain of 1912–14. The upper class in England will not rally to unionism's cause, as it did then; hundreds of thousands will not gather in Hyde Park to hear whoever is leading Ulster unionism at the time – as they did for Edward Carson; 2 million people will not sign an 'Ulster is British' petition; no political party will try to force an election on the sole issue of support for north-east Ulster Protestants, as they did both at that time and in 1886.

The second observation returns to 1886, recalling the words of one A. C. Dicey, who at that time was the leading unionist intellectual polemicist against Irish self-rule. Even Dicey placed limits on his resolve. He ended his book, *England's Case Against Home Rule*, as follows:

If the time should come when the effort to maintain the unity of the State is too great for the power of Great Britain, or the only means by which it is found maintainable are measures clearly repugnant to the humanity or the justice or the democratic principles of the English people – if it should turn out that after every effort to enforce just laws by just methods our justice itself, from whatever cause, remains hateful to the mass of the Irish people – then it will be clear that the Union must for the sake of England, no less than of Ireland, come to an end.[33]

9

The Twilight of Ulster Unionism

Tuesday, 15 June 2010, was one of the British parliament's better days in its long and often torturous relationship with the people of Ireland. That afternoon in the House of Commons, the prime minister, David Cameron, reported on the Saville Inquiry into what had become known as Bloody Sunday. On that day, thirty-eight years and four-and-a-half months before then, the British army's Parachute Regiment had shot dead thirteen anti-internment demonstrators in the Bogside district of Derry, a fourteenth later dying of his wounds.

Finally, Lord Saville and two other members of his team had produced their report, declaring that the killings were both unjustified and unjustifiable. Cameron accepted this judgement, noting that Saville had concluded that soldiers of the Parachute Regiment had opened fire without warning or being fired on, that they had shot people who were running away, that none of the dead had been armed, and that some were shot while lying in the road wounded or when going to the help of others. 'I am deeply sorry', he said, accepting that ultimately the British army was the responsibility of the British government, and that therefore so were the deaths. Cameron quoted Saville's judgement that Bloody Sunday 'was a tragedy for the bereaved and the wounded, and a catastrophe for the people of Northern Ireland'.

The themes of Cameron's statement reappeared five months later, when the House of Commons got round to debating Saville's findings in the Commons. Some Conservatives said the killings did not represent the British army's mission, or that they were the responsibility of a few out-of-control soldiers; some non-Conservatives suggested that the army and the government had been let off too lightly by Saville. But no one questioned that tragic events had happened. Cameron's apology was generally endorsed.

And then the DUP spoke. First was Nigel Dodds, MP for North Belfast, who said: 'Many people in Northern Ireland feel that ... there is a very close focus on this one major incident.' By 'many people', he meant Protestant unionists, who, he insisted, had received 'no justice and no attention' for killings of members of their community. Next came Gregory Campbell, an MP for the city where the killings had occurred. He also referred to the unionist community, many of whose members, he said, believed the Saville report was a political device, the outcome of which had been decided in advance for political reasons. He also sought to excuse the soldiers, saying that when they had gone into the Bogside, they 'were going into an area that was extremely hostile and where they were likely to encounter violence'.

Sammy Wilson, the member for East Antrim, followed. He too complained that Saville had been held for political reasons – to advance the peace process – and also objected that there had been no inquiry into deaths caused by 'terrorists'. Then came Jim Shannon, MP for Strangford, who asked: 'Was the Bloody Sunday inquiry value for money?' Finally, David Simpson, the MP for Upper Bann, avoided the Bloody Sunday killings entirely, preferring to allege Irish government support for the IRA, and saying an inquiry should be held into that.[1]

None of these representatives of Northern Ireland unionism accepted in their speeches that Bloody Sunday had been wrong, or merited the apology offered by their British prime minister – or even that it was, in Cameron's words, 'a catastrophe for the people of Northern Ireland'. Instead, they made it clear that it was very far from being a catastrophe for them, or, they claimed, for the people of Northern Ireland they represented. Empathy with the relatives of Bloody Sunday's victims, or even misgivings about the deaths, were conspicuous by their absence. This was in 2010, twelve years after the GFBA, which it was hoped had initiated a new era of reconciliation in Northern Ireland. The DUP, on that day, had no interest in reconciliation.

Two-and-a-half years later, many loyalists relayed the same message during widespread street protests, and sometimes rioting, over the failure to fly the Union Jack. The immediate political context was the results of the May 2011 council elections, which saw Sinn Féin become the largest party on Belfast City Council – although the Alliance Party held the balance of power between nationalists and republicans, on one hand, and unionists on the other. As it had every right to do, Sinn Féin proposed a motion to remove the Union Jack from its position over Belfast City Hall. Unionists wanted the status quo, with the flag flying every day. Alliance proposed a compromise: that the Union Jack should fly on eighteen designated days each year, mainly on royal birthdays. This was not innovative but was in fact already the policy of some unionist-controlled councils and at the Stormont parliament buildings. The vote on the issue was taken at a Belfast City Council meeting on Monday, 3 December 2012. The Alliance Party motion was carried.

Outside City Hall, a large group of loyalists, mainly from East Belfast, had gathered to protest. They had been encouraged by the DUP, which had distributed 40,000 leaflets in favour of the status quo and attacking the Alliance Party. At the Westminster election of May 2010, DUP leader Peter Robinson had lost the East Belfast seat to Naomi Long of the Alliance Party, so there were political scores to settle. When the outcome of the City Hall vote became known, the rioting began. Five police officers and two security guards were injured in this initial clash, but worse was to follow. Riots outside City Hall and elsewhere in Protestant-dominated areas became a regular feature of Northern Irish life. For a few months, the paramilitary groups, notably the Ulster Defence Association, as well as the Progressive

Unionist Party – which, as we have seen, had links to the Ulster Volunteer Force and Red Hand Commando – were prominent in supporting the protests. This was despite their signatures on the GFBA, whose provisions pledged the careful handling of the use of political symbols – which included, nationalists argued, the Union Jack. By 7 February 2013, 146 police officers had been injured. Protest marches, road-blocks and other forms of protest continued. On 16 February, a Northern Ireland Premiership football match was called off because of a flag protest outside the stadium. According to the Confederation of British Industry, in their first month the protests cost local businesses £16 million.[2] While there were continued protests through 2013, eventually they petered out.

There was more to the flag protests than the Union Jack. An editorial or 'Morning View' in the *Belfast News-Letter* stated that the protests represented 'the frustration of a large section of the Protestant community as it watches the relentless advancement of a [Irish] nationalism that is intolerant of anything British'. On the same page of the same edition, one letter-writer said that unionists were 'the only ones giving way', while another explained:

> I was proud to attend the flag protest at Belfast City Hall on Saturday with fellow grassroots unionists and loyalists … The blame for the situation must be directed at the pan-nationalist front together with the Alliance Party for forcing their latest republican agenda on British citizens … It is clear from speaking to fellow unionists and loyalists that this is the straw that has broken the camel's back and that the Belfast Agreement is well and truly dead in the water. The [Good Friday] Belfast Agreement has provided nothing for unionists and loyalist but has delivered an endless list of concessions to republicans.

The author of the letter, Norman Boyd of Newtownabbey, described himself as an 'Anti-Agreement Unionist', and went on to list twenty-two such 'concessions'. They include the disband-ment of the UDR and the RUC; the inclusion of 'former IRA terrorists in government'; the fact that 'innocent victims of the IRA' had been 'forgotten'; and the 'increasing number of loyal order parades banned or restricted'. He added that 'portraits of Her Majesty the Queen [were] removed' from public offices, and that there was 'media bias against loyalists and unionists'.[3]

From the unionist perspective, these arguments were both relevant and self-evident. For many in the Protestant commu-nity, the GFBA was now becoming the cause of their oppression, having prescribed significant changes in the way society was managed in Northern Ireland. Most importantly, it had targeted the Ulster Protestant senses of entitlement and exclusivity: the assumption that Northern Ireland was their state and that their ancestors had built up 'Ulster' from nothing, so bestowing upon them the right to first choice of jobs and housing, among other privileges. The very notion that Irish Catholics had a right to cultural equality, or to be consulted when it was being decided where Orange marches should go, or where and when their Union flag should be flown, was an affront to their traditions, sentiments and practices.

There were also those within the Protestant community who sought to bring their traditions of exclusivity up to date. One notable development of post-GFBA Northern Ireland was the growth of racism of the British variety. This was summarised in an evidence-based report in 2015 by the left-wing organisa-tion Trademark Belfast, which began: 'At the time of writing, the spectre of racism is haunting Northern Ireland in a way that seems unprecedented in the post-conflict era.' It reported that, 'Despite attempts to brand Belfast as a bright and shiny post-conflict city open for tourism and flows of transnational capital, it is in danger of confirming its reputation as the "race hate capital of Europe".'

The report went on to quote statistics from the Police Service of Northern Ireland showing that, from 2006 to mid-2010, there had been 4,051 race-hate incidents reported, and from mid-2010 to 2014, 3,270 such reports. For one year, 2013–14, this was three times the rate of such incidents in England and Wales – although of course minority-ethnic immigrants had been going there in greater numbers and over a longer period, so greater assimilation and toleration might have been expected. In describing various Northern Ireland incidents, the report recorded the unhappy experiences of individual settlers from Poland, Slovakia, Afghanistan, Pakistan and Nigeria. It also observed: 'existing studies suggest that the majority of racist attacks have taken place in areas that are Protestant and working class', though noting that 'it is also the case that recent migrants tend to live in predominantly Protestant residential areas'.

Nevertheless, said the report: 'Undoubtedly, the legacy of the conflict, patterns of deindustrialisation, social decline and educational underachievement have played a part in fuelling Protestant working-class alienation, a sense of grievance and therefore resentment towards the "Other".'[4] An academic, Richard Reed, who was sympathetic to the Protestant working class also acknowledged that, within that community, racism was 'a problem that [had] been especially prevalent in loyalist areas where attacks [had] targeted both settled ethnic minority communities, such as the tiny Chinese population, alongside recently arrived migrant workers from Eastern Europe'.[5] Reed also noted that, despite some paramilitary organisations having attempted to tackle racism within their own organisations, 'still there is also some evidence the UDA and UVF leaderships haven't always been helpful in countering the attitudes that sustain racist attacks'.[6]

Further evidence of the disproportionately high level of racism in the Protestant community was presented in the *Life and Times* surveys from 2004 to 2017. Whether on the issue of public bodies considering the needs of ethnic minorities, of members of ethnic-minority communities moving into neighbourhoods, or of family members marrying members of ethnic-minority communities, responses from Catholics were more positive than from Protestants. The differences were not great, but they were there. For example, in a survey of 2007, 53 per cent of Catholics said they would be 'very comfortable' with new ethnic-minority neighbours, compared to 43 per cent of Protestants; and, when asked in 2014 if public bodies should consider the needs of minority communities, 73 per cent of Catholics said it was very or fairly important, compared to 57 per cent of Protestants.

While these and other figures vary in the differentials, they all show a greater level of uncertainty and lack of comfort among Protestants than among Catholics with the integration of 'others' within their neighbourhood or society. Of course, hatred of the old enemy persisted. The year 2020 saw a growth in instances of 'KAT' being daubed on walls in Protestant communities: that is, Kill All Taigs (Catholics). The PUP celebrated Christmas in 2020 by putting a 'joke' on their website, in which 'Celtic fan' was code for Catholic: 'What do you call a Celtic fan who is dressed as Father Christmas? A Fenian bastard – don't let the suit fool you.'

Towards the end of 2020, prominent members of the DUP, no doubt aware of growing discontent among their community, were also replaying this old rhetoric, pointing accusing fingers at the traditional Catholic enemy. One was Edwin Poots, not only a DUP member of the Northern Ireland Assembly but the agriculture minister in the Northern Ireland power-sharing executive. He had previously distinguished himself by attacking evolution, insisting that the earth only came into being in 4,000 BC. His father Charlie was a Free Presbyterian – indeed, a close colleague of the Rev. Dr Paisley and a founding member of the DUP – who had stated in 1975 that one way to solve the Troubles would be to 'cut off all supplies including water and electricity to Catholic areas. And I would stop Catholics getting social security.'[7]

In October 2020, his son Edwin was asked about the coronavirus by the *Irish News*. He had noticed, he said, that Covid-19 cases in Irish nationalist areas had outnumbered those in unionist areas by 'around six to one'. When asked by the newspaper if this was not a religiously sectarian statement, implying that Catholics were either more irresponsible than Protestants or somehow attracted Covid's wrath, Poots replied, 'It is not a sectarian statement as most Sinn Féin leaders don't attend the Catholic Church on a regular basis.'[8] Poots's remarks were widely rebutted and condemned by health officials, members of the Official Unionist Party, the Alliance Party, the SDLP and Sinn Féin. There were widespread calls for his sacking from the executive.

Over the next couple of days, the *Irish News* asked Poots's party leader, Arlene Foster, for comment. She declined the invitation, although Gregory Campbell MP defended him. Eventually Poots spoke again. Although it was the *Irish News* that had broken and extensively covered the story, he named a different conspirator: Sinn Féin. It was they, he said, who had tried to 'twist and distort' his words: 'I cherish my Catholic friends and neighbours', he insisted.[9] Mrs Foster did then speak, saying, 'As far as I am concerned that's the end of the matter.'[10]

Foster was asked to comment again in January 2021, when Ian Paisley Jr made an intervention in the House of Commons, saying: 'Today is Holocaust Memorial Day where we remember the victims of the Holocaust … and in Northern Ireland of course we remember the border campaign and the genocide of sectarian murder where the IRA, the Catholic IRA, murdered Protestants at the border.' The chair of the committee to which the remarks were addressed, Conservative MP Simon Hoare, was not impressed by the association of his own faith with the IRA: 'As a practising Roman Catholic myself I would also like to note that I don't think the way the question was phrased was conducive to trying to move things forward.'[11] The next day Paisley defended his words, saying, 'The IRA is/was a sectarian murder machine – its sect identity background was RC.' The

Irish News, as well as quoting an historian refuting the Catholic Church's identification with militant Irish republicanism, asked for a comment on Paisley's assertions from the DUP leadership. No response was forthcoming.[12]

Next, Paisley's fellow DUP MP, Gregory Campbell, updated the targets. On Facebook, on 31 January 2021, he described an edition of BBC's *Songs of Praise* as 'the BBC at its BLM [Back Lives Matter] worst'. The programme had featured the semi-final of the Gospel Singer of the Year Competition. Campbell noted: 'There were five singers, all of them black. There were three judges, all of them black and one presenter who was incidentally, yes black.' The Belfast Multi-Cultural Association, Belfast Islamic Centre and Amnesty International NI were among those who complained.[13] Again, critics outside the DUP urged Foster, as party leader to intervene. Again, as with Poots, she declined.

She had, it must be admitted, other things to think about. She was in a politically precarious position, with her policy of alliance with English Toryism in tatters and her previous acquiescence to the Irish protocol returning to haunt her. When riots broke out over Easter 2021, predominantly in loyalist areas, she too returned to the old ways. She told the Protestant youth to stop fighting the police, insisting that the 'real law-breakers' were Sinn Féin. But it was not Sinn Féin that had drawn the border in the Irish Sea, and everyone knew that. She later said she had used 'clumsy language'.[14] By now, she could not even get her sectarianism right.

Nor could some of her prominent party members choose their allies correctly. When outgoing US President Donald Trump urged his followers to march on Capitol Hill, in what seemed to most observers to be an attempt to prevent the peaceful assumption of power by Joe Biden, Ian Paisley Jr defended Donald Trump. Saying he did not believe that Trump 'provoked the rioters to break the law', Paisley described the outgoing president as a 'good friend'. In September 2020 the run-up to the US election, he had posed for a photograph with fellow DUP MPs holding a flag in public support of Trump's re-election. Sammy Wilson posted the picture of himself, Paul Girvan and Paisley holding a banner that read: 'Trump 2020, Keep America Great'.[15] There was more to this than a simple identification with a fellow right-winger. Paisley's father, the Rev. Dr Paisley, had long been associated with the religious and racist wing of US politics, having gained his doctorate through the Bob Jones University in South Carolina – an evangelical establishment that taught evangelical Christianity, banned black students, and denied Darwinism.

A couple of days before the Easter 2021 riots, Foster's predecessor as DUP leader and first minister, Peter Robinson, intervened with an important article in the *Belfast News-Letter*. In it he stated: 'I can think of no period over my 50 years in politics where unionists have felt more alienated than they are now ... Unionists dwell under a cloud of injustice.' He argued that British culture was being replaced by 'everything Irish', replaying the old conspiracy accusation that British governments give in to republicans out of fear of the return of the IRA. He said that the current anger in the unionist community was unlikely to abate, and might manifest itself beyond peaceful or political protests, and 'be vented more robustly'. He concluded, 'My advice to those who are driving this agenda forward is as short as it is restrained. Take care.'[16]

Robinson, many in Northern Ireland knew, had a history of such melodrama. On the night of 7 August 1986, he had led between 150 and 500 loyalists into the Irish Republic village of Clontibret, in County Monaghan, protesting at the Anglo-Irish Agreement. Two Irish police were beaten by the mob, and local property was damaged. Robinson had been arrested, charged and convicted of a minor offence. In November 1986, he helped to organise Ulster Resistance, Paisley's version of paramilitarism. Sure enough, a couple of days after his article in the *News-Letter*, the riots broke out in Derry, and then Belfast. It would be unfair to blame Robinson for them. He did not now have the necessary influence among the rioters to have motivated them; but certainly he did not help to calm the situation, nor did his article advise restraint.

His words in the *News-Letter* reflected what was now commonplace in unionism of most varieties: they had been undone by the Brits, by the Fenians, by the United States, by the Europeans, by the Catholics, by traitors within their own ranks; they were alone and fragile; of course, none of this was their fault – and, most menacingly, there would be consequences. What might they be? A suggestion was made in a new mural in March 2021, which appeared in the Beersbridge/Castlereagh Road area of East Belfast. It referred to attacks by the IRA, but more pointedly to attacks by loyalists of innocent civilians in massacres at Greysteel, which had seen seven killed, and others at a bookmakers in the Ormeau Road in Belfast that had killed five. I quote it here in full as it was written, including grammatical errors:

> The Provo's fear the reaper
> From the UFF he comes
> The Loyalist executioner
> He brings judgment with his gun
> He strikes when no one expects him to
> From behind his hood cold eye
> The reaper brings still justice
> As another Provo dies
> He brought revenge for the Bann
> In the Ormeau bookies five
> And for the Shankill bombing
> Gray Steel was his reply
> Sometimes his lust is chilling
> As he goes about his task
> The Provo's fear the reaper
> Theres death behind his mask
> Ulster Freedom Fighters[17]

Obviously, this glorification of killing innocent civilians was not a sentiment to which most Northern Ireland Protestants would subscribe. On the other hand, there were unionists who were prepared to associate themselves with those whose killings their own British government condemned. In August 2019 Gregory Campbell MP, Edwin Poots and other prominent unionists posed under a banner in Derry's Fountain estate which prominently included the logo of the parachute regiment, the Bloody Sunday killers. More generally, it is valid to speculate whether the above mural was no more than the ultimate statement of the belief that Catholic lives did matter less, and that, as we have seen, this notion permeated many Protestant and unionist traditions across centuries.

Let us take a less extreme example than killing innocent civilians, in this instance the unionist perception of what Sammy Wilson MP in 1987 called 'a leprechaun language' – by which he meant the Irish language.[18]

Again, Wilson's disparagement could be dismissed as unrepresentative; but unionist and Protestant opposition to equality for the Irish language was not. There was a time, over two hundred years ago, when Protestant ministers of religion were appointed because they spoke Irish, in the hope that they could converse better with Catholics. There are also examples from history of leaders of the Orange Order speaking and supporting Irish; in the Celtic revival of the early twentieth century, the Irish language again attracted the interest and participation of many Irish Protestants.[19]

Of course, many Irish Catholics do see Irish as part of their identity – and the British state's historic intolerance for the language added to such feelings; but this hardly justifies the opposition by unionists to giving equality to Irish in Northern Ireland today. Yet it was on the question of the provision of language equality that the DUP time and again interrupted progress on power-sharing. It was also an opposition that was supported by a significant proportion of the party's voters. A survey for a television programme in January 2020 found that, of those who had cast their vote for Arlene Foster's party at any time in the past five years, 64.5 per cent were totally opposed to an Irish-language act.[20] The unionists objected to Irish because, they said, it represented a cultural attack on their traditions – although in effect its recognition was an example of the cultural equality promised in the GFBA.

Such was the feeling inside the DUP on this that, when Edwin Poots succeeded Foster, he was driven out of office within days because he agreed that the British government should be empowered to legislate on the language if, within a year, the Assembly had not done so. Another 'lundy' was vanquished; the *Daily Mirror*'s 'crackpots' seemed more appropriate than ever.

By now, the DUP was seemingly returning to its sectarian roots, with all hope of a new, modern unionism relegated in the attempt to deflect criticisms of a party that had lost its way. How was it, then, that the DUP's Westminster election manifesto of December 2019 spoke about 'next generation unionism', saying:

> With Northern Ireland's centenary less than two years away, we are seeking to develop a long-term vision for Unionism and Northern Ireland beyond 2021. The Northern Ireland of today differs markedly to how it was at the founding of the state back in 1921, or compared to 1971, or even since the Belfast and St Andrews Agreements. The composition of society is different. Demographics and attitudes have changed. We have new migrant communities. The role of women has transformed. The influence of faith across society is diminishing. Our world feels much smaller as the result of more accessible travel and greater connectivity. The UK has changed and continues to change, as does the Republic of Ireland.

This might seem like the promotion of a unionism seeking a new modernity; indeed, the manifesto went on to call for 'No diminution of workers' rights', action on 'the unfair treatment of women pensioners with a suitable compensatory scheme established [and] legislation to reform the House of Lords'. It even complained that cultural institutions in the UK were too 'English-centric'. But one paragraph heading also demanded: 'Let's Protect Mothers & Unborn Life Again'. The manifesto also called for an increase in defence spending, and 'Bringing Armed Forces Day to Northern Ireland – It is unacceptable that Northern Ireland has never hosted the main national event for Armed Forces Day in the UK.' There was also a call for 'the establishment of an organisation to promote and encourage interaction, dialogue, and practical collaboration around our British identity and developing deeper relationships between all parts of the UK, be they cultural, business, sporting or any other sphere.'

In the real world, it was now becoming fairly obvious that the general 'British identity' was an increasingly dubious concept. There were several indications of this: approximately 50 per cent of the Scottish people supported independence; English nationalism was on the rise (see chapter 8); sympathy in Britain for the Ulster unionist cause was on the wane; and there was growing demand in both northern and southern Ireland for a referendum on partition, as provided for in the GFBA.

The 2019 manifesto was in some places little more than a rehearsal of confused contradictions. In one highlighted section, 'Reasons to vote DUP', the second of six reasons given was: 'For a strong DUP who will not support a Corbyn Government'; and yet some of the manifesto's policies were what could be called Corbynist. In addition to those mentioned above on workers' rights and reform of the House of Lords, these included 'an end to benefits freeze', 'a national living wage of £10.50' (Labour's call was for £10), 'robust action' against companies that failed to comply with the National Living Wage, and 'a prioritisation of the public sector pay rises'.

This suggested the DUP was by now trying to be all things

to all people – although, it must be said, it was chiefly appealing to Protestant people – the first bullet-point of its plea for a mandate was: 'to protect Northern Ireland's place in the United Kingdom'. A consequence of and the aftermath of Brexit was the worst ever Westminster result for unionist parties. Among those who the electorate rejected was deputy leader of the DUP, Nigel Dodds, the outgoing MP for North Belfast, who just two years earlier had proclaimed: 'Today, it is the DUP that stands in the heart of government, not in Northern Ireland, but across the United Kingdom. Our position at Westminster has never been stronger, our support in the country has never been greater' (see chapter 1).

So, what happened? And what will happen next?

In answering these questions, it is important to determine whether the crisis that Ulster unionism faced in, say, the summer of 2021 was a consequence of contemporary circumstances, or something deeper, involving the nature and working-out of its inherent, historic weaknesses. Certainly, the contemporary circumstances were important. Foster's poor leadership; over her deal with May; the naivety of her failed political romance with Johnson and the Conservative right; the DUP's mishandling of Brexit; the duplicity of Johnson and Michael Gove; the farce of Edwin Poots's shortest-ever leadership of the DUP – all are significant and important factors in shaping the nature of the crisis. So too are the demographic changes Northern Ireland is undergoing, leading to the loss of a clear pro-unionist majority for the first time in its history.

Were the consequences of all this avoidable? If there had been a unionist party and philosophy that manged to attract a significant section of the Catholic community, that would have made a huge difference. If such a party had retained the support of its traditional Calvinistic base while still appealing to those who were supportive, or even just tolerant, on such issues as a woman's right to control her own body or gay relationships, that too might have delivered a more optimistic future. If such a party had been able to build an all-class alliance while maintaining unity among unionists, as the old Unionist Party had achieved in the first fifty years of Northern Ireland, then that also would have been helpful. But these were all questionable propositions.

Moreover, it is true that many within unionism, including sections of its leadership, did try to steer the old Unionist Party, and even the DUP, in these directions. The UUP's support for the GFBA and the DUP's for the St Andrews Agreement were the most substantial examples of this. The problem with this was that, even at the time, only 50 to 55 per cent of Northern Ireland's Protestant population had supported the GFBA at the referendum, while many later regretted doing so. Many of these dissatisfied – including the DUP, which opposed GFBA, to most loyalist paramilitaries who supported it – blamed Sinn Féin and its community for going beyond the GFBA over issues like police reforms, Irish-language rights and the flying of the Union Jack. The fact was that issues of cultural equality and respect were part and parcel of the peace process – and, in truth, Sinn Féin had a good deal to complain about when it came to the slowness of the implementation of promises in these and other areas.

It is also the case that even some of the more contentious reforms initiated by the peace process did little more than mildly restrict unionist cultural practices. For example, the Parades Commission – established in 1997, before the signing of the GFBA, to oversee the organising, conduct and routes of parades – imposed conditions on Protestant and Unionist marches only very occasionally. In 2018–19, of 2,523 such marches, the Commission imposed conditions on only 135.[21] But even this was easily interpreted by those, such as the Orange Order and DUP, as too much. For example, in October 2021 the DUP strenuously objected when the Parades Commission banned an Orange march from passing through a mixed area of North Belfast. It also objected when the PSNI placed a row of police Land Rovers at the entrance to the banned route.

'There was no need for such a heavy police response', said the DUP, attacking the PSNI – which by now had become a constant refrain among the party leadership, echoing its protests about the police reforms. In the same vein, it called the Parades Commission an 'unelected and undemocratic quango' and called for its removal.[22]

There is another small piece of evidence revealing the unionist mindset from 2018 to 2021 – or at least that of Arlene Foster. After she was overthrown, the *Irish News* revealed that, for three years, its political correspondent had been trying to secure an interview with her for their newspaper, read mostly by the Northern Irish Catholic community. Each request had been refused by the first minister: apparently she had nothing to say to that newspaper's audience.

The general failure of a significant section of the Protestant community to support the peace process, to welcome social liberalism, to sign up to compromise, or to listen to voices from the Catholic community, was ultimately an indication of broader and deeper attitudes and assumptions, as well as consequences of older political prescriptions. The most obvious of these was the establishment of the Northern Ireland statelet, and the ideas that had informed it.

Ironically, the case can be made that the 1921 settlement was the first legislative stage in the death of Ulster unionism. As we have seen, not only did 'Ulster' lose three counties – by the Ulster unionists' own choice; the first Ulster unionist opponents of Irish Home Rule neither advocated nor supported the establishment of such a polity. To repeat the perception of Dr Kane, Belfast grandmaster of the Orange Order, in 1892, such an idea was 'foolish and treasonable'. This comment was logical: How could unionism mean increasing the political distance between Britain and Northern Ireland, as the establishment of a devolved parliament and a separate, if limited government did?

In modern times there are those who, recognising this rather obvious contradiction, have advocated either complete integration of Northern Ireland with Britain or a state totally separate from both Britain and Ireland. Neither have proved popular, and it is now clear that, while Britain in the last fifty years has for long periods imposed direct rule, no political party there desires this as a permanent arrangement. Nowadays, it would be more trouble than it would be worth. As to independence, the more time that has elapsed since this was advocated in the 1970s, the more broadly it has come to be seen in Britain and Northern Ireland itself as unsustainable.

In an Irish context, what the establishment of Northern Ireland sought to accommodate was the sense of difference and, more importantly, superiority that most Irish Protestants felt and believed themselves to embody. It is interesting to speculate how things might have been different if, in 1921, the unionist political leadership had made attempts to integrate Catholics, instead of discriminating against them. But they did not do so – and when, after too long a time, their British allies insisted that change was necessary, it was either too little, too late, or unionism was too trapped in its culture of exclusivity to commit strenuously to building a new Northern Ireland.

There was always a logic in this. The establishment of the six-county state represented the only way any sort of unionism could survive in Ireland. Within it, unionists could lay the foundations and build the walls to keep out the Irish majority. It was an unquestionably undemocratic act, overseen by a British state in imperial mode. When the integration of the northern Catholic minority was barely thought about, never mind practised, the only hope Northern Ireland had of even a short-term future was for the unionist government that emerged to achieve two things: establish structures that both maintained the material privileges the Protestant community had secured prior to partition, even if for some those privileges were minimal; and build an electoral system tilted in its favour, and oversee repressive laws and security systems that kept Catholics in their place.

This was the siege mentality all over again, sustained by the insistence on Protestant moral and religious superiority that has never really gone away. Even the 'new unionism' or – civic unionism' that was first to emerge in the 1960s, that then reappeared under Trimble, and was, still hinted at in the DUP manifesto of December 2019, was tainted with these same assumptions. They would now be kinder British, but they were still British, with all that this entailed. That included the old sense of colonial and colonialists' superiority and entitlement, the old nudges and winks about the inferiority or Irish natives and their culture. Why should Catholics have equality in jobs and housing? What have *they* done to deserve such bounty? Why should they have signs in the Irish language plastered across Belfast? Why should the Orange Order not be able to march where they want? Why should working-class loyalists not be allowed to build bonfires as high as they can? Why should there be power-sharing with people who are disloyal to the state? Why should they wish to join a priest-ridden southern state that for most of its existence has failed to offer an alternative attraction for the vast majority of northern Protestants, or indeed many northern Catholics.

But that proposition continues to evolve. The hold and influence of the Catholic church has dramatically declined. Today the southern state has more doctors and nurses per head of the population than the UK. In 2021 it was judged by the United Nations to be the second-best place to live in the world. It has higher pensions and unemployment benefits than the UK. It is a socially liberal country that might not persuade northern Calvinists of its worth but will attract others in the Protestant community. A discussion of Irish unity is taking place north and south which recognises that a thirty-two-county Ireland will require promising more than just a southern takeover, aiming instead at a more secular and equal society.[23] Meanwhile, the National Health Service in Northern Ireland seems increasingly unable to shine as the brightest star in unionism's darkening skies. In August 2021, it was reported that it suffered the worst hospital waiting lists in the UK, with one in four of the population awaiting appointments.[24]

At the same time, Northern Ireland and is Protestant community are not as they once were. The Orange Order is now said to be around 30,000 strong – a decline from 100,000 at the start of the Troubles. It no longer enjoys the right to representation in the ruling authority of the leadership of any unionist party, whereas it once occupied one-third of the seats on the ruling body of the UUP. While, at the start of the Troubles, the major unionist party held all of the twelve Northern Ireland seats at Westminster, after the 2019 general election it retained just eight out of eighteen seats, while the two unionist parties received only 42 per cent of the vote. In the 1964 general election, the Ulster Unionist party had won 63 per cent – which itself reflected a 7 per cent decline since the previous election.

There have also been major economic changes. The pillars of the Belfast Protestant economy have shrunk or been pulled down. During the Second World War, the Harland and Wolff shipyard employed 33,000 people. By the summer of 1961, this had declined to 13,000, following a mass sacking that year of 8,000; by the late 1980s, this figure had fallen to 3,000. Today it no longer builds ships and has not done so for nearly two decades. In 2021 the skeleton that remains has just 400 workers. Another stalwart of Protestant employment, Mackies engineering works, which at its height had 7,000 workers, employed just 300 when the receiver was called in in July 2008. The largest manufacturer in Northern Ireland today is Bombardier – an aircraft maker that was once Short Brothers, where, as we have seen, anti-Catholic discrimination was widespread. Today, having suffered recent financial problems, it employs just under 3,000 people.

Outside manufacturing, other industries – notably the state security forces, another employment area traditionally reserved almost exclusively to Protestants – have seen a diminution of

Protestant dominance; 30 per cent of the PSNI now consists of Catholics. As to the more general breakdown of differences between the two communities, young Protestant boys now tend to be the most underprivileged group; although the worst areas of economic deprivation remain Catholic, the differences are very small.

It is now true that the Protestant 'labour aristocracy' has gone – a victim of world-market economics, Thatcherite deindustrialisation and, since the 1990s, a concentrated effort to implement fair employment legislation. The most dramatic decline has taken place in the old centrepiece of the Protestant labour aristocracy, the Shankill area of West Belfast. The 'Greater Shankill Strategic Regeneration Framework', produced for the Greater Shankill Partnership and the Department for Social Development by the Paul Hogarth Partnership in 2008, tells a sad story:

> Analysis confirms that the population continues to decline, that educational attainment remains particularly low, that multiple deprivation persists within many communities and that capital values of properties are far below those of comparable areas … Communities in the Greater Shankill feature highly in any ranking of Northern Ireland places, on the basis of multiple deprivation and on individual measures of need that relate to education and training, ill health, the quality of people's living environment or their economic well-being.

All of this seems a bitter reward for the Shankill's loyalty to the British state, and to the social and economic structures it propped up for one-and-a-half centuries: it seems reasonable to suggest that, as the material conditions generating support for unionism evaporate, the ideology of unionism itself is becoming more vulnerable. A sense of 'Britishness' may persist; but given the way in which Boris Johnson, in particular, lied to the DUP, and broke promises made to the party, it must be wondered just how many more 'betrayals' Ulster Protestants will take. It seems increasingly obvious that they will have more influence in a new Ireland, where they would become a notable minority not so easily ignored as they are in a 'United Kingdom' whose politicians and elites routinely ignore them with little consequence.

Certainly, in the summer of 2021 the DUP was getting the blame from their community for trusting the British too much – opinion polls reported that the party was losing support both to the Alliance Party on its left and to its right-wing unionist competitor Traditional Unionist Voice.

For the more fundamental unionists the imposition by Johnson of a border in the Irish Sea – the Irish protocol in the Brexit agreement – made the DUP guilty by association. So, the DUP reverted to its original brand. The new leader Sir Jeffrey Donaldson endorsed those who were warning of the dire consequences of the protocol, although he had in the past displayed a softer approach, advocating a solution which advocated a 'best of both worlds approach', including respect for the European single market[25] and on other occasions boasting how he was working with Johnson on finding an acceptable solution.[26] Nevertheless, in February 2022 he brought down the executive because, he said, of the protocol, although he had also threatened to bring it down if the British government introduced its long-promised legislation on the Irish language.[27]

At rallies against the protocol in the early months of 2022 the old Paisleyite rhetoric was heard once more and 'lundy' backsliders were denounced. Even Sammy Wilson was heckled at one of these for being a 'traitor', because of a suspected DUP weakness on the protocol. He sought to prove himself otherwise. Just before Russia invaded Ukraine, he compared their threats to do so with the EU's intentions towards Northern Ireland.[28] At another rally, James Bryson, a populist loyalist blogger, spoke of how Northern Ireland was under the 'jackboot' of the EU.[29] The Orange Order then cited past glories, pointing to the UVF gun-running of 1912–14, saying such 'bold' behaviour was needed now.[30] When the UUP withdrew from this programme of rallies protesting at the threatening rhetoric, the window of the party's leader office was smashed. Then, a car was highjacked in a Protestant area of Belfast and its driver forced to drive a suspected bomb to a meeting where the Irish foreign minister was talking. It was a hoax, but it stirred old memories. The police blamed the UVF.

The speeches and antics represented the encouragement and manipulation of the traditional insecurities of the Protestant community; conjuring the spectre of imagined enemies, and the employment once more of Calvinistic 'end is nigh' prophecies. It had some effect. In the May 2022 Assembly election the DUP recovered some of the ground opinion polls had indicated they were losing to Traditional Unionist Voice, but as they buried any semblance of 'new unionism' they also lost ground to the Alliance Party.

Most dramatic of all, Sinn Féin topped the poll. They won 29 per cent of the vote, compared to their nearest rivals, the DUP, who received just 21.3 per cent, a fall from 28.1 per cent in 2017. This was the first time a nationalist party had won an election to a Northern Ireland parliament. Overall, the votes of the main unionist parties declined 3.3 per cent to 40.1 per cent, although independent unionists won a further 0.8 per cent. Anti-partition parties won 40.7 per cent. The Alliance Party enjoyed an increase of first preference votes of 4.5 to 13.5 per cent. In terms of seats, non-unionist parties won 53 out of the 90 seats, although neither unionist nor nationalist parties won a majority.

The growth in support of the border-neutral Alliance Party was an important development. While it is easy to dismiss Alliance as middle-of-the-road and middle class, and a party with unionist roots, its growth made those roots all the more significant because Alliance drew most of its votes from ex-unionists. Accordingly, it can be argued we are seeing the re-birth of the Protestant liberalism which two and a half centuries ago was commonplace in Belfast, and which in its most activist and radical form had, in the 1790s produced the United Irishmen.

Sinn Féin and Alliance had already come together to oppose Brexit and to support women's right to control their own bodies, marriage equality, and acceptance of the Irish protocol. Herein was the suggestion of a new partnership. Certainly, combined with the rise in support for Irish nationalism it meant unionism was no longer a majority ideology in the six north-eastern counties of Ireland. Maybe, after all, the prophecies of unionist doom did, this time, have a grounding in reality; maybe the traditional Orange insistence that 'united we stand, divided we fall' was now not just a warning but an actuality.

It is not that simple. To return to the start of this discussion, Northern Ireland unionism is not and never has been a 'crackpot' ideology. It has been based on the retention of privilege – which, though it may not be ethical, is understandable. Its sense of superiority over 'others' offers a self-assurance that is easy to embrace – in Ireland as in many other communities and cultures. Its bowing down to the British state despite the many 'betrayals' may be humiliating – but what choice did it have if it wanted its own six-county mini-state to survive, especially since British troops were also present to protect unionists if need be?

Many in the unionist community may continue to cling to a world-view informed by theology; but the nature of that theology at least offers reassurance that God is on their side as they continue to lose friends and influence. If they continue to insist that a world outside is conspiring against them, then at least that gives them a sense of togetherness, of a people under siege. In truth, they have indeed been under siege since 1968.

Many Protestants, in and out of uniform, have been killed, chiefly by the IRA, and the unwillingness of the Protestant community to forgive and forget such crimes is easy to understand. Irish republicanism is seen as the enemy, and this myopia inhibits Ulster Protestants from developing the 'protest' side of

Protestantism to respond to the social and economic conditions in which they live. Instead, there is still a widespread sense that the old ways are best: in the words of their favourite anthem, *The Sash My Father Wore*, 'It is old but it is beautiful and its colours they are fine.'

All of this casts doubt on whether a substantial proportion of northern Protestants would today welcome a future in a new Ireland. But substantial support for it is not necessary; the type of majority the 'Remain' vote won in the Brexit vote in Northern Ireland would be enough to secure Irish unity, and an end to six-county unionism. Even now, its majority support in Ulster's capital of Belfast – once the predominantly industrial heart of the Protestant working class – has been lost. Moreover, there is more questioning of the old ways than before: a majority of the Protestant community may not welcome the changes the 'peace process' has delivered, but a significant minority do. Recent research by political scientist Jonathon Tonge revealed that almost a fifth of DUP voters had migrated to the liberal, border-abstentionist Alliance in the Westminster election of December 2019.[31]

Religious belief is also in decline, though some estimates suggest this applies more among Catholics than Protestants. In 2009, *Life and Times* reported that 43 per cent of the Northern Ireland population described themselves as Catholic, another 43 per cent as belonging to various Protestant religions, and 12 per cent as having 'no religion'. In 2021 these figures were 28 per cent, 35 per cent and 27 per cent, respectively.[32] A further suggestion of changing times can be found in recent interviews with members of the Protestant community conducted by journalist Susan McKay for her book *Northern Protestants: On Shifting Ground*, which suggests a growing breadth of identity and attitudes among those she interviewed – though she was explicitly searching for a new diversity.

And yet the Northern Ireland of 2021 has yet to achieve the reconciliation promised or hoped for when the GFBA was signed. This impression is supported by the so-called 'peace walls', built during the Troubles to protect the Catholic and Protestant communities from attacks by the other side. A Peace Barrier programme – formally the Peace Walls programme – was launched in 2012. Created by the International Fund for Ireland (IFI), its goal was 'to help residents arrive at a position where they feel it is safe and appropriate to discuss and consider the removal of Peace Walls in their area', which the IFI felt was hardly an ambitious aim.[33] More than £7.5 million was spent on the initiative to the end of 2021. The final removal of the barriers was made an explicit objective of the power-sharing executive in 2013, when it was pledged that they would be consigned to history by 2023. But this will not happen. In a 2019 survey commissioned by the IFI, 76 per cent of Peace Wall residents said they were strongly in favour of barriers being removed – but within the lifetime of their children or grandchildren. More tellingly, only 19 per cent supported the walls coming down immediately.[34]

Meanwhile, on the Protestant side, those behind the barriers and within the working-class community who contribute to, and even benefit from them, community distrust and tension continue to prosper. A BBC Northern Ireland report in December 2020 reported that the police and MI5 estimated that loyalist paramilitary groups were still amassing around £250,000 a month from payments by more than 12,500 members. Both the UDA and UVF had continued to recruit members, despite calling a ceasefire more than twenty-six years ago. Security assessments claimed that there were around 7,500 people in the UVF and 5,000 in the UDA. They were involved in drug rackets, prostitution and protection.[35]

There are thus contrary indications, and sometimes conflicting interpretations, of what the future will hold. The old Orange tradition remains strong, but a re-emergence of the old Belfast 'Protestant' liberal tradition is detectable. The eventual reunification of Ireland seems the most likely prospect, not just because the demographics and the balance of political forces are moving in that direction, but also because Ulster unionism in all its various manifestations has run out of answers to Ireland's British questions. The reversion to stridency and threats evident in the DUP's 2022 Assembly election campaign and the accompanying anti-protocol rallies summed up the historic negativity of unionism and its contemporary failure to offer an alternative to this. Unionism never has been an optimistic or progressive philosophy, but today it has little to offer but echoes of the drumbeats of the past. That only seven out of its 30 candidates in the Assembly election were women, contrasting with Sinn Féin's 19 out of 34, was illustrative of its traditionalism.

Only a fool would predict that a new Ireland would put an end to division, prejudice and inequality; on the other hand, only the visionless would object to the prospect of a new start for the people of the thirty-two counties of Ireland – including the Protestants of Ulster.

Acknowledgements

First and foremost, I am greatly in debt to Verso, both for publishing this book and for taking a great deal of care in its production. This began with Leo Hollis, my editor, whose encouragement and suggestions for improving the book from its first draft were sustaining and enormously helpful. The copy editing was undertaken by Charles Peyton. Charles was meticulous, conscientious, and spotted my carelessness more often than I had a right to expect. He improved the book greatly.

Thanks to Nadine Finch, Dorothy Macedo and Susan O'Halloran for reading and advising on a first draft of this book, and to them and Di Parkin for editorial advice. Thanks to Dr Niall Meehan for a constant supply of information and for his comments on the book's concept. Thanks to James Anderson for also commenting on the concept. Thanks to Fearghal Mac Bhloscaidh for allowing me to quote from his research when it was at a pre-publication stage.

I am also indebted to Angela Birtill, Richard Chessum, Alana Heaney, Austin Harney, Amanda Nichols, Laura Sullivan, and Mick Sullivan for conversations relating to the subject matter of the book.

Thanks to my family, Mary Margaret, Iona, Lauren and Sean for comments, support and patience.

I would like to acknowledge the CAIN and Divided Society websites, especially helpful during the pandemic, and the staff at the British Library, the National Archive in Kew, and the Bodleian Library in Oxford for doing what they do so well.

I am responsible for any mistakes.

Finally, thanks to the members of the Woodberry Down and Walthamstow book club for pointing out the quotation from Irmgard Keun used for the epigraph.

Notes

Abbreviations used:
CPA: Conservative Party Archives, Bodleian Library, Oxford.
CPNIC: Conservative Party Northern Ireland Committee (CPA)
NA: National Archives, Kew, London.
PDHC: Parliamentary Debates, House of Commons (Hansard).
PDHL: Parliamentary Debates, House of Lords (Hansard).

1. 'Crackpots'

1 *Irish News*, 15 June 2021.
2 The DUP's support at Foster's fall (May 2021) was 16 per cent. This compared to 35 per cent in September 2017 (*Lucid Talk* opinion polls) and 28.1 per cent at the Assembly election in 2016. For support for unionism in general, see throughout.
3 *Guardian*, 21 June 2017.
4 *Observer*, 2 July 2017.
5 *Economist*, 17 June 2017.
6 *New York Times*, 10 June 2017.
7 See 'Plague Monks' at totalwarwarhammer.fandom.com.
8 *Observer*, 18 June 2017.
9 *The Times*, 16 June 2017.
10 Ibid.
11 *Daily Telegraph*, 12 June 2017.
12 *Daily Telegraph*, 14 June 2017.
13 *Guardian*, 26 June 2017.
14 PDHL, 27 June 2017.
15 *Daily Telegraph*, 14 June 2017.
16 Michael Gove, *The Price of Peace* (London: Centre for Policy Studies, 2000), pp. 4, 5, 14.
17 Ibid., p. 35.
18 *Irish News*, 4 July 2016.
19 Mydup.com, 12 June 2017.

20 *Belfast Telegraph*, 28 June 2018.

21 *Belfast News-Letter*, 24 June 2017.

22 *Daily Telegraph*, 13 June 2017.

23 *Daily Telegraph*, 11 June 2017.

24 *Daily Telegraph*, 10 June 2017.

25 *Irish News*, 11 April 2019.

26 *Daily Telegraph*, 14 June 2017.

27 'Arlene Foster: Brexit brinkmanship rooted in a border childhood', *Guardian*, 8 December 2017, theguardian.com.

28 *Irish News*, 8 July 2017.

29 Northern Ireland BBC website, 10 July 2017.

30 *Irish News*, 10 July 2017.

31 *Irish News*, 11 July 2017.

32 Ibid.

33 Both speeches, mydup.com/archive, 25 November 2017.

34 *Belfast News-Letter* website: newsletter.co.uk, 13 February 2018.

35 *Spectator*, 23 March, 2019.

36 *Sun*, 30 March 2019.

37 *Guardian*, 7 December 2018.

38 *Belfast News-Letter* website, 6 January 2018.

39 The sample of those questioned included 1,542 people. Lord Ashcroft Polls, 30 August–2 September 2019.

40 Both speeches, PDHC, 11 July 2019.

41 David Cameron, *For the Record* (London: William Collins, 2019), p. 305.

42 'Press Release: May's "Precious Union" Has Little Support in Brexit Britain', Centre on Constitutional Change, 9 October 2018.

2. The Precious Union

1 Kevin Haddock-Flynn, *Orangeism: A Historical Profile* (Leicester: Matador, 2019), p. 159.

2 Ibid., p. 160.

3 *The Standard Orange Song Book*, Armagh Guardian Office, 1848.

4 Haddock-Flynn, *Orangeism*, p. 235.

5 R. F. Foster, *Randolph Churchill: A Political Life* (Oxford: OUP, 1981), p. 143.

6 Lewis Perry Curtis, *Coercion and Conciliation in Ireland* (Princeton/London: Princeton University Press, 1963), p. 64.

7 Foster, *Randolph Churchill*, p. 252.

8 Winston Churchill, *Lord Randolph Churchill, Volume 2* (London: Macmillan, 1906), p. 31.

9 Haddock-Flynn, *Orangeism*, p. 254.

10 This and subsequent speech quotes compiled from Churchill, *Randolph Churchill*, pp. 62–3 and speech of Thomas Sexton, PDHC, 1 September 1886.

11 Foster, *Randolph Churchill*, p. 257.

12 Curtis, *Coercion and Conciliation*, p. 98.

13 This is well covered in J. A. Jackson, *The Irish in Britain* (London: Routledge & Kegan Paul, 1963).

14 This and the following from PDHC, 12 April 1886.

15 PDHC, 4 June 1886.

16 PDHC, 9 April 1886.

17 George C. Brodrick, *Home Rule and Justice for Ireland* (Oxford: E. Baxter, 1886), p. 10.

18 Joseph Chamberlain, *Home Rule and the Irish Question: A Collection of Speeches Delivered between 1881 and 1887* (London: National Radical Union, 1887), p. 162.

19 Ibid., p. 206.

20 Ibid., p. 207.

21 Brodrick, *Home Rule and Justice for Ireland*, p. 8.

22 English Radical Union, *A Unionist Policy for Ireland* (London: English Radical Union, 1888), p. vi.

23 PDHC, 1 June 1886.

24 Richard Jay, *Joseph Chamberlain: A Political Study* (Oxford: OUP, 1981).

25 PDHC, 10 May 1886.

26 'History of Orangeism', at orangeheritage.co.uk.

27 PDHC, 17 May 1886.

28 This and the following, *Report of the Belfast Riots Commission*, House of Commons, 1887.

29 PDHC, 1 September 1886.

30 Quoted in Michael de Nie, 'Ulster Will Fight: The British Press and Ulster', *New Hibernia Review* 12: 3 (Autumn 2008).

31 *John Bull*, 27 February 1886.

32 *John Bull*, 19 June 1886.

33 *Belfast News-Letter*, 25 June 1992.

34 Belfast News-Letter, *The Ulster Unionist Convention* (Belfast: Belfast News-Letter, 1892), p. 18.

35 Ibid., pp. 23–6.

36 Ibid., p. 36.

3. The Appearance of Northern Ireland

1 J. C. Beckett, *The Making of Modern Ireland* (London: Faber & Faber, 1966), pp. 426–7; Alan F. Parkinson, *Friends in High Places:*

Ulster's Resistance to Irish Home Rule, 1912–14 (London: Ulster Historical Foundation, 2012), p. 43.

2 J. J. Lee, *Ireland 1012–1985: Politics and Society* (Cambridge: CUP, 1989), p. 7.

3 Beckett, *Making of Modern Ireland*, p. 424.

4 Both quotes and voting details in Geoffrey Bell, *The Protestants of Ulster* (London: Pluto, 1976).

5 PDHC, 18 February 1907.

6 PDHC, 14 March 1907.

7 PDHC, 18 April 1907.

8 The dates in this list are as in PDHC.

9 A. T. Q. Stewart, *The Ulster Crisis: Resistance to Home Rule, 1912–14* (London: Faber & Faber, 1967), p. 47.

10 George Dangerfield, *The Strange Death of Liberal England* (London: Macgibbon and Kee, 1935, this edition, 1966), p. 80.

11 *The Times*, 29 July 1912.

12 Both quotes from Dangerfield, *Strange Death of Liberal England*, p. 89.

13 Stewart, *Ulster Crisis*, p. 55.

14 Parkinson, *Friends in High Places*, p. 59.

15 Ibid., p. 61.

16 Union Defence League, *Irish Facts* 1: 1 (April 1907).

17 *Irish Facts*, April 1912.

18 Parkinson, *Friends in High Places*, p. 238.

19 Dangerfield, *Strange Death of Liberal England*, p. 47.

20 Parkinson, *Friends in High Places*, p. 161.

21 Stewart, *Ulster Crisis*, p. 135.

22 Daniel M. Jackson, *Popular Opposition to Irish Home Rule in Britain* (Liverpool: Liverpool University Press, 2009), p. 242.

23 Geoffrey Bell, *Hesitant Comrades: The Irish Revolution and the British Labour Movement* (London: Pluto, 2016).

24 Michael Farrell, *Arming the Protestants: The Formation of the Ulster Special Constabulary, 1920–27* (London: Longwood, 1983), p. 21.

25 See Fearghal Mac Bhloscaidh, 'The Red Triangle', in Terry Dunne and John Cunningham, eds, *Spirit of Revolution* (Dublin: Four Courts, forthcoming).

26 Kieran Glennon, 'Facts and Fallacies of the Belfast Pogrom', *History Ireland*, September/October 1920. See also the November/December 1920 and January/February 1921 editions of *History Ireland* for comments on Glennon's article. None of these challenged his overall interpretation or figures.

27 Beckett, *Making of Modern Ireland*, p. 450.

28 See Bell, *Hesitant Comrades*, pp. 116–24.

29 *New Statesman*, 16 July 1913.
30 *Forward*, 8 July 1911.
31 James Connolly, 'Ireland, Karl Marx and William', *Forward*, 20 June 1911.
32 *Forward*, 27 May 1911.
33 James Connolly, 'The Exclusion of Ulster', *Forward*, 11 April 1914, in P. Beresford Ellis, *James Connolly: Selected Writings* (London: Penguin, 1973), p. 283.
34 All quotes from *Belfast Evening Telegraph*, 30 April 1914.
35 Paul Bew, Peter Gibbon and Henry Patterson, *Northern Ireland, 1921–2001: Political Forces and Social Classes* (London: Serif, 2002), p. 60.
36 Robbie McVeigh and Bill Rolston, *Ireland, Colonialism and the Unfinished Revolution* (Belfast: Beyond the Pale, 2021), pp. 213, 222.
37 Ibid., p. 223.
38 For this and details of the riots, see Michael Farrell, *Northern Ireland: The Orange State* (London: Pluto, 1976), pp. 136–42.
39 UK Government, Ministry of Defence, *Operation Banner: An Analysis of Military Operations in Northern Ireland*, prepared under the direction of the chief of the General Staff, London, 2006, paras 202, 206–8.

4. Betrayals

1 *Observer,* 20 October 2019.
2 PDHC, 23 October 2019.
3 PDHC, 21 October 2019.
4 *Irish News,* 18 October 2019.
5 *Guardian*, 5 December 2017.
6 *Spectator*, 20 November 2018 (website, speech in full).
7 Ibid.
8 Text of a Speech by Brian Faulkner, the Prime Minister of Northern Ireland, 24 March, 1972, cain.ulster.ac.uk/.
9 PDHC, 24 March 1972.
10 Vanguard, *Ulster a Nation*, Belfast, Vanguard, April 1972.
11 *Revivalist*, January 1974.
12 *UWC Journal* 1, undated (c. June 1975).
13 Speech dated 30 September 1972, enochpowell.net.
14 *Loyalist News*, 19 May 1975.
15 *Voice of Ulster*, June 1982.
16 PDHC, 26 November 1985.
17 PDHC, 27 November 1985.
18 Ibid.

19 PDHL, 26 November 1985.
20 *Irish Times*, 2 January 2003.
21 PDHC, 27 November 1985.
22 Ibid.
23 RTE Archives, 'Tomás Mac Giolla Addresses the Workers' Party Annual Conference in Dublin', 12 April 1986, at rte.ie.
24 Arthur Aughey, *Under Siege: Ulster Unionism and the Anglo-Irish Agreement* (Belfast: Blackstaff, 1989).
25 *Revivalist*, March, 1986.
26 PDHC, 26 November 1985.
27 PDHC, 27 November 1985.
28 Margaret Thatcher, *The Downing Street Years* (London: Harper-Collins, 1993), p. 385.
29 Ibid., p. 403.
30 *Ulster Patriot* 5 (1990).
31 *Ulster Review* 4 (1991).
32 *Leading the Way* 5 (1995).
33 See Geoffrey Bell, *Troublesome Business: The Labour Party and the Irish Question* (London: Pluto, 1982), chapters 5 and 6.

5. Tories Out, DUP In

1 *Visit by Members of the Ulster Unionist Council*, April 1960, NVA 7/1/1, CPA.
2 PDHC, 8 November 1961.
3 PDHC, 15 June 1967. See also 2 March 1967, 28 February 1967, 6 March 1967, 21 March 1967, 18 April 1967, 4 July 1967 and 23 November 1967.
4 PDHC, 6 May 1967.
5 PDHC, 22 February 1965.
6 PDHC, 14 July 1964.
7 Conservative Research Department, *Northern Ireland: A Background*, 24 March 1971, CPA.
8 Speech by Biggs-Davison, 1 December 1969, in Jeremy Harwood, Jonathan Guinness and John Biggs-Davison, *Ireland – Our Cuba?*, Monday Club (1970).
9 Conservative Party Northern Ireland Committee, 26 July 1974, CRD/4/15/1–5, CPA.
10 CPNIC, 30 October 1975, CPA.
11 CPNIC, 18 May 1976, CPA.
12 *Belfast News-Letter*, 4 November 1976.
13 John Biggs-Davison, *The Strategic Implications for the West of the International Links of the IRA in Ireland*, Foreign Affairs Research

Institute, September 1976, Conservative Policy on Northern Ireland, NA CJ4/1443.

14 Northern Ireland Office Memo, 15 September 1976, Conservative Policy on Northern Ireland NA, CJ4/1443.

15 Statement to Saville Inquiry by Lord Carver, Chief of the General Staff (KC8), 24 July 1999.

16 Transcripts of Saville Inquiry, Day 282, p. 83.

17 Ibid., p. 88.

18 Ibid., Day 291, pp. 40–1, 14.

19 Conservative Party Northern Ireland Committee, 16 October 1975, CPA.

20 For an interesting account of this, see Colin Coulter's two articles in *Irish Studies Review* 23.4 (2013) and 25.1 (2015).

21 David Cameron, 24 July 2008, Conservative Party website.

22 See Ed Moloney, *Paisley: From Demagogue to Democrat* (Dublin: Poolbeg, 2008), p. 231.

23 *Revivalist*, June/July 1976.

24 *Protestant Telegraph*, 5 October 1964.

25 *Protestant Telegraph*, 20 January 1968.

26 *Protestant Telegraph*, 13 April 1968.

27 Sydenham Defence Association, as in *Protestant Telegraph*, 10 June 1972 (emphasis in original).

28 *Revivalist*, June/July 1973.

29 See below, chapter 7.

30 'Ian Paisley "Broke Rules" over Maldives Family Holiday,' 29 September 2020, bbc.co.uk.

31 *Irish Times*, 26 May 2016.

32 *Belfast Telegraph*, 8 January 2018.

33 NA, CJ4/4218. 288/421/12, 18 August 1982.

34 *Irish News*, 6 September 1989; *Belfast News-Letter*, 3 September 1991; *Daily Express*, 1 June 1992; *Irish Times*, 12 January 2000.

35 *Irish News*, 2 March 2017.

36 'Sammy Wilson: I Still Think Man-made Climate Change Is a Con', 31 December 2008, belfasttelegraph.co.uk.

37 Interviews by Fintan O'Toole, *Magil,* 30 November 1985.

38 *Belfast Telegraph*, 1 September 2012.

39 *Irish News*, 11 December 2015.

40 PDHC, 8 July 2019.

41 PDHC, 8 January 2020.

42 *Life and Times*, 2021.

43 Jonathan Tonge, Maire Braniff, Thomas Hennessey, James W. McAuley and Sophie A. Whiting, *The Democratic Unionist Party: From Protest to Power* (Oxford: OUP, 2014) – religion figures, p. 139; class figures, p. 67.

6. What About the Workers?

1 Eamonn McCann, *War and an Irish Town* (London: Pluto, 1974), p. 39.

2 All quotes from Liam Baxter, Bernadette Devlin, Michael Farrell, Eamonn McCann and Cyril Toman, 'Discussion on the Strategy of Peoples Democracy', *New Left Review* I/55 (May–June 1969).

3 *Free Citizen*, 7 August 1970.

4 Peoples Democracy, *Fascism in the Six Counties* (Belfast: Peoples Democracy, 1973).

5 Michael Farrell, ed., *Twenty Years On* (Dingle: Brandon, 1988), pp. 71–2.

6 Bernadette Devlin, *The Price of My Soul* (London: Pan, 1969), p. 156.

7 W. F. Monypenny, *The Two Irish Nations: An Essay on Home Rule* (London: J. Murray, 1913), p. 19.

8 Ibid., pp. 13–14.

9 Ibid., p. 11.

10 Ibid., pp. 11–12.

11 Brendan Clifford, *The Economics of Partition* (Belfast: Athol, 1992 [1972]), p. 95.

12 Ibid., p. 9.

13 For example, in James Connolly, 'Labour and the Proposed Partition of Ireland', *Irish Worker*, 14 March 1914; P. Beresford Ellis, *James Connolly: Selected Writings* (London: Penguin, 1973), p. 275.

14 Peter Gibbon, *The Origins of Ulster Unionism* (Manchester: Manchester University Press, 1975), p. 72. Emphasis in original.

15 Ibid., p. 145.

16 Conor Cruise O'Brien, *States of Ireland* (London: Hutchinson Radius, 1972), p. 302.

17 Ibid., p. 164.

18 Ibid., p. 296.

19 Ibid., pp. 298–303.

20 For O'Brien and revisionism, see Niall Meehan, *The Embers of Revision* (Cork: Aubane Historical Society, 2017).

21 Tom Nairn, *The Break-Up of Britain* (London: Verso, 1977), p. 237.

22 Ibid., pp. 231, 233.

23 Ibid., p. 226.

24 Ibid., p. 240.

25 Ibid., p. 253.

26 Ibid, p. 253.

27 For example, *Workers Weekly*, 8 March 1986.

28 David J. Smith and Gerald Cambers, *Inequality in Northern Ireland* (Oxford: OUP, 1991), p. 161.

29 Ibid., p. 244.
30 Ibid., p. 242.
31 Ibid., p. 198.
32 *Standing Advisory Committee on Human Rights Household Survey*, 1990.
33 For more on Sloan and Crawford, see Geoffrey Bell, *The Protestants of Ulster* (London: Pluto, 1996), pp. 74–9.
34 For more on this tradition, see Roger Courtney, *Dissenting Voices* (Belfast: Ulster Historical Foundation, 2013).
35 Paddy Devlin, *Yes We Have No Bananas: Outdoor Relief in Belfast, 1920–39* (Belfast: Blackstaff, 1981); Sean Mitchell, *Struggle or Starve: Working-Class Unity in Belfast's 1932 Relief Riots* (Chicago: Haymarket, 2017).
36 PUP, 'The Principles of Loyalism', 2002, at pupni.com.
37 Quotes in Richard Reed, *Paramilitary Loyalism* (London: Manchester University Press, 2005), pp. 77–8.
38 Ibid., p. 78.
39 *Combat* 2: 2 (1975).
40 *Combat*, April 1975.
41 Reed, *Paramilitary Loyalism*, pp. 110–11.
42 Peter Shirlow, *The End of Ulster Loyalism?* (Manchester: Manchester University Press, 2021), pp. 200–6.
43 Susan McKay, *Northern Protestants: On Shifting Ground* (Belfast: Blackstaff, 2021), p. 175.
44 Progressive Unionist Party Press Statement, 13 November 2019, at pupni.com.

7 The Not-So-Good Friday

1 *Irish News*, 8 September 2020.
2 Barry White, 'The Peace Process: A Question of Definition', in Dominic Murray, ed., *Protestant Perceptions of the Peace Process in Northern Ireland* (Limerick: Centre for Peace and Development Studies, 2000), chapter 6.
3 Ibid.
4 For a good account of this, see Paddy Devlin, *Straight Left: An Autobiography* (Belfast: Blackstaff, 1993).
5 All quotes from Ian Paisley Jr, *Peace Deal?* (Belfast Democratic Unionist Party, 1998).
6 *Orange Standard*, May 1998.
7 Jeffrey Donaldson, 'The Northern Ireland Peace Process: Blurring the Lines Between Democracy and Terrorism', *Friends of the Union*, November 1999, at friendsoftheunion.uk.

8   *Leading the Way* 5 (undated but 1998).

9   *Combat*, Special Agreement edition (undated but 1998).

10   *Burning Bush* 28: 5 (May 1998).

11   See 'Key Issues – Elections in Northern Ireland', cain.ulster.ac.uk.

12   Gove, *The Price of Peace*, pp. 8–9.

13   Henry Patterson, 'Unionism after Good Friday and St Andrews', *Political Quarterly* 83: 2 (April–June 2012).

14   Jonathan Powell, *Great Hatred, Little Room: Making Peace in Northern Ireland* (London: Vintage, 2008), p. 9.

15   Dennis Kennedy, 'Political Reality and the Belfast Agreement', in Patrick Roche and Brian Barton, *The Northern Ireland Question: Perspectives on Nationalism and Unionism* (Tunbridge Wells: Wordzworth, 2020), p. 350.

16   William Matchett, *When Winning Is Losing*; Roche and Barton, *Northern Ireland Question*, p. 190.

17   Brendan O'Leary, *A Treatise on Northern Ireland, Volume 3: Consociation and Confederation* (Oxford: OUP, 2019), p. 193.

18   Dean Godson, *David Trimble and the Ordeal of Unionism* (London: HarperCollins, 2004), p. 141.

19   'Press Statement from Ian K. Paisley on the Patten Report', 9 September 1999, CAIN Web Service, cain.ulster.ac.uk.

20   Godson, *David Trimple*, pp. 482, 486.

21   Gregory Campbell, 'The Peace Process and Protestants', in Dominic Murray (ed) *Protestant Perceptions of the Peace Process in Northern Ireland*, (Limerick, University of Limerick, 2000).

22   For more on Vanguard, see Garry Watson, '"Meticulously Crafted Ambiguities": The Confused Political Vision of Ulster Vanguard', *Irish Political Studies* 28: 4 (2013).

23   Godson, *David Trimble*, p. 53.

24   Gary Kent, 'The Trimble Enigma', in *Times Change*, Winter 1996–97.

25   Godson, *David Trimble*, p. 358.

26   Patterson, 'Unionism after Good Friday and St Andrews', p. 250.

27   Gregory Campbell, 'The Peace Process and Protestants', in Murray, *Protestant Perceptions*.

28   Powell, *Great Hatred, Little Room*, p. 272.

29   Peter Mandelson, *The Third Man: Life at the Heart of New Labour* (London: HarperPress, 2010), p. 291.

30   Ibid., p. 302.

31   O'Leary, *Treatise on Northern Ireland, Volume 3*, pp. 194–6.

32   Ibid., pp. 204–5.

33   Richard Humphreys, *Beyond the Border: The Good Friday Agreement and Irish Unity After Brexit* (Newbridge: Merrion, 2018).

34   *Irish News*, 20 July 2020.

35   *Irish News*, 2 December 2020.

36 Duncan Morrow, 'Nothing to Fear But ...? Unionists and the Northern Ireland Peace Process', in Murray, *Protestant Perceptions*, chapter 1.
37 *Éire-Ireland* 39: 1 & 2 (Spring/Summer 2004), pp. 189–214.

8. The Twilight of British Unionism?

1 *Irish Times*, 8 December 2018.
2 *Belfast Telegraph*, 1 February 2019.
3 *Irish News*, 11 December 2020.
4 Quoted in Diarmaid Ferriter, *The Border: The Legacy of Anglo-Irish Politics* (London: Profile, 2019), p. 129.
5 *Belfast News-Letter*, 10 June 2016.
6 *Revivalist*, June 1975.
7 *Belfast News-Letter*, 16 June 2016.
8 Matthew Goodwin and Oliver Heath, 'Brexit Vote Explained: Poverty, Low Skills and Lack of Opportunities', Joseph Rowntree Foundation, 31 August 2016, at jrf.org.uk.
9 *Economist*, 30 June 2020.
10 *Economist*, 17 April 2021.
11 *Guardian*, 12 April 2021.
12 Paul Dixon, '"A Real Stirring in the Nation": Military Families, British Public Opinion and Withdrawal from Norther Ireland', in Graham Dawson, Jo Dover and Stephen Hopkins, *Northern Ireland Troubles in Britain: Impacts, Engagements, Legacies and Memories* (Manchester: Manchester University Press, 2017).
13 The Channel 4 poll is from Geoffrey Bell, 'The British Question', in Dawson, Dover and Hopkins, *Northern Ireland Troubles in Britain*. For all other figures see 'Polls of Opinion and Attitude in Northern Ireland, 1973–2004', cain.ulster.ac.uk, which contain other results showing the same pattern.
14 *New Statesman*, 4 August 2021.
15 David Miller, ed., *Rethinking Northern Ireland: Culture, Ideology and Colonialism* (London: Routledge, 1998).
16 Ibid., p. xix.
17 Ibid., p. 5.
18 Ibid., p. 15.
19 Ibid., p. 25.
20 Brendan O'Leary, *A Treatise on Northern Ireland, Volume 1: Colonialism; Volume 2: Control; Volume 3: Consociation and Confederation* (London: OUP, 2019).
21 O'Leary, *Treatise on Northern Ireland, Volume 1*, p. 19.
22 O'Leary, *Treatise on Northern Ireland, Volume 3*, p. 309.

23 Ibid., p. 407.
24 Anne Cadwallader, *Lethal Allies: British Collusion in Ireland* (Cork: Mercier, 2013).
25 Mark McGovern, *Counterinsurgency in Northern Ireland* (London: Pluto, 2019).
26 Ibid., p. 167.
27 *Irish News*, 13 December 2020.
28 Both newspapers, 14 July 2021.
29 *Irish News*, 15 July 2021.
30 *Irish News*, 11 March 2021.
31 *Irish News*, 15 July 2021.
32 As well as the texts quoted throughout, see Kevin Meagher, *A United Ireland: Why Unification Is Inevitable and How It Will Come About* (London: Biteback, 2016); and Paul Gosling, *A New Ireland, a New Union, a New Society: A Ten-Year Plan?* (Paul Gosling, 2018).
33 A. C. Dicey, *England's Case Against Home Rule* (London: Richmond, 1886), p. 287.

9. The Twilight of Ulster Unionism

1 All comments, PDHC, 3 November 2010.
2 This summary is largely derived from CAIN Web Service, 'A Background Note on the Protests and Violence Relating to the Union Flag at Belfast City Hall, December 2012–January 2013', at cain.ulster.ac.uk.
3 Editorial and letters, *Belfast News-Letter*, 11 December 2012.
4 All quotes and statistics from Robbie McVeigh, 'Racism and Racist Attitudes in Northern Ireland', Trademark, 2015, at community-relations.org.uk.
5 Richard Reed, *Paramilitary Loyalism* (London: Manchester University Press, 2005), p. 158.
6 Ibid., p. 159.
7 *Irish News*, 19 October 2020.
8 *Irish News*, 20 October 2020.
9 *Irish News*, 22 October 2020.
10 Ibid.
11 *Irish News*, 28 January 2020.
12 *Irish News*, 29 February 2021.
13 *Irish News*, 8 February 2021.
14 *Irish News*, 14 April 2021.
15 Both incidents, *Irish News*, 6 January 2020.
16 *Belfast News-Letter*, 26 March 2021.
17 Quoted in *Irish News*, 21 April 2021.

18 *Irish News*, 3 November 1987.
19 Roger Courtney, *Dissenting Voices* (Belfast: Ulster Historical Foundation, 2013).
20 *Irish News*, 8 January 2020.
21 Parades Commission, *Annual Report, 2018–19*.
22 *Irish News*, 6 October 2021.
23 See, for example, the work of Ireland's Future. From December 2020 to October 2021 months, it published four notable documents addressing different elements of the unity discussion: *A Principled Framework for Change* (Dec 2020), *Advancing the Conversation* (Jan 2021), *Planning for a Strong Economy in a New Ireland* (March 2021), and *Rights, Citizenship and Identity in a United Ireland* (October 2021).
24 *Irish News*, 27 August 2021.
25 *Irish News* website, 22 February 2022.
26 PDHC 20 May 2020.
27 *Irish News*, 7 January 2022.
28 *Irish News*, 21 February 2022.
29 *Irish News*, 26 March 2022.
30 *Irish News*, 25 April 2022.
31 *Irish News*, 6 March 2020.
32 *Northern Ireland Life and Times Survey*, 2009, 2022, arc.ac.uk.
33 International Fund for Ireland, Annual Report 2013, p. 16.
34 International Fund for Ireland, Annual Report 2019, p. 17.
35 *Irish News*, 3 December 2020.

Index